SOLAR DRYERS–
their role in post-harvest processing

CONTRIBUTORS:

B.BRENNDORFER

L.KENNEDY

C.O.OSWIN BATEMAN

D.S.TRIM

Tropical Development & Research Institute,
127 Clerkenwell Road, London EC1R 5OB, U.K.

G.C.MREMA

Sokoine University of Agriculture,
P.O.Box 3003, Morogoro, Tanzania.

C.WEREKO-BROBBY

Commonwealth Science Council,
Marlborough House, Pall Mall, London SW1Y 5HX, U.K.

COMMONWEALTH SCIENCE COUNCIL

COMMONWEALTH SECRETARIAT

Marlborough House, Pall Mall, London SW1Y 5HX

© Copyright 1987
First edition 1985

Printed and published by
The Commonwealth Secretariat

May be purchased from
Commonwealth Secretariat Publications
Marlborough House
London SW1Y 5HX

ISBN 0 85092 282 8

CONTENTS

FOREWORD

The Solar Crop Drying Project (SCDP) of the African Energy Programme (AEP), as initiated by the Commonwealth Science Council (CSC), has the objective of improving traditional methods of sun drying crops and commodities in Africa by the development and introduction of appropriate solar drying techniques. The progress of SCDP since its inception in 1979 is documented in CSC reports CSC (81) AEP-4 and CSC (82) AEP-10. The research programme has been funded from local (national) sources and by the Overseas Development Administration (ODA) of the United Kingdom.

In 1983 the Tropical Development and Research Institute (TDRI) was appointed by CSC to participate in the SCDP by the provision of information and advice on solar crop drying technology. Following a consultant's visit to the researchers in all 7 countries participating in the SCDP; Gambia, Ghana, Kenya, Mauritius, Tanzania, Uganda and Zimbabwe, it was recommended that a Training Workshop be held to overcome shortcomings that were identified in certain areas of solar drying technology. This recommendation was accepted by CSC and the Workshop was held at the Jacaranda Hotel, Nairobi from 19-30 November 1984.

The objectives of the Workshop were:

(i)   to provide basic information and instruction on solar crop drying techniques encompassing the range of disciplines involved,

(ii)   to promote the three stage concept of initial project evaluation, experimental investigation, and project extension as a methodology for successful projects,

(iii)   to strengthen links and improve liaison between researchers by means of case studies, discussion periods and design projects.

The Workshop Co-ordinators were Mr D S Trim and Mr B Brenndorfer of TDRI. Dr G C Mrema, Principal Co-ordinator for the SCDP was in attendance throughout and Dr C Y Wereko-Brobby of CSC was present during the second week. There was a total of 18 delegates from 9 African countries. In addition to those from the 7 countries participating in the SCDP, funded by the ODA, there were delegates from both Zambia and Malawi funded by the International Development Research Centre (IDRC).

The lecture notes for the Workshop were prepared by the Chemical Engineering Section of TDRI in consultation with other sections of the Institute. The first 17 lectures were presented jointly by Mr Trim and Mr Brenndorfer; the lecture on 'Economic Project Appraisal' was given by Dr Wereko-Brobby and the lecture 'Extension of Solar Crop Drying Technology' was presented by Dr Mrema. These lectures, amended in the light of discussions at the Workshop, form the basis of this publication. All diagrams for the manual were drawn by Mr D Green of TDRI.

The intention of the Commonwealth Science Council in organizing and funding the workshop was that the participants from many African countries will widen their appreciation of the many factors relevant to their national Solar Crop Drying Projects currently operating as part of the African Energy Programme.

This manual is intended to provide an introduction to basic theories of drying, an outline of the principal operating features that can be used to classify the many designs of solar dryer developed to date, and a detailed account for the construction and operation of the three most popular types of solar dryer. Information is included on the theory and design of flat-plate solar collectors which are an integral part of many dryers. It is important to realise that solar drying, or any drying technique for that matter, is not an operation carried out in isolation and therefore sections have been included on pre-drying processes and techniques, methods of quality assessment and analysis, and storage and packaging techniques.

Recommendations on experimental methodology for the evaluation, development and extension of solar drying techniques are also provided, together with notes on basic economic considerations. Worked examples of drying theory, dryer design and economic analysis are provided.

Commonwealth Science Council
Marlborough House
Pall Mall
London SW1Y 5HX
UK

November 1985

SYMBOLS

Symbol	Description	Units
A_c	collector area	m^2
a_w	water activity	-
C_p	specific heat of air at constant pressure	$J\ kg^{-1}K^{-1}$
D	diffusion coefficient	m^2s^{-1}
D_a	average annual depreciation	-
d	diameter	m
f	fanning friction factor	-
f_{ca}	effective transmissivity absorptivity product of cover and absorber	-
G_a	mass flowrate per unit collector area	$kg\ m^{-2}s^{-1}$
G_d	mass flowrate per unit cross-sectional area of duct	$kg\ m^{-2}s^{-1}$
g	acceleration due to gravity	$m\ s^{-2}$
H	height	m
h	heat transfer coefficient	$W\ m^{-2}K^{-1}$
h_a	absolute humidity	-
h_{as}	adiabetic saturation humidity of the air	-
h_b	bed depth	m
h_i	absolute humidity of air entering dryer	-
h_o	absolute humidity of air leaving dryer	-
h_s	saturation humidity	-
I	initial incremental amount invested	-
I_c	insolation incident upon collector	$W\ m^{-2}$
I_d	total daily insolation	$kJ\ m^{-2}day^{-1}$
I_h	insolation on horizontal surface	$W\ m^{-2}$
I_s	insolation on sloping surface	$W\ m^{-2}$
k	thermal conductivity	$W\ m^{-1}K^{-1}$
L	characteristic linear dimension	m
M_c	moisture content, dry basis	-

M_o	mass of commodity at time $t = 0$	kg
M_t	mass of commodity at time t	kg
m_a	molecular mass of air	g mole^{-1}
m_w	molecular mass of water	g mole^{-1}
N	day length	h
n	Day number; 1 on January 1st 365 on December 31st	-
NPV	Net Present Value	-
Nu	Nusselt number $\dfrac{hL}{k}$	-
O	average annual incremental cash flow	-
P_a	total atmospheric pressure	Pa
P_o	vapour pressure of pure water	Pa
P_s	saturated vapour pressure	Pa
P_w	partial pressure of water vapour	Pa
PS	percentage absolute humidity	-
R	incident radiation	W m^{-2}
R_a	radiation absorbed per unit area	W m^{-2}
R_{ac}	accounting rate of return	-
R_e	radiation emitted per unit area	W m^{-2}
R_h	hydraulic radius	m
R_t	energy transfer by radiation	W m^{-2}
Re	Reynolds number $\dfrac{\rho v.L}{\mu}$	-
Re_h	modified Reynolds number $\dfrac{4.\rho v. R_h}{\mu}$	-
RH	relative humidity	-
T	temperature (absolute)	K
t_d	drying time	s
U_L	collector heat loss coefficient	W m^{-2} K^{-1}
U_o	overall heat transfer coefficient	W m^{-2} K^{-1}

Symbol	Description	Units
V	volumetric air flowrate	$m^3 s^{-1}$
V_c	volumetric air flowrate per unit collection area	$m s^{-1}$
v	air velocity	$m s^{-1}$
W	moisture evaporated	kg
x	distance from particle surface	m
α	absorptivity	-
α_b	absorptivity of black body	-
β	slope angle - the angle between the horizontal plane and the plane of the surface in question	degrees
ΔH_L	latent heat of evaporation	$kJ kg^{-1}$
ΔP	pressure drop	Pa
ΔT	temperature change	$^\circ C$
δ	declination angle	degrees
ε	emissivity	$W m^{-2}$
η_c	collection efficiency	-
η_d	system drying efficiency	-
η_p	pick-up efficiency	-
Θ	angle of incidence of radiation on a sloping surface	degrees
Θ_h	angle of incidence of radiation on a horizontal surface	degrees
μ	viscosity	$kg m^{-1} s^{-1}$
ρ	density	$kg m^{-3}$
σ	Stefan-Boltzmann constant	$W m^{-2} K^{-4}$
ξ	transmissivity	-
ϕ	latitude	degrees
ω	hour angle - angular displacement of the sun	degrees
γ	surface azimuth angle - orientation with respect to North-South axis	degrees

ABBREVIATIONS

AACC	AMERICAN ASSOCIATION OF CEREAL CHEMISTS
AEP	AFRICAN ENERGY PROGRAMME
AOAC	ASSOCIATION OF ANALYTICAL CHEMISTS
ASAE	AMERICAN SOCIETY OF AGRICULTURAL ENGINEERS
ASME	AMERICAN SOCIETY OF MECHANICAL ENGINEERS
BED	BUREAU ENERGY DEVELOPMENT
CSC	COMMONWEALTH SCIENCE COUNCIL
CSIRO	COMMONWEALTH SCIENTIFIC, INDUSTRIAL & RESEARCH ORGANISATION
DCF	DISCOUNTED CASH FLOW
db	DRY BASIS
EEC	EUROPEAN ECONOMIC COMMUNITY
FAO	FOOD AND AGRICULTURE ORGANIZATION
HDPE	HIGH DENSITY POLYETHYLENE
IDRC	INTERNATIONAL DEVELOPMENT RESEARCH CENTRE
IRR	INTERNAL RATE OF RETURN
ISES	INTERNATIONAL SOLAR ENERGY SOCIETY
LDPE	LOW DENSITY POLYETHYLENE
LED	LIGHT EMITTING DIODE
NPV	NET PRESENT VALUE
ODA	OVERSEAS DEVELOPMENT ADMINISTRATION
OPP	ORIENTATED POLYPROPYLENE
PCA	PERCHLORIC ACID
PRT	PLATINUM RESISTANCE THERMOMETER
PS	PERCENTAGE SATURATION PERCENTAGE ABSOLUTE HUMIDITY
PVDC	POLYVINYL DICHLORIDE
PVF	POLYVINYL FLUORIDE
RH	RELATIVE HUMIDITY
SCDP	SOLAR CROP DRYING PROJECT
STP	STANDARD TEMPERATURE AND PRESSURE
TBA	THIOBARBITURIC ACID
TDRI	TROPICAL DEVELOPMENT AND RESEARCH INSTITUTE
TMA	TRIMETHYLAMINE
TVB	TOTAL VOLATILE BASES
UN	UNITED NATIONS
UNESCO	UNITED NATIONS EDUCATIONAL, SCIENTIFIC AND CULTURAL ORGANIZATION
UNIDO	UNITED NATIONS INDUSTRIAL DEVELOPMENT ORGANIZATION
USDA	UNITED STATES DEPARTMENT OF AGRICULTURE
wb	WET BASIS
WHO	WORLD HEALTH ORGANIZATION
WVTR	WATER VAPOUR TRANSMISSION RATE

1. INTRODUCTION

1.1   Background

The preservation of surplus crops and foodstuffs can be regarded as one of the first and most important techniques of food processing. Traditionally, since the early days of civilization, man has had to set aside or store a sufficient proportion of his agricultural produce (or fish) obtained during the growing season to feed himself until the next harvest.

The early civilizations developed in the warmer and sunnier areas of the world, and sun drying was an obvious choice as a method of preserving foodstuffs. It is worth recalling that sun drying is nature's way of preserving seeds produced by plants during the growing season such that they are in a viable state for germination the following spring.

We now have at our disposal many ways of preserving commodities. These include the salting and brining of fish, meat and vegetables, the sugaring of fruit, drying of grain and many other foodstuffs, and as developed over the last century or so, canning, freezing, chilling, and freeze drying techniques. In each region the techniques selected depend on many factors; the nature of the foodstuff, climatic conditions, availability of materials and the degree of technology available to the processor are some of the factors that spring readily to mind. Sun drying however is still by far the most widely practised agricultural processing operation in the world; the Food and Agriculture Organisation (FAO) stated that in 1968 255 million tonnes of agricultural produce were dehydrated by solar energy.

Due principally to ever increasing labour costs, improving quality standards and the sometimes uncertain climate there has been a trend towards artificial dryers in the highly industrialised countries. These dryers are capable of providing a high quality product independent of the weather and with a low labour requirement. They are not, however, intrinsically suitable for the small-scale farmer or for the majority of agro-industries in African countries. They are capital intensive and in the main tend to be designed for a large throughput of a single product in some cases are designed for continuous (24 hours per day) operation. Because of their size and complexity they are incompatible with the requirements of a farmer with relatively small quantities of crops to be dried for short seasons throughout the year. In addition, they invariably require a source of power and also a supply of skilled labour for operation and, more importantly, for maintenance of the equipment.

In the context of this manual the term sun drying is used to denote the spreading of the commodity in the sun on a suitable surface, hanging it from eaves of buildings, trees and suchlike, or as in the case of cereal crops, drying on the stalk by standing in stooks or bundles. Whilst it is a technique which requires little in the way of capital or expertise and one that can give a product of acceptable quality in a reliable climate, sun drying does have many limitations. Loss of moisture can be intermittent and irregular and the rate of drying is generally low so increasing the risk of spoilage during the drying process. The final moisture content of the dried product can be high, because of low air temperatures and high relative humidities, which can result in spoilage during subsequent storage.

- 1 -

At best, product quality is likely to be variable with part of a batch being over-dried and part under-dried and with probable contamination by dust and infestation by insects. During the time of drying the crop is liable to theft or damage because of the shallow bed depths necessary, relatively large areas of land or other surfaces are required upon which to spread the crop. There is also a need for labour to be on hand scare away would-be predators. The direct exposure to sunlight, or more precisely ultra-violet radiation, can greatly reduce the level of nutrients such as vitamins in the dried product.

1.2   Potential of Solar Drying

Solar drying relies, as does sun drying, on the sun as its source of energy. Solar drying differs from sun drying in that a structure, often of very simple construction, is used to enhance the effect of the insolation. This could, for example, be a simple box covered with clear plastic sheet to trap the sun's heat. In many cases solar drying is a sensible alternative to sun drying for the African farmer and is particularly so when it supplements or replaces artificial drying.

Compared with sun drying, solar dryers can generate higher air temperatures and consequential lower relative humidities which are both conducive to improved drying rates and lower final moisture contents of the dried crop. As a result the risk of spoilage is reduced, both during the actual process and in subsequent storage. The higher temperatures are also a deterrent to insect and microbial infestation. Additionally, protection against dust, insects and other animals is enhanced by drying in an enclosed structure. All of these factors contribute to an improved and more consistent product quality. Furthermore, as the throughput per unit area is increased due to the higher drying rates and also to the higher bed loadings possible, the demand for suitable land is reduced. Solar dryers can also be relatively waterproof, minimizing the requirement for labour to be on hand in case of rain or to move the crop under cover at the end of the day.

In many cases solar drying is an effective alternative, in whole or in part, to artificial drying although not capable of a comparable throughput or of providing such consistent product quality. Although a source of motive power is required for some types, considerable savings in energy costs are still possible. Comparatively unskilled labour can be used to construct, operate and maintain solar dryers utilizing materials that are readily and cheaply available in rural areas or alternatively existing drying or storage buildings can be modified to incorporate a solar collector to supplement conventional fuel supplies.

Solar drying can also be a feasible alternative to those natural convection dryers that use wood or agricultural waste products as fuel. The saving of wood would probably be the main attraction of solar dryers in this context.

However, despite this apprarent attractiveness, solar drying is still far from being a widely used technology. Apart, perhaps, from the incorporation of solar collectors into grain drying and storage silos in North America, there is not one instance of the widespread and widely acceptable use of solar dryers for the drying of crops and foodstuffs. Although solar drying has received appreciable research interest worldwide in universities and technical institutes this has been mainly in the form of thermodynamic studies, a comparison of sun and solar drying rates, or in very recent years, computer modelling techniques, all performed in an academic environment. In many cases scientific evaluation of the quality of the solar dried product is conspicuous by its absence. Perhaps the principal and most important failing of many projects is a lack of appreciation of the environment for which the dryer is intended. The final design is frequently inappropriate and the subsequent transfer of technology from researcher to end-user is anything but effective.

Another undesirable characteristic of many studies is the lack of a multi-disciplinary approach to the problem to which solar drying may be the solution. In many cases, research is carried out by, for example, mechanical engineers or physicists without reference to food scientists, nutritionists, economists or extension workers who are familiar with the local situation, and to some extent, the tendency has been that a dryer is designed and then an application sought. The true measure of success in the development of new technology is its widespread acceptance and use by the end-user and to ensure this it is essential that he is consulted in the initial evaluation of a project.

2. EVALUATION OF SOLAR DRYING POTENTIAL

2.1   Introduction

As with any other research project, before a start is made on the building and testing of a solar dryer the advantages and also disadvantages of solar drying a particular commodity must be evaluated. It should not be thought that the utilization of a free energy source is invariably economically attractive or socially desirable. It is strongly recommended that the researcher make strenuous efforts, in co-operation with extension agencies and other organisations, to determine as accurately as possible the quantity of commodity(s) that potentially could be dried. It is obviously advantageous that the dryer be used for as long a period during the year as is practically possible. Towards this aim it is not necessary that the owner or operator should harvest or catch all of the commodity since it may be more beneficial and socially desirable that the solar dryer be operated on a community basis or by a co-operative of local farmers or fishermen.

2.2   Estimation of Commodity Production

The first questions that have to be answered relate to the quantity of the commodity that may be available for drying. In order to determine this, the following should be established:

-   the quantity of 'fresh' commodity produced in the growing season by:

    (i)   a farmer (or fisherman),

    (ii)   the organization, i.e. co-operative society or group in which the farmer participates,

    (iii)   each district,

    (iv)   the country,

-   the number of producers providing:

    (i)   0-100 kg of fresh commodity,

    (ii)   100-250 kg,

    (iii)   250-500 kg,

    (iv)   500-1,000 kg,

    (v)   more than 1,000 kg.

-   the total quantity handled by the co-operative societies or groups,

-   the duration of the harvesting season:

(i)   for a farmer,

(ii)   within a district,

-        the amount of commodity harvested in a day,

-        the likely increase or decrease in the production of the commodity in the
         years ahead.

It is appreciated that this information may be difficult to obtain particularly for
crops such as fruits and vegetables that are in the main consumed by the
producer or within the village, etc., and do not enter any centralized form of
purchasing, marketing or suchlike.

2.3   Present Drying Practices

It may well be that the commodity is being dried already, perhaps by traditional
techniques such as simple sun drying, or possibly with some form of artificial
dryer, or even processed in some other way.

If alternative drying practices are being carried out then the following facts
should be established:

-        how much of an individual farmer's crop is dried?

-        is any processing carried out after harvest and prior to drying?

-        the moisture content of the commodity:

         (i)   before drying;

         (ii)   after drying?.

         (Alternatively, what is the wet to dry ratio, i.e. the weight of the
         commodity prepared for drying to its weight when dry?)

-        the size, shape and other important features of the commodity prior to
         drying?

-        the actual techniques used to dry the commodity. Every effort should be
         made to obtain this information as precisely as possible. If at all possible
         the costs of this operation should be established.

-        the problems experienced with these techniques, i.e. high capital or
         operating costs, high labour requirement, poor product quality, etc.

-        post-drying processing operations carried out prior to sale or storage.

-        the means of storage of the dried commodity before further processing,
         sale or consumption.

By asking these questions it can be seen that a deal of information can be
gathered on which design of a dryer can be based.

2.4   Product Quality Considerations

The quality of the dried product is of considerable importance. This can be so in many different ways; for dried fruit and vegetables sold to the local consumer the main quality factor is the general appearance of the dried material whereas for commodities such as spices or pyrethrum the content of extractable constituent is the main aspect of quality. For dried grain the moisture content is of particular importance. Some knowledge of the importance of quality can be gauged from the following:

-    the features of the dried product that determine its selling price, i.e. appearance, colour, size, shape, moisture content, purity, extractable constituent, degree of contamination, microbiological quality,

-    the methods by which the quality factors are evaluated, i.e. by visual examination or laboratory analysis,

-    the relationship between product quality and selling price.

2.5   Markets for the Dried Commodity

As with any development of a new or improved product, knowledge must be gained at an early stage of the market either as it presently exists for the current product or its potential for an improved product. It is appreciated that such information may well be difficult to obtain in certain areas, particularly from rural communities. It is important though that attempts be made to do so particularly for determining the level of technology and the economic boundaries for the subsequent technical development of a solar dryer.

Information must be sought concerning the following:

-    the (envisaged) outlets or markets for the dried commodity:

(i)   self-consumption,

(ii)   local sale,

(iii)   sale to large towns at some distance from the producer, either by the producer or via a third party,

(iv)   export,

(v)   further processing.

-    consumer acceptability of the product. This is of particular importance when the dried product is not currently available or is unknown to the potential market,

-    marketing mechanisms or organizations for bringing producer and buyer/consumer together,

-    the price currently obtainable for the fresh (or unprocessed) commodity. This may vary widely from season to season or from district to district,

\-   the price that can be obtained for the dried product.

A situation that may well be encountered is that there may be a possible alternative operation for the utilization of the fresh commodity. It could be that surpluses of commodity are sold to a local entrepreneur for sale elsewhere or another preservation operation is carried out, e.g. pickling of vegetables, jam-making from fruits. If this is the case, as for an alternative drying process, as much information as possible should be obtained particularly with regard to its economic viability.

2.6   Project Viability

If sufficient information concerning the above topics is obtained then it will be possible to make preliminary conclusions about the potential viability of some type of solar drying operation for the economic preservation of the commodity. It may also be possible to draw conclusions about the attractiveness of solar drying relative to other processing operations. In the situation where the dried commodity is unknown then it may be necessary to carry out preliminary drying trials to produce sufficient quantity of the product to enable some indications of its acceptability and market potential to be obtained.

At this stage efforts should be made to determine whether there has been any previous research carried out, either nationally or in other countries, on drying the commodity in question.   Similarly, efforts should be made to ascertain whether solar drying techniques have been investigated within the country for use with other commodities. If such research has been conducted it is strongly recommended that contact be made with the researchers or organizations involved to avoid any unnecessary duplication of research and to benefit from the results so obtained.

3. PRE-DRYING PROCESSING OPERATIONS

Introduction

Pre-drying processes are necessary for most commodities in order to prepare the commodity in a suitable form for drying, storage and its intended end-use. For instance, grading apricots to remove bruised/damaged fruit is conducive to a high quality dried product. Chipping cassava to reduce the particle size (and hence increase the surface area) is essential to achieve sensible drying times. Blanching and sulphiting of potatoes is necessary to inhibit development of off-colours and off-odours during drying and storage.

Before various operations are considered in detail it is imperative to stress the need for correct harvesting of crops (or, catching and handling of fish). For instance, fruit should be hand picked, not shaken from trees, when "eating ripe" and still firm. Over-ripe fruit not only suffer physical damage during transportation, but during subsequent processing it can, for example, absorb an excess of sulphur dioxide during sulphiting and become dark and unattractive. Conversely, under-ripe fruit is slow in taking up sulphur dioxide and turns out an inferior product. There is therefore little sense in preparing and drying crops which have been harvested at the wrong time or using an inappropriate method. It is also very important that post-harvest operations should be carried out as soon as possible after harvesting to minimize the extent of spoilage.

3.1 Hygiene

The need for good hygiene during all processing operations cannot be over-emphasized. Good housekeeping, in particular the washing of hands, regular cleaning of equipment, and rapid disposal of waste materials goes a long way to preventing contamination of the dried product. Adequate provision of preparation equipment, for example, sharp (stainless steel) knives, availability of potable (or chlorinated) water and power (if required), plenty of room for working, and suitable labour which has been trained in processing procedures and the need for hygienic conditions, together with correct siting of the processing site are other factors which contribute to hygienic working conditions.

3.2 Cleaning

Following harvesting and transportation to the drying site the first pre-drying operation is usually cleaning, although this is not an essential operation for all commodities. Cleaning serves to remove dirt, leaves, twigs, stones, insects, insecticidal residues and other contaminants. Cleaning may be required under statues that protect public health. However, other important advantages accrue, since removal of contaminants reduces spoilage rates, improves the efficiency of peeling equipment and other processing machines, and protects machines against damage from foreign material.

Small-scale washers can be purchased but it is generally more cost-effective to wash manually in a purpose built tank made from concrete, plastic, or in clay pots. Mattei (1984) describes the manufacture of a washer-peeler for cassava made from an old oil drum.

Industrially, mechanical grading machines are also used to remove objects such as twigs and stones but for small scale operations these are generally picked out by hand. Industrial washers involve continuously tumbling the commodity on vibrating screens or other units equipped with parallel rolls, discs, or brushes, or in rotating horizontal drums constructed of bars, rods, slats, or coarse screens, together with sprays of water directed on the tumbling commodity. The tumbling action loosens adhering soil and the water sprays wash it away.

3.3   Grading and Sizing

The grading operation is very important in the production of high quality foodstuffs. However, it should be noted that the operation can be made much easier (and losses reduced) if correct harvesting procedures are followed. Grading may be performed at the time the commodity is received at the drying site, but is sometimes done after cleaning when the physical characteristics of the commodity are better exposed. Factors that may be considered in grading are size and shape, colour, texture, density, chemical composition, blemishes, and insect infestation. Maturity, colour, flavour, and defects largely determine the quality of the finished product and therefore grading is second in importance to correct harvesting for producing high quality dried products. Usually final market requirements effectively specify the grading requirements of the finished product as well as the raw commodity. It should be stressed that during grading (and other operations) the commodity should be handled gently to prevent physical damage. Grading is often a manual process, even on an industrial scale, but mechanical grading machines have been developed for some commodities. Peas are graded for maturity by brine flotation after being graded for size and blanched. Potatoes are also graded by brine flotation when total solids content is a factor in the quality specification of the dried product.

Sorting into lots according to size or shape benefits subsequent operations as follows:

(i)   blanching, sulphiting (or sulphuring) and drying operations can be better controlled;

(ii)   the finished product has greater uniformity, and

(iii)   maximum performance and yields are obtained for peeling and cutting machines that are set to a particular size of material.

For small quantities of commodity manual sizing is more appropriate than mechanical methods – this is similar to that described for washing.

3.4   Peeling

Many fruits and vegetables require peeling prior to drying. Since a thick skin presents a physical barrier to moisture, removal aids the drying operation. However, care must be taken not to remove too thick a layer in case valuable nutrients are lost, e.g. peeling a thick layer from potatoes or ginger removes most of the vitamins and minerals. Losses in yield can also be important if not properly controlled. Freshness is important – sometimes shrivelled or corky skins develop and require special peeling treatment. Manual peeling is the cheapest and simplest method for small-scale operations. However, small-scale peelers have been developed, such as the washer-peeler (Mattei, 1984) previously mentioned. For larger throughputs there are generally three types; mechanical, chemical and thermal.

The simplest mechanical peelers used for vegetables use abrasion techniques; the vegetables being rotated against abrasive surfaces such as carborundum while being sprayed with water. This tends to be a wasteful procedure, but nevertheless it is widely used for root vegetables. Lye peeling, steam peeling and flame peeling are other peeling methods used on an industrial scale.

Raisins and prunes can be treated with lye (dilute sodium hydroxide solution), the purpose being not to 'peel' but merely to 'check' the skin to allow more rapid drying rates. Shelling of nuts is sometimes necessary before drying. Partial drying of nuts is sometimes carried out to ease extraction of the kernel.

3.5   Coring, Pitting and Trimming

The procedure and applicability of these is dependent on the commodities. For example, carrots, other root vegetables, and onions are topped and rooted; cabbage and apples are cored, bell peppers are cored and seeded and peaches and apricots are pitted.

3.6   Cutting and Slicing

Unless the commodity is small, it is necessary to reduce its size in order to achieve uniform blanching and sulphiting, sensible drying times and in a form which is ready for use when reconstituted. Fruits and vegetables may be cut into cubes, slices, strips, rings, shreds, and wedges. Cutting with a knife is the simplest and cheapest method, but can lead to non-uniformity in the product which may not be satisfactory for particular market specifications. Several types of machines are manufactured for cutting, ranging in size from small hand operated batch-type devices to large automatic and continuous equipment.

A common type of chipper for cassava and other root vegetables, originally developed in Malaysia (Anon (1974)) consists of a steel framework supporting a feed hopper and a rotor cutting disc, and a petrol or diesel engine. The cutting disc (approximately 1 m in diameter) is fitted with four equi-spaced, corrugated blades and rotates at about 500 rpm. The petrol or diesel engine can be replaced by an electric motor or by the power take-off from a tractor. Such a chipper driven by a 2 kW engine, can produce around one tonne of cassava chips per hour (Coursey et al (1981)).

Fish, are usually cut or split by hand, the various cuts depending on the type and size of fish. Very small fish can be left intact for drying, larger ones can be split along the backbone, gutted and opened out, or filleted.

3.7   Blanching

Blanching or scalding in water or steam is essential for many foodstuffs to be preserved by drying primarily to control or prevent the actions of enzymes and to reduce the initial concentration of micro-organisms. The undesirable effects of enzyme activity are discolouration, off-flavours and distintegration of tissue (Voirol (1972)). Although the precise nature of off-flavour development has not yet been established, changes due to enzymic oxidation appear to be involved. Discolouration, that is, the formation of alien brown or purple colours, always occurs when, for example, cut apples or potatoes are exposed to the air. Enzymes are known to catalyse the oxidation of phenols to quinones which in turn form coloured compounds. Peroxidase, polyphenol-oxidase, and ascorbic acid oxidase are the three main enzymes of importance in enzymic oxidation.

Blanching involves subjecting raw commodities to boiling or near-boiling water temperatures for short periods. The principal function of blanching is to inactivate enzymes but the operation also partially cooks the tissues and renders the cell membranes more permeable to moisture transfer. More rapid and complete drying is obtained and the texture is improved when the blanched and dried product is rehydrated. During blanching, the micro-organism count in foodstuffs is substantially reduced (Weiser et al (1971)); sometimes the food becomes practically sterile. However, during exposure to the non-sterile conditions that can exist in subsequent processing operations, the product can easily become recontaminated.

Enyzme systems in foodstuffs are extremely complex and vary with different commodities. Most of these are progressively inactivated at temperatures above $70°C$ and completely deactivated at around $90°C$. Sometimes exposure of one or two minutes in the blanching vessel is sufficient, but longer times are usually used to ensure complete inactivation. Peroxidase is one of the most heat-resistant enzymes, the test for this being used to indicate the adequacy of blanching (Appendix 2).

As a general rule, when the products of enyzme-catalysed reactions in foodstuffs are undesirable, blanching is used to eliminate them. Foodstuffs that do not require blanching are onions, garlic and other seasoning materials, fruits that are sulphured before drying, fish and grain.

During the blanching process, the time of exposure to the heating medium required for a given commodity depends upon several factors.

(i)   Piece size - to obtain enzyme inactivation all parts of the material should reach a temperature of at least $90°C$. Longer blanching times are required for larger pieces to allow penetration of heat to the centres. However, care should be taken, for if the piece is too large its outer surface becomes cooked.

(ii)   Temperature - suitable uniform temperatures must be maintained throughout the blancher. In mountainous regions, where the barometric pressure is lower, immersion times must be increased to compensate for the lower boiling temperature of water.

(iii)   Depth of load - heat must penetrate into the centre of the bed of material
          so that all pieces will reach the desired temperature.

(iv)   Blanching medium - blanching in water usually requires less time than
          blanching in steam at the same temperature, because of the rapid
          application of heat to each piece in the liquid medium, as against the
          relatively slow penetration of steam into the bed of pieces.

Blanching can either be carried out in water or steam.   Water blanching is
basically the immersion of the commodity in a container of boiling or near
boiling water for the necessary time.   Care must be taken to avoid over-
blanching which leads to loss of texture and diffulties in subsequent drying. On a
small-scale the easiest method is to use a muslin bag or wire basket for
immersion which not only ensures the same immersion time, but keeps all pieces
together in an environment.   The water blancher needs to be such that when
charged with commodity the water temperature does not fall below 90°C. The
blanching temperature can be reduced by the use of additives such as citric acid,
ascorbic acid, sodium sulphite, etc. to the blanching water.

Steam blanching is often preferred to water blanching because there is a smaller
loss of nutrients by leaching and in some vegetables the dried product has an
enhanced storage life.   It basically consists of subjecting the prepared
commodity to steam. If the commodity is on trays there need be no direct
handling of the commodity between blanching and drying, thus handling of the
commodity between blanching and drying, thus aiding hygiene. On a small-scale
this can be carried out by placing the tray in the upper section of a tank or
chest, the lower section of which contains vigorously boiling water, and covering
with a lid. The tray should not come into direct contact with the boiling water.
Industrially, a continuous line of trays passes along via a conveyor through a
tunnel and is subjected to jets of steam from above and below.

Steam blanching times are usually a few minutes longer than water blanching
times. The steam blancher should be large enough to house the tray or tiers of
trays and contain enough boiling water to produce a continuous supply of steam,
particularly just after charging the blancher.

Since blanching times can vary considerably for both steam and water these
should be determined using the peroxidase test (Appendix 2).

3.8   Use of Additives

Substances added to food during processing can be sub-divided into two main
categories, those of non-nutritive value, and those adding nutritive value.
Substances added primarily for the nutritive value, such as vitamins and
minerals, will not be considered further. It is recognized, however, that in
certain instances substances added to food to impart a desired quality or for
some other functional purpose may also be of nutritional value. Generally small
quantities of non-nutritive substances, such as sulphur dioxide (SO_2) or benzoic
acid, are added to improve appearance, flavour, texture, or storage properties.
A report of a joint FAO and World Health Organization (WHO) Expert
Committee on Food Additives has been published (Anon (1956)) which summarizes
the general principles relating to the use of food additives.

In some countries, lack of suitable storage facilities and the inadequacy of transportation and communications may increase the requirement for additives; e.g. in tropical areas where high temperatures and humidities favour microbial activity, and increase the rate of development of oxidative rancidity, a wider use of anti-microbial agents and anti-oxidants than that of a more temperate climate may be justified. It is recognized that the increased risks associated with the increased use of some food additives must be weighed against the benefits gained from preventing food losses and making more food available in areas where it is needed. In such circumstances food additives might be used to supplement the effectiveness of traditional processing methods rather than to replace them. In assessing the need for an additive, attention should be given to its technological usefulness and its safety when used.

Of the many non-nutritive additives used prior to drying, only the main ones will be considered. Table 3.1 shows the maximum permitted levels of various additives for dried products.

3.9   Sulphuring Techniques

The main purpose of SO_2 is to reduce non-enzymic browning during drying and storage. It also helps to preserve certain nutrients, e.g.,β, – carotene and ascorbic acid, in food during drying, but causes large losses of thiamine. Further, it is effective in controlling microbial and insect activity, and in protecting delecate flavours in foods (Desrosier (1959)).

Non-enzymic browning is a Maillard type reaction - the condensation of reducing sugars with amino acids, which is a process accelerated by heat, and which is responsible for much of the darkening occuring during and storage (McBean et al (1970)).

There are two methods of providing SO_2 to commodities; sulphuring and sulphiting. Sulphuring is more commonly used for fruits and sulphiting for vegetables.

Sulphuring involves burning elemental sulphur in a sulphur chamber to produce SO_2 which permeates into food tissues. A sulphur chamber consists of an enclosure, with adjustable vents, housing perforated trays stacked one above the other. Figure 3.1 shows a typical small-scale sulphur chamber. The amount of sulphur used and the time of exposure depend upon the commodity, its moisture content, other pretreatments, and the permitted levels in the final product. In the case of apples, for example, the sliced material is exposed for between 30 minutes and 2 hours. Generally, for fruits, about 3.5 to 4 kg of sulphur per tonne of fresh fruit is sufficient.

Sulphiting involves introducing SO_2 into the commodity by the use of sulphite salts such as sodium sulphite or sodium metabisulphite, either by adding them to the blanching water or, when steam blanching is employed by either spraying a sulphite solution on to the commodity or by soaking it in a cold solution following blanching. Blanching in a sulphite solution is particularly useful since it combines two operations into one. The concentration of sulphite salts and time of dipping, spraying or blanching again depends on the commodity. Solution concentrations for spraying applications are typically 0.2 to 0.5% (as SO_2)

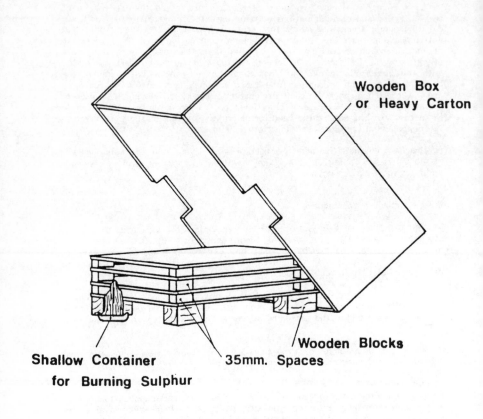

Wooden Box
or Heavy Carton

Wooden Blocks

35mm. Spaces

Shallow Container
for Burning Sulphur

Figure 3.1   Sulphur Chamber

whereas a 0.8% solution is recommended by Jackson & Mohammed (1969) for a soaking time of one minute.

TABLE 3.1   Maximum Permitted Levels of Additives for Dried Foods, United Kingdom (Anon, (1979)).

Food	Preservative	Level mg kg^{-1}
Coconut, dessicated	Sulphur Dioxide	50
Fruit:		
Figs	Sulphur Dioxide Sorbic Acid	2,000 500
Prunes	Sulphur Dioxide Sorbic Acid	2,000 1,000
Others	Sulphur Dioxide	2,000
Vegetables:		
Cabbage	Sulphur Dioxide	2,500
Potato	Sulphur Dioxide	550
Others	Sulphur Dioxide	2,500

3.10   Salting Techniques

Salt is most frequently used in the drying of fish and meat but also in fruit and vegetable preservation. Common salt (sodium chloride) is used as an additive primarily to inhibit microbial attack (Section 14.14) but also to reduce enzymic browning and discolouration, to achieve some moisture removal by osmosis and to a lesser extent, to prevent the undesirable effects of 'hard' water on the texture of vegetables during blanching.

With fish, salt is rubbed into the flesh or the fish are placed in very concentrated brine. In this way, water is removed and salt passes into the flesh, thereby achieving some moisture removal by osmosis. Since most bacteria cannot survive in salt concentrations above 6%, salting will therefore reduce bacterial activity (Clucas (1981)). For other commodities with different bacterial infections the relationship between salting and growth rate is variable, and some (halophilic) bacteria can survive in salt concentrations of 15% or more.

Fish can be salted in three basic ways (FAO 1981)):

(i)   Kench curing where solid salt is rubbed into the fish flesh, the fish then being stacked while the salt penetrates the flesh and the exuded moisture drains away.

(ii)   Pickling, which is similar to kench curing except that the moisture exuded from the fish is not allowed to drain. The fish become immersed in a very salty pickle of exuded fluids.

(iii)   Brining, where fish are soaked in a concentrated salt solution.

Kench curing is suitable for lean fish such as cod, but cannot be used successfully for fat fish such as sardine or anchovy, for which pickling is used. Brining can be used for both lean and fatty fish (Waterman (1976)). Trim and Curran (1983) successfully pickled fish overnight with a salt to fish ratio of one to three and brined other batches for one hour.

There are three main types of salt used by the fish processing industry:

(i)   solar salt, made by solar evaporation of sea and salt lake water:

(ii)   brine evaporated salt, prepared through the evaporation by artificial heat of strong brine, usually pumped from mines;

(iii)   rock salt, mined from underground deposits.

The purity of salt varies considerably from 99.9% to less than 80%. In addition to contaminants such as dust, sand and water, the principal chemical impurities are calcium and magnesium chlorides and sulphates, sodium sulphate and carbonate, and traces of heavy metals such as iron and copper. These impurities have various attributes depending on the use to which the salt is put. For instance, minute quantities (as little as 0.2 $mg.kg^{-1}$) of copper has been shown to result in a characteristic and troublesome brown discolouration of salted cod.

Salt is used for the temporary storage and handling of some cut fruits and vegetables, for example, apples or potatoes, to inhibit enzymic browning following preparation for drying. When free from large amounts of iron and copper impurities, salt has definite anti-oxidant effects of its own and also has the property of enhancing the inhibition of oxidation by other anti-oxidants such as sulphurous acid, sulphites and ascorbic acid. For this reason mixtures of salt and anti-oxidant are usually more effective than either alone. Salt also inhibits the activity of oxidising enzymes such as polyphenoloxidase involved in oxidative discolouration of peeled, cut or injured tissue of apples, potatoes and other products. Where salt absorption from brines is not harmful, or even desirable, temporary storage and handling in brines is useful for preventing discolouration following preparation.

During blanching salt can be used to prevent the undesirable effects of hard water on the texture of peas and beans. The addition of 2 to 4% of salt to hard water results in marked softening of skins of these products. Salt water blanching has also been used to prevent absorption of calcium and magnesium salts from hard water and to reduce losses by leaching of soluble constituents.

3.11   Sugaring Techniques

Sugar has been used in the past in small amounts to protect the quality of dried fruits and vegetables. However, in more recent times, the main use of sugar in conjunction with dried products is the removal of water by osmosis prior to drying (Ponting et al (1966)). The phenomenon of osmosis is the diffusion of a solvent through a semi-permeable membrane from a dilute to concentrated solution until an equilibrium concentration is reached. The solute is unable to diffuse through the membrane in the reverse direction, or only very slowly, so that the net result is transfer of water to the concentrated solution. The process of osmosis can be used to remove water from a dilute solution contained within a semi-permeable membrane by surrounding the membrane with a more concentrated solution. Transfer of water by osmosis is applicable to fruits since they contain sugars in solution and their cellular surface structure acts as an effective semi-permeable membrane. By immersing fruit in a concentrated sugar solution water can be removed to the extent of over 50% of the initial fruit weight, thereby greatly reducing the evaporative load on the dryer.

It should be noted that the product obtained by osmotic drying followed by solar drying is different to that obtained by solar drying alone.

Some of the advantages of osmotic drying are:

(i)   during osmosis the material is not subjected to a high temperature over an extended time, so heat damage to colour and flavour are minimized,

(ii)   a high concentration of sugar surrounding the material prevents discolouration by enzymic browning. Hence a good colour can be obtained in the dried product without chemical treatments, such as sulphiting,

(iii)   for fruits, as water is removed by osmosis, some of the fruit acid is removed along with it. This lower acid content, combined with the small amount of sugar added to the fruit during osmosis, produces a blander and sweeter product than ordinary dried fruit.

Some of the disadvantages are:

(i)   the decrease in acidity mentioned above may be a disadvantage in certain products. If this is the case, the acidity can be maintained by adding a fruit acid to the osmotic solution,

(ii)   a thin film of sugar is left on the surface of the fruit after drying, which may be undesirable. However, this can be reduced by a quick rinse in water after osmosis,

(iii)   Sugar treated fruit which has been dried to a very low moisture content can become rancid after storing for several weeks, which may be caused by the greater retention of flavour oils in osmotically treated fruit. To counter this it may be necessary to add an anti-oxidant during packaging.

The concentration of solutions and time of soaking is dependent on the material, initial moisture content and desired level of water removal. Osmotic drying of bananas has been conducted (Hope et al (1972)) by soaking slices for 18 hours in a 67% sugar solution, stirring occasionally, which removed about 40% of the original moisture, followed by one hour soak in a 60% sugar solution containing 1% SO_2, and finally a rinse in cold water to reduce subsequent stickiness.

3.12   Other Additives

There are many more food additives, many of which are not applicable to dried products and many of which are usually only used for industrial operations. Whether other additives are considered may depend on product specifications and legislation.   Degradation of chlorophyll takes place when green tissues are heated in the presence of acid.   During blanching, since the contents of plant tissues are acid, the pH of the blanching water falls, and when green vegetables such as cabbage are blanched, it is necessary to add sodium carbonate solution to maintain the pH of the liquor at 7.3 - 7.8 to prevent chlorophyll degradation.

Firming agents can be used when tissues soften during processing (Desrosier, 1959).   For instance, pectic substances are present in the cell walls of plant materials conferring rigidity; this cell wall structure partially collapses during heating as in blanching.   The addition of calcium salts establishes a calcium pectate gel which supports the tissues and maintains the structure.   Calcium salts are used industrially for many fruits in concentrations below 0.1%.   As with all additives, care must be exercised in the use of firming agents, as excess quantities may reduce rather than improve the desired quality characteristics.

Ascorbic acid and citric acid have been used to retard enzymic browning or oxidation during processing.   Jansen (1958) proposed the use of sulphydryl compounds to inhibit oxidative enzymes in apples. Makower (1960) investigated the chemical inactivation of enzymes in vegetables before drying.   Coating carrots with a 2.5% corn starch suspension as an alternative to sulphiting is practiced industrially. Benzoic acid and sorbic acid or their potassium or sodium salts are used to prevent mould and yeast growth.

4. THE MECHANISMS OF DRYING

Despite considerable research a complete understanding of the mechanism of drying has yet to be fully developed. This is particularly true of crops and foodstuffs with the possible exception of grains. However, it is generally accepted that there are two basic phenomena involved in the drying operation, viz:

(i)   evaporation of moisture from the surface,

(ii)   migration of moisture from the interior of a particle to the surface.

It is shown below how each of these phenomena control the drying process and what external factors have the greatest influence upon them.

4.1   Surface Evaporation of Moisture

It can be considered that moisture evaporates from a wet surface in much the same way as it evaporates from a free water surface, e.g. a puddle of water. As long as the surface remains completely wetted the rate of evaporation is constant and the factors affecting the rate of drying are the same as those affecting the rate of evaporation from a free water surface, its temperature and its humidity.

The rate of evaporation is proportional to the difference between the saturated vapour pressure of water at the surface temperature, P_s, and the partial vapour pressure of the water in the adjacent air, P_a. The vapour pressure, P_s, increases with increase in air temperature at constant humidity whereas P_a increases with humidity at any fixed temperature. In practical terms the warmer the air the greater the difference $P_s - P_a$ and hence the greater the rate of evaporation; the more humid the air the smaller the difference $P_s - P_a$ and hence a lower rate of evaporation.

The degree of movement of air over the particle surface is also of great importance. As moisture leaves the surface it passes to the air immediately adjacent to it. This increases the humidity of the surrounding air which in turn will slow down the rate of evaporation for although P_s is constant, P_a is rising. Thus unless the air surrounding the particle is replaced by fresh, relatively dry air, an equilibrium will be reached between the particle and the air and evaporation will not continue. In practice this is rarely the case since even under very low natural convection there is sufficient movement of air for evaporation to proceed. Increasing the air velocity (e.g. by use of a fan) will markedly increase the rate of evaporation as the surface of the commodity will be in contact with relatively dry air at all times. In practice there is a limit to how much the air velocity should be increased for as air velocities become higher there is steadily less gained by further increases in velocity.

Much of the heat necessary for evaporation of moisture from a particle is supplied from the air by convection but conduction and radiation of heat to the particle can also be important, particularly so for those solar dryers with the drying chamber exposed to the sun. Material dried on metal trays can receive appreciable heat via conduction through the tray bottom.

4.2   Internal Migration of Moisture

Although several mechanisms for moisture migration have been proposed [(Van Arsdel (1973), Perry & Chilton (1973)], it is supposed that there are two principal controlling mechanisms, diffusion and capillary flow.

From basic physics it can be realized that the temperature of the particle, its moisture content (or moisture gradients) and the physical dimensions of the particle are the most important factors affecting the rate of moisture migration but the internal structure and composition of the material are also of importance.

The general equation for diffusion of liquid through a porous solid is:

$$\frac{\partial M_c}{\partial t} = D \frac{\partial^2 M_c}{\partial x^2} \qquad (4.1)$$

where M_c = moisture content, dry basis

t   = time

D   = diffusion coefficient

x   = distance from the particle surface

This equation shows that the change in moisture content with time is proportional to the change in moisture gradient across the particle from interior to surface. In practical terms it can be appreciated that the rate of drying decreases in particle size.

Equation 4.1 has been solved by Sherwood (1929) and has been applied with fair success to the drying of grain and some other crops. Recent articles by Chirife & Cachero (1970), Chirife (1971), Suarez et al (1980), Farinati & Suarez (1984) and Kitic & Viollaz (1984) are good examples of the applicability of this technique.   Chirife (1971) amongst others has shown that the diffusion coefficient increases with increase of temperature.

4.3   Drying Rates

The most informative means of illustrating information on drying mechanisms is by drying rate curves, rather than the drying curves. A drying curve (Figure 4.1) is a plot of moisture content against time whereas a drying rate curve (Figure 4.2) is a plot of the rate of drying, i.e. the change in moisture content with time, against the moisture content or, in some cases, time.

At this point it is necessary to consider the relative effects of the two drying mechanisms in terms of which one controls the drying process. In the initial stages of drying the rate of moisture migration from the interior of the particle to the surface is sufficiently high to maintain the surface in a completely wetted condition.   Under these circumstances the rate of drying of the particle is controlled by the rate of evaporation from the surface (which is therefore

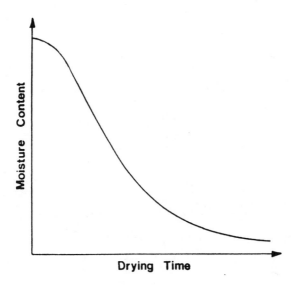

Figure 4.1   Drying Curve

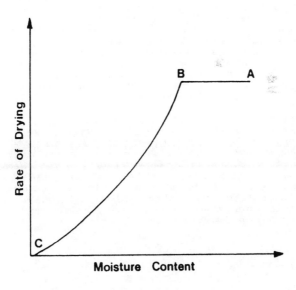

Figure 4.2   Drying Rate Curve

termed the rate controlling mechanism) which, as outlined previously, is controlled by the condition of the air adjacent to the surface. This results in a constant rate period of drying as shown as part AB of the curve in Figure 4.2. The point B at which the drying rate starts to decrease is termed the critical moisture content. Below the critical moisture content the rate of drying decreases tending to zero at the equilibrium moisture content. This period of drying is termed the falling rate period, part BC in Figure 4.2. If the initial moisture content is less than the critical moisture content then obviously there is no constant rate period. This is frequently the case with crops and foodstuffs.

Figure 4.3 illustrates four of the commonly encountered drying rate curves. Figure 4.3.A shows a constant rate period followed by diffusion controlled drying throughout the falling rate period. If a higher air velocity were used (at the same temperature) it would generally be observed that drying would be more rapid in the constant rate period but there would be little change seen in the falling rate period. This indicates that air velocity only has a significant effect when drying is controlled by moisture evaporation from the commodity surface.

Figure 4.3.B is a similar but slightly more complex curve for a different commodity. It should be noted that at the lower air flow rate the drying rate is lower during the constant rate period as would be expected where surface evaporation is the rate controlling process. During the falling rate period (of both curves) there are two distinct zones, the first of which (at the higher moisture content) shows dependency on air velocity since the gradients of the two curves are different. Such a situation can be portrayed by imagining a particle the surface of which is completely wet at the start of drying. As evaporation proceeds the particle becomes in places surface dry with some wet spots remaining. At this intermediate stage the rate of drying is governed partly by the rate at which moisture can evaporate from the wet spots and partly by the rate of internal migration of moisture within the particle. As drying proceeds the proportion of the surface of the particle that is dry increases and the rate of drying becomes less dependent upon air velocity. Eventually the surface of the particle becomes completely dry and internal moisture migration becomes the rate controlling process. It is at this point, T, that the two curves merge into one. If at this point T the temperature of the air were increased then the rate of drying would increase as intra-particulate moisture movement becomes more rapid as the temperature increases.

According to Sherwood (1929) Figures 4.3.C and 4.3.D are typical of rate curves where the removal of water vapour is largely the rate controlling process in the falling rate period. Figure 4.3.C is typical of the drying of thick but relatively porous materials, such as fish, where the zone of moisture evaporation tends to retreat into the material as drying proceeds. Initially air velocity and humidity have an important but decreasing effect throughout the falling rate period, but as dryness is approached the rate of drying is controlled by the rate of vapour transfer through the material. In Figure 4.3.D the drying rate is controlled by surface evaporation and will be affected by changes in air temperature, humidity and velocity as in the constant rate period.

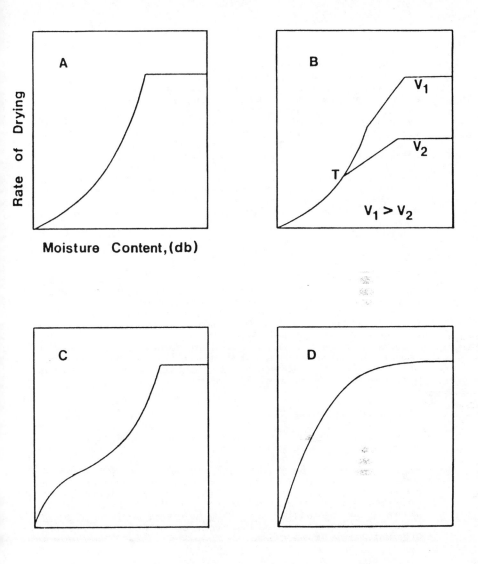

Figure 4.3   Typical Rate of Drying Curves.

(Sherwood , 1936)

On the above basis some broad generalizations can be made. A constant rate of drying will be obtained only if the initial moisture content is greater than the critical value. In such cases the drying rate is controlled by the rate of surface evaporation and is affected by humidity, velocity and to the lesser extent air temperature, and unaffected by the particle thickness. In the falling rate period internal migration mechanisms may be expected to control the drying. The rate will depend largely on the temperature, will vary inversely with the particle thickness and will be unaffected by the humidity of the air (except insomuch as it determines the equilibrium moisture content) and the air velocity.

In practice this means that initially when the moisture level is above the critical moisture content, the use of a high air velocity and moderate temperature will optimize the energy input. In the latter stages a low air flow with a high air temperature will provide more rapid drying than a high air flow with a low temperature.

4.4.   Particle Size

From the comments above it can be appreciated that, in the constant rate period, the greater the surface are the greater the rate of evaporation. Consider for example a 20mm cube of material and compare it with eight 10mm cubes. The combined volume of the 8 smaller cubes is identical with that of the single large cube but their aggregate surface area, 4,800 mm^2, is double that of the larger cube. The aggregate rate of drying from the smaller cubes will therefore be double that of the large cube. In the falling rate period with drying controlled by moisture migration, the drying rate will also be greater for the smaller cubes since the (maximum) distance over which moisture must migrate before it reaches the surface has been reduced by half.

4.5   Efficiency of Drying

A means of assessing the thermodynamic performance of drying operations is considered extremely useful for two reasons.

Firstly, it enables a comparison, albeit somewhat crude, to be made between the performance of two (or more) dryers. Secondly, and more importantly, it provides a means of assessing just how well (or poorly) a dryer is operating under certain conditions. For solar dryers there are three criteria which can be used to do this. As will be shown later these criteria enable the separate components of a solar drying system to be assessed individually and action taken, if necessary, to improve their performance.

(i)   System Drying Efficiency η_d

This parameter is defined as the ratio of the energy required to evaporate the moisture to the energy supplied to the dryer. For a solar collection the heat supplied to the dryer is the insolation upon the collector. Mathematically the system drying efficiency is calculated from the formula:

$$\eta_d \quad = \quad \frac{W . \Delta H_L}{I_c A_c t} \qquad (4.2)$$

where W = Mass of moisture evaporated (kg) in time t

 ΔH_L = Latent heat of evaporation of water (at temperature of the dryer) (kJ kg^{-1}) (See Appendix 1)

 I_c = Insolation on collector surface (W m^{-2})

 A_c = Collector area (m^2)

The system drying efficiency is a measure of the overall effectiveness of a drying system and as such it is commonly quoted. However, it does not lend itself for comparative factors; the particular commodity being dried, the air temperature and the mode of air flow are some of the more obvious. For natural convection dryers values of 10-15% are typical whereas for forced convection dryers higher values of 20-30% can be expected.

(ii) Collection Efficiency η_c

This parameter is considered in greater detail in Section 6. In practical terms it is a measure of how effectively the energy available in the insolation incident upon a collector is transferred to the air flowing through the collector.

(iii) Pick-up Efficiency η_p

This parameter is more useful for evaluating the actual evaporation of moisture from the commodity inside the solar dryer. It is a direct measure of how efficiently the capacity of (heated) air to absorb moisture is utilized. The pick-up efficiency is defined as the ratio of the moisture 'picked up' by the air in the drying chamber to the theoretical capacity of the air to absorb moisture. Mathematically it can be expressed as:

$$\eta_p \quad = \quad \frac{h_o - h_i}{h_{as} - h_i} \qquad (4.3)$$

where h_o = absolute humidity of air leaving the drying chamber

 h_i = absolute humidity of air entering the drying chamber

 h_{as} = adiabatic saturation humidity of the air entering the dryer

The calculation of the pick-up efficiency necessitates the use of the the psychrometric chart. A description of the features and usefulness of this chart is given in Appendix 3. Figure 4.4 is a simplified version of the chart and can be used to demonstrate the calculation of the pick-up efficiency.

The condition of the inlet air at temperature T_i and absolute humidity h_i is represented as point I. The outlet air condition, temperature T_o and humidity

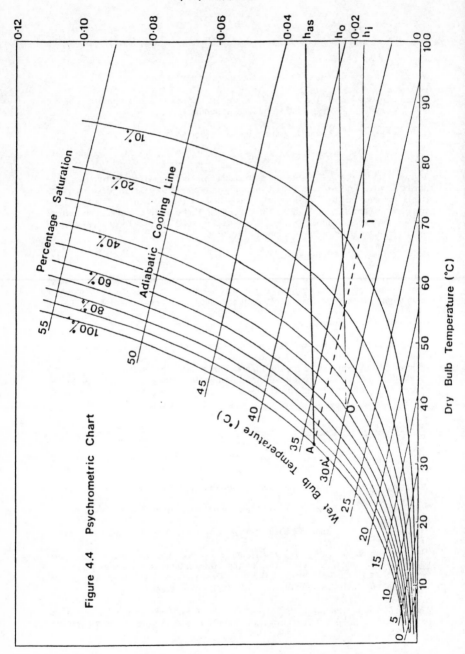

Figure 4.4 Psychrometric Chart

Humidity kg/kg

Dry Bulb Temperature (°C)

Wet Bulb Temperature (°C)

Percentage Saturation

Adiabatic Cooling Line

h_{as}

h_o

h_i

-26-

h_o is shown as point 0. The adiabatic saturation humidity of the inlet air is obtained by following the adiabatic cooling line (otherwise known as a line of constant enthalpy) to its intercept upon the saturation curve, point A.

It is not always easy to directly measure the humidity of the inlet air. However, measurement of the relative humidity (RH) of ambient air (prior to the collector) usually poses few problems. Since the absolute humidity of air does not change as the air is heated (although the relative humidity does change) measurement of ambient air RH enables the absolute humidity, h_i to be established.

The pick-up efficiency can also be calculated from the formula:

$$\eta_p \quad = \quad \frac{M_o - M_t}{V.\boldsymbol{\rho}.t\,(h_{as} - h_i)} \tag{4.4}$$

where M_o = Mass of commodity at time t = o (kg)

M_t = Mass of commodity at time t (kg)

V = Air flow rate $(m^3 s^{-1})$

$\boldsymbol{\rho}$ = Air density $(kg\ m^{-3})$

t = Drying time (s)

Use of this equation obviates the need to measure the outlet air humidity, h_o. Examples of the calculation of system drying efficiency and pick-up efficiency are given in Appendix 7.

The value of pick-up efficiency likely to be experienced with solar dryers can vary widely depending principally on the ease with which moisture evaporates from the commodity being dried. For example, in the early stages of drying of a very moist commodity such as fruit or vegetables, drying is relatively easy and therefore a high pick-up efficiency would be expected. Conversely in the drying of grain with a low moisture content drying is relatively slow and a low pick-up efficiency would be expected. Care must be taken therefore when assessing pick-up efficiencies to take into consideration the initial and final moisture contents over the drying period in question and the nature of the commodity being dried. The pick-up efficiency is perhaps most useful for evaluating the performance of two or more dryers with the same commodity.

If generalizations can be made then perhaps a value for the pick-up efficiency of 30%, as an average over the whole drying period, would be good. It should be noted that outlet air with a RH of 100% does not necessarily imply a pick-up efficiency of 100%; a dryer invariably performs non-adiabatically such that the outlet air will be represented as point A' in Figure 4.4.

Of these three efficiencies the most useful in the practical sense are the collection efficiency and the pick-up efficiency. The former enables an assessment of the performance of the collector to be made and the latter of how efficiently the (solar) heated air is utilized to dry the commodity, i.e. drying performance. It is therefore possible to evaluate separately the performance of the collector and the drying operation and take appropriate action to re-design or modify if necessary. For example, should collection efficiency be shown to be low, then attention can be paid to collector modification, etc. with the actual drying operation remaining unaltered if the pick-up efficiency is satisfactory.

5. SOLAR RADIATION

5.1 The Solar Constant

Though the level of insolation at ground level varies greatly with time of the year, time of day, and atmospheric conditions, the level of extra-terrestrial radiation remains fairly constant. Many measurements have been made of the intensity of extra-terrestrial radiation. This parameter is called the Solar Constant and its value as stated by Duffie and Beckman (1980) is 1,353 W m^{-2}. The energy in extra-terrestrial solar radiation varies with the wavelength as shown in Table 5.1.

TABLE 5:1   Composition of Extra-terrestrial Solar Radiation According to Wavelength (Duffie and Beckman (1980))

Wavelength (10^{-6}m)	0 - 0.38	0.38 - 0.78	0.78 - 00
Fraction in range	0.0700	0.4729	0.4571
Energy in range (Wm^{-2})	95	640	618

5.2 Terrestrial Radiation

The effect of absorption, mainly by ozone, water and carbon dioxide molecules, and scattering by dust particles, air molecules and water vapour is to both lessen the total amount of radiation per unit area and also to alter the proportion of the different wavelengths present in the radiation. The result of this is to decrease greatly the amount of ultra-violet radiation (that of wavelength less than 0.3×10^{-6}m) due to absorption by ozone and to decrease the amount of infra-red radiation reaching the earth's surface. The overall result of this absorption is that nearly all terrestrial radiation lies in the range of wavelength 0.3×10^6m - 3.0×10^{-6}m.

5.3 Beam and Diffuse Radiation

As a result of scattering by dust particles, air molecules and water vapour insolation at ground-level consists of two components; these being diffuse and beam radiation. Diffuse radiation is the scattered radiation which comes from the whole sky. Beam radiation is that radiation which comes in a beam directly from the sun and which casts a distinct shadow. Total radiation is the sum of beam and diffuse radiation. The relative proportions of beam and diffuse radiation vary with atmospheric conditions. The proportion of diffuse radiation in the total radiation can range from about 10% for a clear day to 100% on a very cloudy day. Further information is given by Duffie and Beckman (1980) and Kreider and Kreith (1981).

5.4 Direction of Beam Radiation

As well as the effect of absorption and scattering by the atmosphere the effect of relative movement of the sun and earth must be taken into account when designing solar dryers and collectors.

The position of the sun in the sky is, for a given location, dependent upon the time of day and year. The daily movement of the sun - rising in the East in the morning to its highest point at mid-day and then setting in the West - is due to the rotation of the earth about its own axis.

The change in climate with the seasons is a result of the tilt of the earth's axis and its orbit about the sun. The period taken to complete one orbit is a year. The angle of tilt of the axis to the plane of the orbit is approximately 23.5° as shown in Figure 5.1. The hemisphere (north or south) which is angled towards the sun at a particular time during the orbit around the sun will be receiving sunlight more directly and for a greater time each day than the other hemisphere.

From the point of view of an observer on the earth's surface the changes in sun position with time of year can be outlined as shown in Figure 5.2. On June 22 the sun is at its most northerly point and appears directly overhead at mid-day on the Tropic of Cancer (23.5°N). As a result the northern hemisphere receives a relatively large amount of sunlight at this time of year. As the year progresses the sun appears to move south giving longer periods of daylight in the southern hemisphere but less in the northern hemisphere. On September 22 the sun is directly overhead the equator and both hemispheres receive similar amounts of insolation. The sun continues to move south until December 22 when it is directly overhead the Tropic of Capricorn (23.5°S). On this date the northern hemisphere has its shortest period of daylight and the southern hemisphere its longest. Having reached its most southerly point the sun then moves northwards, crossing the equator again on March 21 and is again overhead at the Tropic of Cancer on June 22 to complete its yearly cycle. A good application of this concept is to be found in Kenya. TDRI has designed a coffee dryer which will be built and operated at two different locations, with different harvesting seasons. In one location the major crop is picked in November and December. From the explanation of the movement of the sun it is clear that at this time of year the sun is directly overhead near the Tropic of Capricorn. Thus to maximize the level of insolation on the collector, the collector must face south. At the other location the main crop is picked in April and May when the sun is in the northern hemisphere. For this dryer the solar collector faces north, again to maximize the level of insolation upon it.

When designing and predicting the performance of solar dryers and collectors it is often useful to have more precise knowledge of the direction of insolation in relation to the slope of the collector or dryer than the above description affords. Insolation data are most often gathered from an instrument measuring the intensity of radiation on a horizontal surface. However, this is not the same as the intensity of radiation on a sloping surface. The relation between the two is given by the expression:

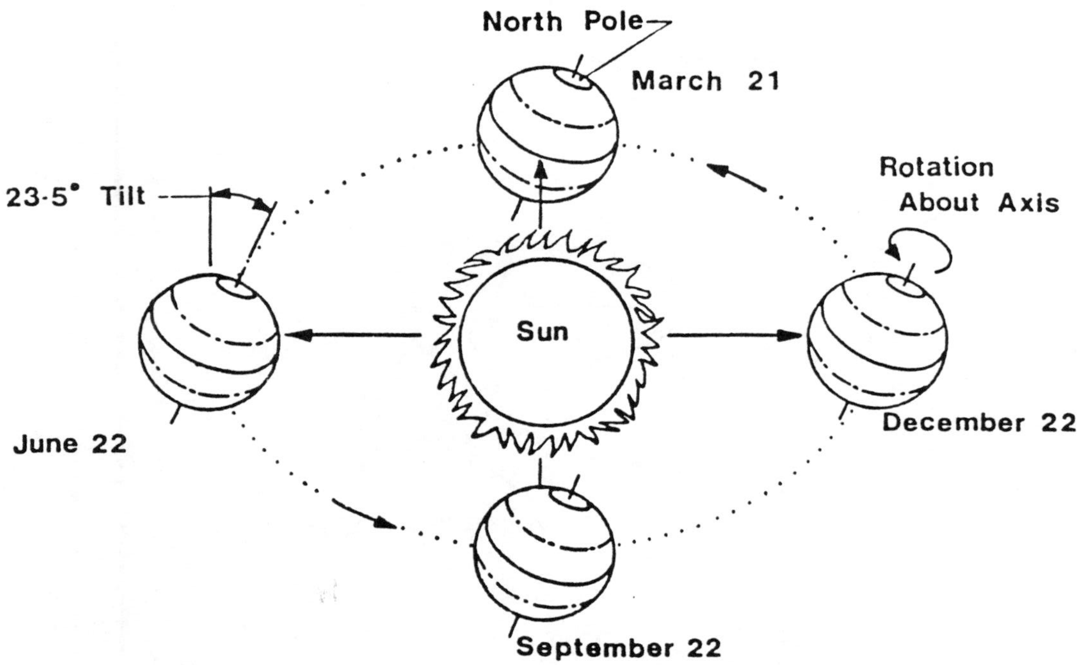

Figure 5.1   The Earth In Its Yearly Orbit About The Sun

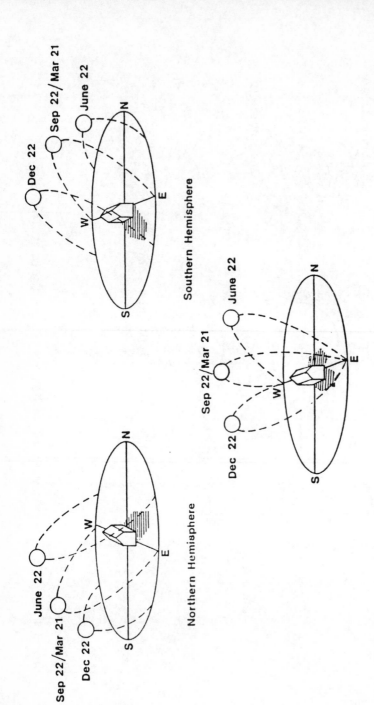

Figure 5.2   The Sun's Position As Seen From The Earth.

$$I_s = I_h \frac{\cos \theta}{\cos \theta_h} \qquad (5.1)$$

where I_s = insolation on sloping surface (WJ m^{-2})

       I_h = insolation on horizontal surface (WJ m^{-2})

       θ = angle of incidence of radiation on the sloping surface

      θ_h = angle of incidence of radiation on horizontal surface

In figure 5.3 the intensity of insolation on the sloping surface will be greater than that measured on a horizontal surface as the insolation is more direct on the sloping surface.

The angle of declination δ, that subtended by the sun and the plane of the equator at solar noon, (as shown in Figure 5.4) ranges from -23.45° (December 21) to 23.45° (June 21). It is negative when the sun is south and positive when the sun is north of the equator and can be calculated from the expression:

$$\delta = 23.45 \sin(0.9863(284 + n)) \qquad (5.2)$$

where n = Day number; 1 on January 1, 365 on December 31.

The angle of incidence, θ on a plane of slope β can be determined from the expression:

$$\begin{aligned}
\cos \theta = \ & \sin \delta \sin \emptyset \cos \beta - \sin \delta \cos \emptyset \sin \beta \cos \gamma \\
& + \cos \delta \cos \emptyset \cos \beta \cos \omega \\
& + \cos \delta \sin \emptyset \sin \beta \cos \gamma \cos \omega \\
& + \cos \delta \sin \beta \sin \gamma \sin \omega
\end{aligned}$$

where $\emptyset$ = latitude, - ranges from -90° to 90°, north positive, south negative (where test is situated)

      β = slope angle - the angle between the horizontal plane and the plane of the surface in question

      γ = surface azimuth angle, - for a structure this can be considered as its orientation with respect to a north-south axis. The angle varies from -180° to +180°, zero is due south, east is negative and west positive.

      ω = the hour angle, - is the angular displacement of the sun east or west. It is zero at solar noon (when the sun is due north or south) and changes 15° per hour. Morning is negative, afternoon is positive.

A useful concept when using insolation data in calculations for prediction of performance in solar dryers and collectors is that of the average day of the month. This is defined as the day for which the extra-terrestrial radiation is

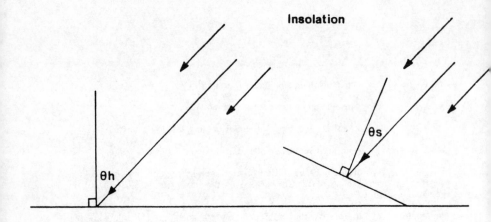

Figure 5.3   Insolation on a Sloping Surface

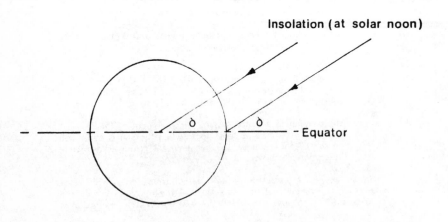

Figure 5.4   Angle of Declination

-34-

closest to the average for that month. A list of average days for each month and their day numbers is given in Table 5.2.

TABLE 5.2   Average Day for Each Month

Month	Day of Month	Day of Year	Month	Day of Month	Day of Year
January	17	17	July	17	198
February	16	47	August	16	228
March	16	75	September	15	258
April	15	105	October	15	288
May	15	135	November	14	318
June	11	162	December	10	344

An example of the use of equation 5.3 is given in Appendix 7.

5.5   Calculation of Daylength

The daylength N can be determined from the following equation (Duffie & Beckman (1980)):

$$N \quad = \quad 0.133 \cos^{-1}(-\tan \emptyset \tan \delta) \tag{5.4}$$

5.6   Radiation Absorption and Emission

The laws of electromagnetic radiation absorption and emission play an important part in collector performance. Before these laws can be properly considered some definitions are needed.

The absorptivity, α , of a surface can be defined as the fraction of incident radiation which is absorbed by the surface. Values for absorptivity range from zero for a perfectly reflecting surface, to unity for a blackbody.

A blackbody is a theoretical body which has the following properties:

(i)   it absorbs all radiation incident upon it,

(ii)   the level of radiation emitted from a blackbody is a function of temperature only.

For a blackbody exposed to a constant level of radiation, R, the amount of energy absorbed per unit of the blackbody, R_a, is given by:

$$R_a \quad = \quad \alpha_b.R \tag{5.5}$$

where α_b = absorptivity of a blackbody

By definition $\alpha_b = 1$
and hence $R_a = R$

Absorption of energy will cause the temperature of the body to rise, until at equilibrium the amount of radiation emitted, R_e, equals the amount of radiation absorbed, hence

$$R_e = R_a = R \qquad (5.5)$$

The emissivity, ε, of a body as a ratio of the radiation emitted by the body to the radiation which would be emitted by a blackbody at the same temperature. As for absorptivity values of emissivity range from zero to unity for a blackbody.

The rate at which energy is radiated from a blackbody is proportional to the fourth power of its absolute temperature T,

$$R_e = \sigma T^4 \qquad (5.7)$$

where σ = Stefan - Boltzmann constant, $5.67 . 10^{-8} W m^{-2} K^{-4}$

The rate at which energy is radiated from a non-blackbody is given by the equation:

$$R_e = \varepsilon \sigma T^4 \qquad (5.8)$$

Equation 5.8 shows clearly that the energy emitted from a body increases rapidly with its temperature.

The energy transfer R_t between two blackbodies at temperature T_1 and T_2, T_1 being the greater temperature, is given by:

$$R_t = \sigma (T_1^4 - T_2^4) \qquad (5.9)$$

For a non-blackbody at temperature T_1 and emissivity, ε, facing the sky at a (sky) temperature of T_s the nett energy radiated by the body is given by:

$$R_e = \varepsilon \sigma (T_1^4 - T_s^4) \qquad (5.10)$$

Whillier (1963) suggested a value of sky temperature as 10°F (5.5°C) below ambient temperature.

Consideration must be given to a further optical property of materials important in performance of flat plate collectors, this is the transmissivity, τ, of clear material used for the collector cover(s). This is defined as the fraction of the radiation incident upon a clear cover which is permitted to pass through the cover. The ideal cover will permit the passage of sunlight but not the longer infra-red wavelengths which are emitted by the absorber surface.

A more detailed discussion of these laws is given by Zemansky (1968).

6. SOLAR COLLECTORS

Solar collectors are employed to gain useful heat energy from the sun's radiation. They are almost invariably used to heat either air or water and may be either of the concentrating type or of the (non-concentrating) flat plate type. Concentrating collectors use a specially shaped focusing reflector thus increasing the intensity of radiation on the absorbing surface and can attain higher temperatures than flat plate collectors. For the purpose of crop drying, flat plate air heating collectors can provide the desired temperature elevation and are a more appropriate solution than the more complex concentrating collectors.

6.1   Flat Plate Solar Collectors

The basic components of flat plate solar collectors are an absorbing surface which receives insolation and an air duct, one side of which is formed by the absorber. Other elements which are frequently used in flat plate collectors are clear covers placed above the absorber to reduce heat loss from the absorber, and insulation as shown in Figure 6.1. For the many applications where a relatively high air flow is required a fan is used to blow air through the collector.

Although natural convection systems are widely used, very little detailed information is available about the air flow rate, temperature increase and overall efficiency for even the simplest natural convection flat plate solar air heater. However, Macedo and Altemani (1978) have investigated to some extent the relative performance of four natural convection collectors.

There are two stages in which the energy of the sun's radiation is transformed to thermal energy in the drying air. Firstly, the radiation must be absorbed on the absorber surface thus heating the absorber plate. This heat is then transferred to the air by contact between air and absorber plate. By viewing the solar collector in this way its design and performance in relation to ambient conditions can be appreciated.

6.2   Absorber Performance

There are several factors affecting the amount of energy absorbed by the absorber plate.

(i)   The level of insolation; clearly the higher the insolation, the greater the energy absorbed. For this reason some knowledge of typical insolation levels is needed for proper sizing of a collector. It must be borne in mind that isolation levels can vary considerably from place to place and at different times of year.

(ii)   The angle between incident insolation and the absorber plate surface. Ideally, the absorber plate should be perpendicular to the insolation. As the angle of insolation varies with time of day and throughout the year this ideal condition cannot always be satisfied. Methods of calculation for determining the direction of insolation have been reviewed already in Chapter 5. It should be noted that the angle subtended by the transparent cover is not important.

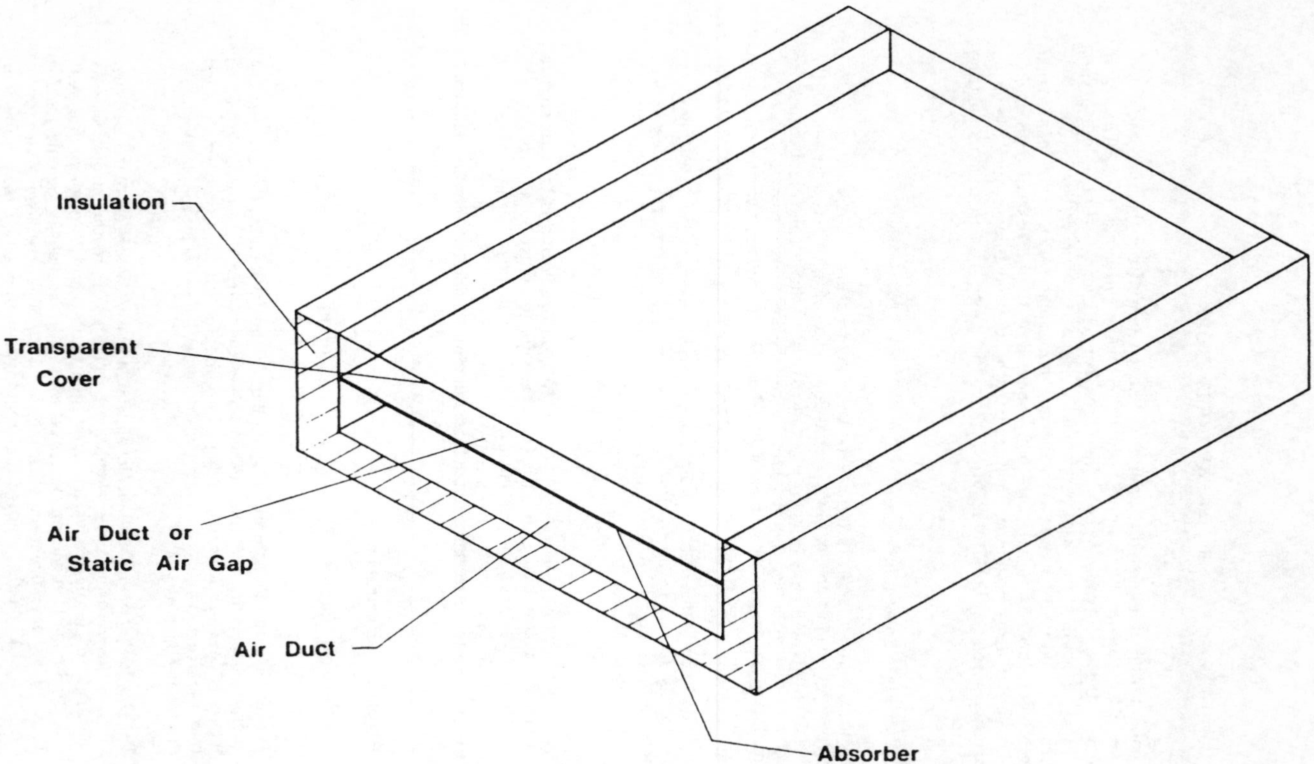

Figure 6.1   Schematic   Diagram   of   a   Solar   Collector

Insulation

Transparent
Cover

Air Duct or
Static Air Gap

Air Duct

Absorber

(iii)   The absorptivity of the absorber surface. The greater the absorptivity of the absorber surface the higher the proportion of incident radiation that will be absorbed.

(iv)   The transmissivity of the cover material (if a cover is used). Data for some commonly used materials are given in Table 6.1.

6.3   Heat Transfer from Absorber to Air

The rate at which the energy absorbed by the absorber is transferred to the air is controlled by the patter of air flow over, below or around the absorber plate. At low velocities, as in natural convection collectors, the air flow pattern will be laminar (stream line) resulting in poor heat transfer between the absorber plate and the air. As velocity increases (by using a fan) the air flow becomes more turbulent and heat transfer improves. Therefore for a high collection efficiency high volumetric flow rates in narrow ducts are best.

Volumetric flow rates and duct depth are limited by two factors. Firstly, high volumetric flow rates although giving good collection efficiency will also lead to low temperature increases, and secondly, high volume flow rates in narrow ducts will result in high pressure drops. Some guidelines to suitable air velocities are given later.

Collection efficiency is defined as the ratio of heat received by the drying air to the insolation upon the absorber surface and is calculated from the equation:

$$\eta_c \quad = \quad \frac{V.\rho.\Delta T.C_p}{A_c.I_c} \times 100 \ \% \qquad (6.1)$$

where V = volumetric flowrate of air ($m^3 \ s^{-1}$)

ρ = Air density (kg m^{-3})

ΔT = Air temperature elevation ($^\circ$C)

C_p = Air specific heat (J $kg^{-1} \ K^{-1}$)

A_c = Collector area (m^2)

I_c = Insolation on collector surface (W m^{-2})

It is important to note that equation 6.1 is a definition and as such should not be used to predict the performance of a collector. If a collector performs with a given efficiency under certain conditions this does not mean that it will perform with the same efficiency under different conditions.

Consideration must also be given to ways of limiting heat losses from the collector either by radiation from the absorber or heat loss to the surrounding air. Radiation of energy from the absorber can be limited either by using an absorber with a low emissivity or by using a cover which although transparent to

Table 6.1   Properties of Cover Materials

Material	Transmissivity % Light	Transmissivity % IR	Thickness mm	Weight per unit area kg m^{-2}	Maximum Operating Temperature °C	Durability/Weatherability
Polymethylmethacrylate	91	1	3.2	3.7	60-95	Outdoor longevity 10 – 20 yrs
Polycarbonate	84	6	3.2	3.8	121-123	Outdoor longevity 5 – 7 yrs
Poly Vinyl Fluoride Tedlar	91	43	0.1	0.14	108 177*	Not damaged by sunlight
FEP Teflon Suntek	96 95	13	0.05	0.1	205	Outdoor longevity 30 yrs
Fibre-reinforced polyester Sunlite Premium	83	6	0.1	1.5	93	Outdoor longevity 20 yrs Good shatter resistance
Polythene	86	77				1 year life
PVC Novolux	84	4	0.8			
Polyester Mylar	87	18	0.1			
PET	85		0.025	0.034	100*	
Float Glass	83	2	3.9	9.8		
Low Iron Glass	88	2	3.1	7.8		

* For short periods only

a large proportion of the sun's radiation, will not permit the longer wave radiation from the absorber to pass through. The air gap between the transparent cover and the absorber also acts as a barrier to heat loss from the absorber to ambient air by convection, especially if this air is static. Insulation around the collector also serves to minimize heat loss by convection and conduction.

6.4   Types of Flat Plate Collectors

The simplest type of flat plate collector for both natural and forced convection sytems is the bare plate collector as shown in Figure 6.2. This consists simply of an air duct, the uppermost surface of which acts as the absorber plate. This type of collector is widely used in crop drying operations and buildings having corrugated sheet roofs are frequently converted to collectors in this manner.

There are four principal variations of the single cover flat plate solar collector, mainly applicable for forced convection systems. These collectors vary in the path which the air takes when passing through the collector as also shown in Figure 6.2.

Where a single cover flat plate collector cannot provide the required air temperature rise, further covers may be added to decrease heat losses. Due to the higher temperatures in double and triple-covered collectors more insulation is required than for single cover and bare plate collectors and the air flow is invariably below the absorber plate to minimize heat loss to the surroundings.

One further type of flat plate collector worthy of mention is that with a porous, high surface area absorber (Macedo and Altemani (1978)). The absorber area of this type of collector is increased by inserting in the air space additional blackened metallic elements viz gauze, meshes, swarf or iron chippings. Absorbers of this type give intimate contact between the air and the absorber surface and hence good heat transfer.

6.5   Selection of Collector Type

The main factor governing the choice of solar collector type is the temperature increase required. Some general guidelines to this choice are as follows.

(i)   For temperature increases up to approximately 10°C a bare plate solar collector is most suitable due to its simplicity. Since heat losses from the absorber plate in bare plate collectors can be considerable it is especially important that there is good heat transfer between the absorber plate and the air in the duct. For this reason it is recommended that a higher air velocity is used for bare plate collectors than for covered plate collectors. For the former an air velocity of approximately 5 m s^{-1} is recommended (Peterson (1980)). The use of higher air velocities is limited as these will lead to higher pressure drops requiring more powerful fans.

(ii)   For a greater temperature rise it becomes necessary to limit heat losses from the absorber by the use of transparent covers. For temperature rises of up to approximately 35°C single cover collectors are more effective overall than double or triple covers.

Key:

Cover   Casing

Absorber Plate   ——→ Air Flow

Bare Plate

Single Front Pass

Single Back Pass

Double Pass

Parallel Pass
(or Covered Plate)

Figure 6.2   Principal Types of Flat
Plate Collectors

(Davidson , 1980)

These general temperature guidelines are given in an easily interpreted form in Figure 6.3. It should be noted that these guidelines are derived from research in North America and will vary from country depending on insolation levels and costs of fuel and materials.

The choice of which of the types of single cover collector to use is made on the basis that as the temperature difference between ambient and heated air increases the need to insulate the air duct becomes greater. At the lower end of this range the single cover front pass collector is suitable as it is the simplest of the single cover collectors. At the upper limit of this range the extra insulation of the static air gap above the absorber plate of the back pass collector provides the most efficient solution. The double pass and parallel pass collectors are more efficient than back pass collectors in the lower part of this range but become less efficient as the temperature elevation increases. Double and parallel pass collectors are more complex in their construction than the single pass collectors.

Air velocities for single or multiple cover collectors should be in the range from 2.5-5 m s^{-1}. At higher temperatures a double covered collector with flow below the absorber plate is the best solution. As the required temperature gain increases, the choice of material for the covers and the absorber becomes more critical. Extra covers not only decrease the heat losses due to convection but also decrease the amount of insolation incident on the absorber. The emissivity of the absorber and the infra-red transmissivity of the covers also have greater effect as the temperature of the absorber increases. The mechanical properties of construction materials at the elevated temperatures encountered, especially if plastic sheet is to be used as an inner cover, must also be considered as must the durability of plastics at these temperatures.

Additionally, factors such as the availability of and cost of materials and how the proposed collector fits in with available space must be considered. If the collector is to be part of an existing structure then this also will affect which type of collector is to be built.

6.6   Prediction of Collector Performance

Considerable research has been carried out on forced convection solar collectors and some researchers have developed empirical equations based on principles of heat transfer.

As part of his work on grain drying Buelow (1961) developed empirical equations for predicting the temperature rise for bare plate collectors and also for parallel pass single cover collectors.

These equations are:

(i)   for the bare plate collector

$$\Delta T = 0.019\ I_c\ (1 - \exp(-0.041/V_c)) \qquad (6.2)$$

Figure 6.3   Recommended Collector Type for various temperature elevations

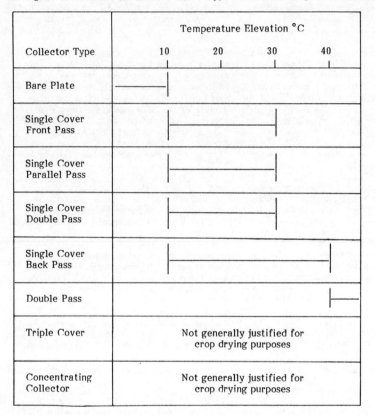

NB   This chart should only be used as a general guideline

(ii)   for the single cover parallel pass collector

$$\Delta T = 0.064 \, I_c \, (1 - \exp(0.011/V_c)) \qquad (6.3)$$

where V_c = Volumetric flow rate divided by collector area (m s^{-1})

These equations are represented graphically in Figure 6.4. By combining these equations with the equation for calculating efficiency of a collector (Equation 6.1) predictions of collector efficiency can be made. It should be noted that equations 6.2 and 6.3 are only strictly valid for the range of air flow rates investigated by Buelow. Another equation which can be used to predict collection efficiency is that proposed by Whillier (1964). This equation is based on the same theoretical principles as Buelow's equation but is rather more flexible and does make allowance for varying absorber emissivity and heat losses; unfortunately it is also somewhat more complicated than Buelow's equations.

Whillier's equation is:

$$\eta_c = \frac{1}{(1 + U_L/h)} (1 - \exp(-U_o/G_a C_p)) \cdot \frac{G_a \cdot C_p}{U_o} \cdot f_{ca} \qquad (6.4)$$

where U_L = collector heat loss coefficient (W m^{-2}K^{-1})
      h = heat transfer coefficient between absorber plate and flowing air (W m^{-2}K^{-1})
      U_o = overall heat transfer coefficient (W m^{-2}K^{-1})
      G_a = mass flow rate per unit collector area (kg s^{-1} m^{-2})
      f_{ca} = effective transmissivity absorptivity product of cover and absorber ($f = \tau\alpha$)

The data required to use this equation are provided in Tables 6.2, 6.3 and 6.4.

The equation

$$Nu = 0.02 \, Re^{0.8} \qquad (6.5)$$

where Nu = $\dfrac{hL}{k}$

      Re = $\dfrac{v \cdot \rho \cdot L}{\mu}$

      h = heat transfer coefficient (W m^{-2} K^{-1})

      L = characteristic dimension (m)

      k = air thermal conductivity (W m^{-1} K^{-1})

      v = air velocity (m s^{-1})

      ρ = air density (kg m^{-3})

      μ = air viscosity (kg m^{-1}s^{-1})

can be used to calculate values of the heat transfer coefficient between the absorber plate and flowing air, h.

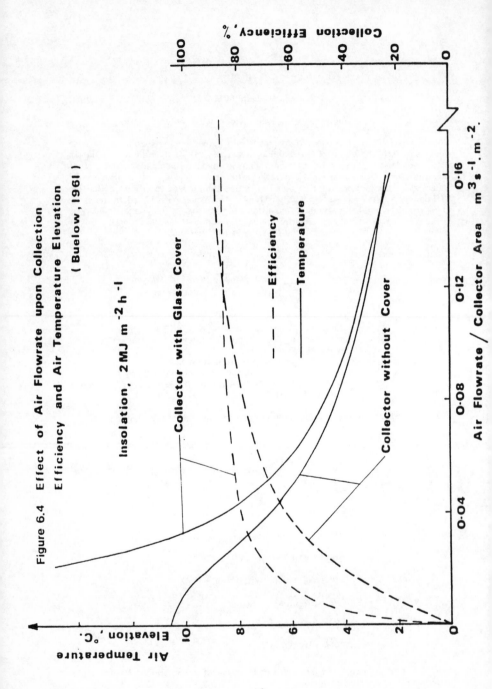

Figure 6.4 Effect of Air Flowrate upon Collection Efficiency and Air Temperature Elevation (Buelow, 1961)

- 46 -

Table 6.2   Data for prediction of collector performance (Whillier, (1964))

	f_{ca}	U_L	U_o	U_o/GC_p
No cover	0.9	22.2	11.2	0.274
Single cover glass (k = 0.2)	0.88	6.99	5.3	0.131
Single cover glass (k = 0.6)	0.83	6.99	5.3	0.131
Single Tedlar cover	0.82	8.12	6.0	0.146
Double cover glass (k = 0.2)	0.78	4.43	3.7	0.91
Double cover glass (k = 0.6)	0.74	4.43	3.7	0.091
Double cover One glass (k = 0.2) over 1 Tedlar	0.79	5.25	4.3	0.103
Double cover Tedlar	0.84	5.44	4.4	0.107

The assumptions have been made in determining these values are:

(i)   Air flow rate = 40.8 x 10^{-3} kg m^{-2}s^{-1},

(ii)   Heat transfer coefficient h = 22.7 W m^{-2}K^{-1},

(iii)   Rear and edge heat losses are 10% of upward heat loss,

(iv)   Glass thickness = 2.5 mm, Tedlar thickness = 0.1 mm,

(v)   Absorptivity of absorber = 0.95,

(vi) f_{ca} is taken as 0.85 of the effective transmissivity-absorptivity product at normal incidence,

(vii)   Sky temperature taken as approximately 5°C below ambient, wind speed 5mph (2.2 m s^{-1}).

The values above are a specific air mass flow rate and heat transfer coefficients. To obtain efficiencies for different mass flow rates and heat transfer coefficients, the correction factors given in Tables 6.3 and 6.4 should be used.

Table 6.3   Correction Factors for Varying Air Flow Rates (Whillier (1964))

To obtain the corrected value of efficiency, multiply the efficiency as determined from equation 6.4 by the correction factors as below:

Air flow rate G. 10^{-3} kg m^{-2} s^{-1}	1.36	6.80	13.6	40.8	68.0	136
No cover	0.14	0.57	0.78	1.00	1.06	1.10
One cover	0.26	0.73	0.88	1.00	1.03	1.05
Two covers	0.34	0.79	0.91	1.00	1.02	1.03
Three covers	0.42	0.84	0.93	1.00	1.01	1.02

Table 6.4   Correction Factors for Varying Heat Transfer Coefficients (Whillier (1964))

To obtain the corrected value of efficiency, multiply the efficiency as determined from equation 6.4 by the correction factors as below:

Heat transfer coefficient, h $W m^{-2} K^{-1}$	11.4	22.7	34.1	45.4	68.2	90.9
No cover	0.67	1.00	1.20	1.33	1.49	1.59
One cover	0.80	1.00	1.09	1.14	1.20	1.23
Two covers	0.85	1.00	1.06	1.10	1.13	1.15
Three covers	0.88	1.00	1.04	1.07	1.10	1.11

6.7 Collector Orientation and Slope

The insolation on any collector, no matter what its slope or orientation, will vary over the period during which it is used. Consequently the heat output of the collector will also vary. Since the designer must match the heat output of the (fixed) collector to the drying load the question arises what value or level of insolation to use when determining the size of the collector. Whatever value is selected, it is obviously a compromise between an excessively large collector on the one hand and the risk of not generating enough heat on the other. Optimum values can be determined, but these involve quite complicated mathematical procedures and are, to some extent, site specific. In the absence of full analytical facilities, a good rule of thumb is to design for the peak of the harvest season. Whilst this will in some instances give an oversized collector for a large part of the season, it does ensure that sufficient energy is available when it is most needed. The collector is designed such that it is perpendicular to the insolation at solar noon on the day selected as representing the peak of the harvest. Depending on the time of year and location, the collector should, ideally, face either directly South or directly North.

Using the sign convention given in Section 5 the angle of slope is given by:

$$\beta = (\phi - \delta) \qquad\qquad (6.6)$$

The declination angle δ can be found either from equation 5.2 or from Figure 6.5. A positive value of β means that the collector should be South facing and a negative value that it should be North facing. Table 6.5 provides an example of the calculation of slope angle for collection at two African locations. It should be noted that when using equation 5.3 to calculate the angle of incidence only the magnitude (modulus) of angle β (from equation 6.6) is used.

In many cases due to local constraints it will not be possible to adhere exactly to direct North or direct South facing requirements. This will affect the level of insolation on the collecter, I_s, which as stated previously varies through the season. To show the general effect of slight changes in orientation, Table 6.6 and 6.7 have been computed using equation 5.3.

Table 6.6 shows data for a South facing collector at a latitude of 25°N for use over a drying season lasting from the beginning of February to the end of June. The optimum slops of the collector is 16°; selected such that insolation is perpendicular to the collector surface at solar noon on April 15, the middle of the drying season. Insolation upon a horizontal surface is assumed to remain constant over the drying season. The level of insolation upon the collector on April 15 is given a nominal value of 100 and used as a basis of comparison with the insolation level upon the surface at other times (February 15 and June 15) and also with insolation levels upon surfaces of identical slope but with different orientation. Table 6.7 show similar data for a North facing collector on the Equator for use over the same drying season. In this situation the optimum collector slope is 9°.

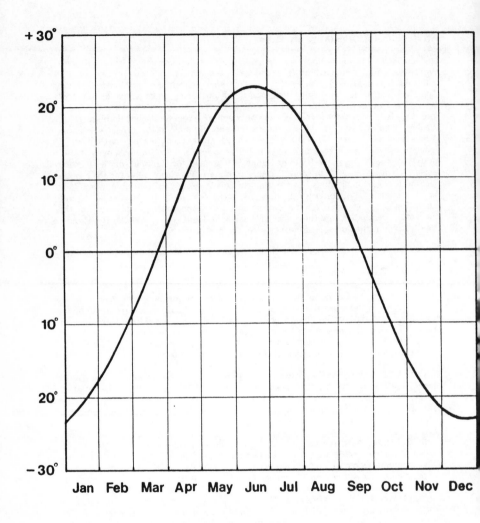

Figure 6.5   Monthly Variation of Angle of Declination

Table 6.5: Examples of the Determination of Slope Angle

Location	Latitude ø	Time of peak harvest	Declination	Slope	Facing Direction
Khartoum	+15	Mid April	+10	+5	South
		Mid October	-10	+25	South
Lusaka	-15	Mid April	+10	-25	North
		Mid October	-10	-5	North

Table 6.6: Surface Insolation Levels for a South Facing Collector at a Latitude of 25°N

Collector Slope = 16°

Date	Orientation (surface azimuth angle)	Relative level of insolation
Feb 15	0	113.6
	± 15	112.8
	± 30	110.7
	± 45	107.4
April 15	0	100
	± 15	99.7
	± 30	99.0
	± 45	97.8
June 15	0	93.4
	± 15	93.3
	± 30	93.3
	± 45	93.1

Table 6.7: **Surface Insolation Levels for a North Facing Collector on the Equator**

Collector Slope = 9°

Date	Orientation (surface azimuth angle)	Relative level of insolation
Feb 15	180	93.8
	± 165	93.9
	± 150	94.3
	± 135	94.9
April 15	180	100
	± 165	100
	± 150	99.7
	± 135	99.2
June 15	180	104.1
	± 165	103.9
	± 150	103.2
	± 135	102.1

The following points emerge from Tables 6.6 and 67. Firstly it is perhaps surprising that relatively large changes in orientation have little effect upon I_s, the difference is rarely more than 5% for a change in orientation of $\pm$ 45°; secondly, I_s can be greater at other times of drying season (eg February 15 in Table 6.6) than at the day upon which the determination of collector slope is based; and thirdly, there are situations where the sun moves from a position North of a North facing collector to a position South (or vice versa) of the collector during the drying season, deviation in collector orientation will actually increase I_s (eg February 15 in Table 6.7).

Similar calculations to those performed for Tables 6.6 and 6.7 can be carried out for various slopes. Such calculations would show two main points: firstly, that small deviations ($\pm$ 5°) in collector slope do not have a great effect on the level of insolation on the collector surface, and secondly, that as slope increases so does the effect of incorrect orientation.

A final point worth noting is that all values given in Table 6.6 and 6.7 are mid-day values and do not give any indication of how insolation would vary over each day. The orientation of the collecter will affect the distribution of insolation over the day, the most even distribution will be given by a North or South facing collector.

An example of the design of a collector is presented in Appendix 9.

6.8   Clear Cover Materials

Desirable properties of clear covers are:-

(i)   high transmissivity in the visible range of the spectrum,
(ii)   low transmissivity of infra-red radiation,
(iii)   stability at the operating temperature. All materials used must be able to
        withstand the temperatures attained under stagnation conditions, ie on a
        hot sunny day when no air is flowing through the collector,
(iv)   durability of weatherability,
(v)   strength and resistance to breakage,
(vi)   low cost,
(vii)   low weight per unit area.

Glass is the traditional clear cover and has good transmissivity for visible radiation and is virtually opaque to infra-red radiation. Glass is also stable at the temperatures encountered and durable. The disadvantages of glass are its low shatter resistance, high cost and weight which increases the cost of the supporting structure.

The use of plastic sheet has in the past been limited by the poor weatherability and stability of plastics in the conditions found in solar collectors. However, plastics have recently been developed which overcome these problems, examples of these are polyvinylfluoride films (PVF) such as Tedlar, fibre reinforced polyester (Kalwall, Sun Lite Premium), acrylic and polycarbonate sheets which are either intrinsically stable to UV radiation or have been made stable by use of additives. Plastic covers weight as little as 10% of the weight of glass covers, for example, 1 m^2 of PVF sheet of thickness 1 mm weighs less than 3 kg compared to over 30 kg for a 5 mm thick glass sheet of the same area. Other materials such as acrylic and polycarbonate sheet of the same thickness as glass sheet weigh about half as much as glass for the same area. Plastics also have the advantage of easier installation than glass especially when available in thin film form.

6.9 Absorber Materials

Desirable properties for the absorbers in solar collectors are:

(i)   high absorptivity of incident radiation,
(ii)   low emissivity,
(iii) good thermal conductivity in the case where air flow is below the absorber,
(iv)   stability at the temperatures encountered during operation and under stagnation conditions,
(v)   durability,
(vi)   low cost,
(vii) low weight per unit area.

In collectors where the absorbing medium is of a porous nature it is also desirable that the absorber gives little resistance to the passage of air.

One of the more commonly used absorbers is black-painted metal sheet, frequently this is corrugated galvanized iron. This has the advantages in most places of being readily available, relatively cheap and easy to use. Other suitable absorbers are black plastic sheet, painted rocks, ash and charcoal.

In the rare cases for drying purposes, when the required temperature elevation exceeds $40°C$ the use of selective absorbers becomes more attractive. Selective absorbers are materials which have a high absorptivity but a low emissivity of long-wave radiation ie infra-red, much more so than materials like black paint. Values of absorptivity and emissivity of some absorber materials are given in Table 6:8. From the Stefan-Boltzmann equation for radiation from a hot body it can be seen how absorber emissivity becomes more important as temperature increases. Information on selective absorbers can be found in papers by Christie (1970), Keller (1970), McQueen at al (1980) Nahar and Garg (1981) and Ramakrishna Rao et al (1978).

Table 6.8   Properties of Surface Coatings

Coating	Substrate	Absorptivity	Emissivity	Max Temp.	Durability
Black Nickel	Iron, Copper, Zinc/Aluminium,	0.85–0.96	0.05–0.15	288°C	medium
Black Chrome	Nickel/Aluminium, Copper, Iron	0.82–0.96	0.04–0.15	427°C	very good
Black Copper	Copper	0.85–0.95	0.10–0.15	316°C	
Copper Oxide	Copper Iron, Aluminium	0.87–0.9	0.08–0.16		
Anodic Aluminium	Aluminium	0.90–0.96	0.10–0.23		
Metal Carbide	Copper, Glass	0.82–0.93	0.02–0.05		
PbS Paint	Any	0.90	0.30		
Selective Paint (Coralur)	Most	0.93	0.30		
Black Paint	Any	0.95–0.97	0.95–0.97		

7. SOLAR DRYER CLASSIFICATION

TDRI have found it appropriate to classify solar dryers based upon the following criteria:

(i)   whether or not the drying commodity is exposed to insolation,

(ii)   the mode of air flow through the dryer,

(iii)   the temperature of the air circulated to the drying chamber.

7.1   Exposure to Insolation

Based upon this criteria solar dryers can be termed either <u>direct</u> or <u>indirect</u>. Direct dryers are termed those in which the crop is exposed to the sun and indirect dryers those in which the crop is placed in enclosed drying chambers and thereby shielded from insolation. In direct dryers heat transfer to the drying crop is by convection and radiation and therefore the rate of drying can be greater than for indirect dryers. For dates, exposure to sunlight is considered essential for the required colour development in the dried product, and for arabica coffee in Kenya a period of exposure to sunlight is deemed sacrosanct for the development of full flavour in the roasted bean. On the other hand with some fruits the ascorbic acid (Vitamin C) content of the dried product is considerably reduced by exposure to sunlight and colour retention in some highly pigmented commodities can also be adversely affected if they are dried in the sun.

7.2   Mode of Air Flow

There are two possible modes of air flow, <u>natural</u> convection or <u>forced</u> convection. The former is reliant upon thermally induced density gradients for the flow of air through the dryer whereas for forced convection dryers the air flow is dependent upon pressure differentials generated by a fan. The latter is obviously capable of providing a much greater air flow and therefore suitable, if not essential, for dryers with large throughputs. Another advantage of forced convection dryers is that the air flow is independent of ambient climatic conditions and is easily and accurately controllable for most applications. Forced convection is essential for the drying of deep beds of grain wherein the relatively high pressure drops through the depth of the grain bed would preclude the use of natural convection. A further advantage of forced convection dryers is that their high air flows and therefore the high velocities through flat plate solar collectors are, as noted in the previous section, conducive to high collector efficiencies.

However, forced convection dryers possess one basic shortcoming; they require a source of motive power for the operation of the fan except in those rare cases where wind power or photo-voltaic power generation is a feasible proposition. In many areas in African countries such sources of power are rarely available or, at best, unreliable and expensive. The capital cost of equipment necessary to provide forced convection is high compared with the minimal costs for natural convection dryers. Scarce foreign exchange is often needed to pay for the fans and the source of motive power. Additionally, the running costs of forced convection dryers, namely those of power and mechanical maintenance and repair, and the difficulties in obtaining such spare parts as are necessary are other potential disadvantages to the application of forced convection solar dryers in rural areas.

7.3 Circulated Air Temperature

The air entering the drying chamber of a solar dryer can either be at the ambient temperature or at some higher temperature; the elevation in temperature of the air being achieved by its passage through a solar collector prior to the drying chamber. Dryers that employ a separate solar collector and drying chamber have an inherent tendency towards greater efficiency as both units can be designed for optimum efficiency of their respective functions. Conversely, dryers in which the collector and the drying chamber are combined are invariably a compromise. However, a dryer with a separate collector and drying chamber can be a relatively elaborate structure whereas the combined collector and drying chamber can be relatively simple and compact.

7.4 Selection of Dryer Type

Since two basic choices exist for each of these three criteria of classification, it could be supposed that there are eight different types of dryer. However, some of these have proved impractical and of the remainder, three have received the most attention to date from active researchers. These three types are:

(i)   direct dryers employing natural convection with a combined solar collector and drying chamber,

(ii)   direct dryers employing natural convection with separate collector and drying chamber,

(iii)   indirect dryers employing forced convection with separate collector and drying chamber,

However, there are indications that another type of dryer has been investigated in very recent times. This is the indirect dryer employing natural convection with separate collector and drying chamber. An example of this type of dryer as researched in Kenya for the drying of maize (Othieno et al (1981)) is shown in Figure 7.1. However, it is not yet possible to classify this type of dryer as of major importance, comparable with the three types classified above, although this situation may well change in the near future.

Information on this (fourth) dryer type can be obtained from the literature classified as Appendix 11 which also includes references to other dryer types and the commodity groups investigated.

Each of the three principal dryer types will be discussed in subsequent Chapters.

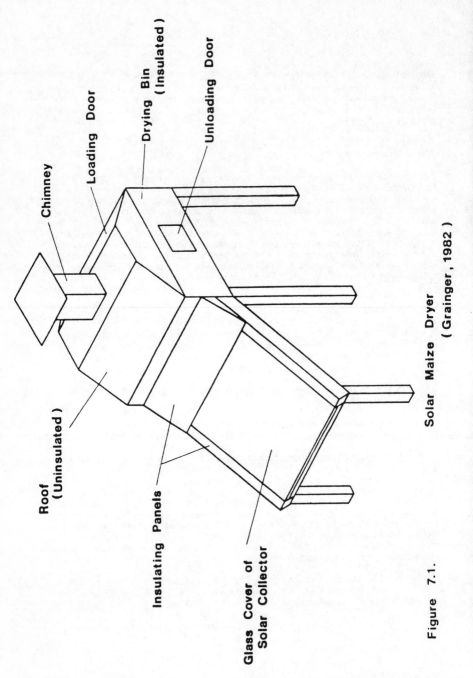

Figure 7.1.

Solar Maize Dryer
(Grainger, 1982)

- 58 -

7.5   Hybrid Dryers

This term is used to denote those dryers in which another form of heating the drying air is used in conjunction with solar heating. Such a system can be used in two ways.   Firstly, solar heating can be the principal source of energy during sunny daylight hours with additional heat, supplied by electricity, solid fuel etc. being used during inclement weather or in some cases at night to maintain continuous drying. Secondly, conventional energy sources are used as the main means of heating the drying air and solar energy is used as a supplement to reduce fuel costs.   The latter system has been extensively researched, particularly in the grain growing areas of the USA.

8. DIRECT DRYERS EMPLOYING NATURAL CONVECTION WITH COMBINED COLLECTOR AND DRYING CHAMBER

8.1 Cabinet Dryer

Within this classification, several variations have been developed. Probably the most widely known variation is the cabinet dryer as pioneered by the Canadian Brace Research Institute (Anon (1965)) and shown in Figure 8.1. Essentially, the basic design consists of a rectangular container, preferably insulated, and covered with a roof of glass or clear plastic. There are holes in the base and the upper parts of the cabinet and rear panels. The interior of the cabinet is blackened to act as a solar absorber. Perforated drying trays are positioned within the cabinet with access to the trays through doors forming the bottom part of the rear of the cabinet.

The operating principle of the cabinet dryer is that insolation passes through the clear cover and is absorbed on the blackened interior surfaces which are thereby heated and subsequently warm the air within the cabinet. The warmed air rises by natural convection and passes through the drying trays and out of the cabinet via the upper holes whilst fresh air enters through the holes in the base.

It is recommended that the length of the cabinet be three times its width to minimize the shading effect of the sides. In any situation the roof should be angled sufficiently to allow water to run off in rainy periods. For portable models the cabinet may be constructed of wood, board or metal for the more sophisticated units and material such as wicker or basket work for more rudimentary models. For permanent (and larger) structures mud, brick, stone or even concrete could be used. The insulation for the base and sides can be wood shavings, sawdust, bagasse, coconut fibre, dried grass or leaves. It is recommended that the insulating layer should be at least 50 mm thick for maximum internal temperatures. Great care must be taken that the insulation material is effectively sealed in place to prevent the ingress of moisture and insects and suchlike. Where insect infestation is troublesome all air holes in the cabinet can be covered with gauze or mosquito netting if these are cheaply available. The drying trays can be constructed of plastic mesh or netting, or even of wicker and basket work, but preferably not metal since this may adversely react with the juices from fruit or vegetable slices. The temperature within the cabinet is regulated by the inlet or outlet holes and by the degree of opening of the access doors.

McDowell (1973) working in Jamaica carried out a considerably amount of work on the development of the cabinet dryer for a large number of tropical crops. His basic dryer is made of clay bricks, mud and wattle or locally produced compressed bricks of earth and cement as shown in Figure 8.2. Plastic sheet is used for the cabinet cover. The entry of air to the bottom of the cabinet is by means of a length of bamboo with regularly spaced holes placed at intervals across the width of the dryer. Air outlet ports are made by leaving gaps in the top layer of bricks. Charcoal fines mixed with clay is an alternative to paint for blackening the interior of the cabinet. Probably the two most important aspects of McDowell's work were the introduction of a means of extending the drying time in inclement weather or at the end of the day, and a method of shading the drying crop or foodstuff from direct exposure to sunlight.

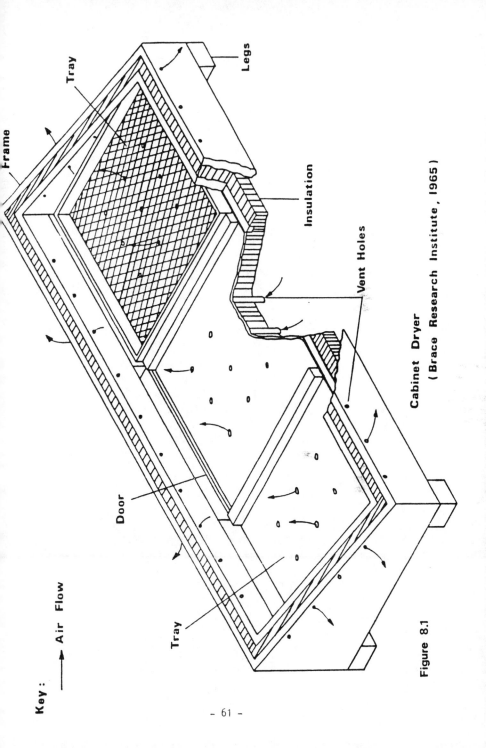

Key:
Air Flow

Frame

Tray

Legs

Insulation

Vent Holes

Door

Tray

Cabinet Dryer
(Brace Research Institute , 1965)

Figure 8.1

- 61 -

N.B. Cabinet Cover Not Shown

Inside of Walls Painted
With Charcoal/Clay Mixture

Bamboo 'Pipes'

Air Distribution Holes

Air Outlets

Brick Walls

Air Inlet

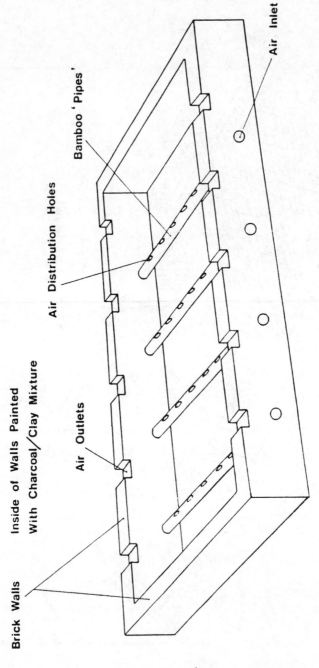

Figure 8.2   Solar Cabinet Dryer. (McDowell, 1973)

The first improvement was by placing a layer of dark-coloured or black-painted stones in the bottom of the dryer which acted as a simple heat store. The second development was the introduction of a black cover (under the clear cover) to reduce loss of colour, vitamin and nutrient loss as a result of direct exposure to sunlight. McDowell used a metal sheet and reported that the air temperatures within the shaded cabinet were similar to those attained under conventional operation. Gomez (1981) used black plastic sheet instead of metal and reported significant improvement in carotene retention of green leafy vegetables compared with those dried exposed to the sun.

Informative results on the use of the cabinet dryer have also been obtained by the following: Bhatia and Gupta (1976) on the drying of apricots in India; Anon (1981) describing the drying of chillies in India; Clark (1981) on the drying and processing of coconut and vegetables in Bangladesh; Kapoor and Agrawal (1973) again in India on the drying of fruit and vegetables; Lawand (1966) also on fruit and vegetable drying but in Syria; Nahwali (1966) on the drying of yams in Barbados; Patterson and Perez (1981) on the development of a dryer using waste materials in the USA.

8.2   Tent Dryer

The second popular version of this type of dryer is the tent dryer originally developed for use with fish at Cox's Bazaar in Bangladesh, (Doe et al (1977).) A sketch of the prototype is shown as Figure 8.3. Essentially, it consists of a ridge tent-like framework covered with clear plastic sheet on the ends and the side facing the sun and black plastic sheet on the side in the shade and on the ground within the tent. The drying rack is positioned centrally along the full length of the tent. The plastic sheet at one end is arranged so as to allow access to the rack as required, but otherwise is fastened shut. The bottom edge of the side of clear plastic is rolled around a bamboo pole which when raised or lowered forms a method of controlling the air flow through and the temperature within the tent. Holes in the apex of both ends permit the venting of the exhaust air.

Fish are particularly susceptible to microbial spoilage and infestation and reduction of drying time is of lesser importance compared with improving quality and reducing losses. In the initial work in Bangladesh drying time was reduced by 25% and the product was larvae-free whereas sun dried fish were heavily infested. It was also found that the tent dryer can be used to disinfest sun dried fish heavily contaminated with larvae. A technically important point emerged in that the optimum method of operation would be two days in the sun for initial drying followed by drying in the solar tent until considered dry since the initial rates of sun drying are commensurate with those of drying in the tent.

The tent dryer has been used for drying fish by Richards (1976) and Anedelina (1978) in Papua New Guinea, and by Pablo (1978) in the Philippines where he also observed a much higher quality product with increased storage life. Pablo also successfully dried fruit in such a dryer.

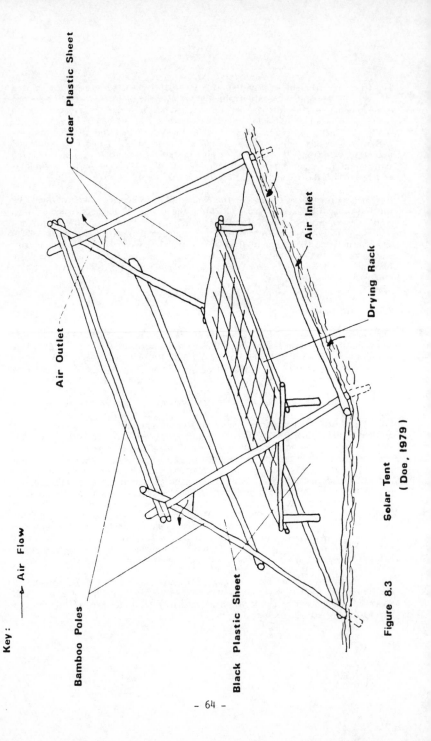

Key: Air Flow

Clear Plastic Sheet

Air Outlet

Air Inlet

Drying Rack

Bamboo Poles

Black Plastic Sheet

Figure 8.3   Solar Tent
(Doe , 1979)

- 64 -

Trim and Curran (1983) used a slightly modified tent for drying fish on the Galapagos Islands of Ecuador. The black plastic sheet on one side was replaced by clear plastic and the drying rack was moved from the centre to along one side. The fish dried in the tent were considered of excellent quality with lower moisture content, and less infestation and dust contamination than sun dried fish. It was also considered that overall, ie, taking into account performance, capital and production costs, the tent dryer was a better proposition for the artisanal fishermen than either the chimney dryer or the cabinet dryer.

The advantages of the tent dryer are its simplicity both of construction and operation and its low cost. The main disadvantage is its susceptibility to damage in windy conditions.

9. DIRECT DRYERS EMPLOYING NATURAL CONVECTION WITH SEPARATE COLLECTOR AND DRYING CHAMBER

9.1   Chimney Dryer

Considerable research on the design and application of the chimney dryer has been carried out at the Asian Institute of Technology at Bangkok in Thailand, (Exell and Kornsakoo (1977), Exell et al (1979), Exell (1980) and Boothumjinda et al (1983)). A sketch of the dryer is shown as Figure 9.1.

The solar collector uses a layer of burnt rice husks or black plastic sheet for the absorber which is covered by clear plastic sheet on an inclined bamboo framework. The drying chamber is a shallow wooden box with a base of either perforated metal or bamboo matting. Loading of the dryer is accomplished through removable panels at the back of the drying chamber. The purpose of the 'chimney' on top of the drying chamber is to provide a column of warm air to increase the draught and hence the flow of air through the dryer. It is made, in the simplest cases, of a bamboo frame covered with black plastic sheet acting as an absorber. The design and sizing of the chimney has been described by Exell (1980); the theory is applied in Appendix 12.

This dryer has been used in field trials to dry one tonne batches of wet paddy. Such a dryer required a collector of approximately $32m^2$ (4.5m x 7m) and a drying chamber of $7m^2$ (1m x 7m). It has been found possible to dry paddy from 20%* to 13% in one or two days except during periods of extended rain. As well as a great saving in drying time and inconvenience to the farmer the quality of the dried grain was much improved; the head yield, i.e. the fraction of uncracked grains after milling, was over 50% but was usually below 40% in paddy that had been sun dried. Germination of solar dried paddy was reported as excellent (Boothumjinda et al (1983)). In the field trials it was found that a dryer could be constructed by 6 men in 3 days at a material cost of just over US$ 100 excluding the bamboo poles which in Thailand can usually be obtained 'free' on the farm.

Costwise, it was estimated that the 'break-even' point could be reached after several batches had been dried. Other agricultural products, eg bananas, fish, peanuts, chillies and fruit pastes were successfully dried during the paddy off-season.

The potential shortcomings of this chimney dryer are its relatively high profile which can pose stability problems in windy conditions and the fact that its surface area is entirely composed of plastic sheet and its replacement can be a relatively expensive undertaking. There has also been some reaction from potential users in that the dryer should be modified in order that it can be dismantled and stored away after use. This, in practice, would prove difficult since removing and replacing the plastic sheet without tearing or holing it would not be an easy task.

---

*   All moisture contents quoted in the text are on a wet weight basis.

Key:

→ Air Flow

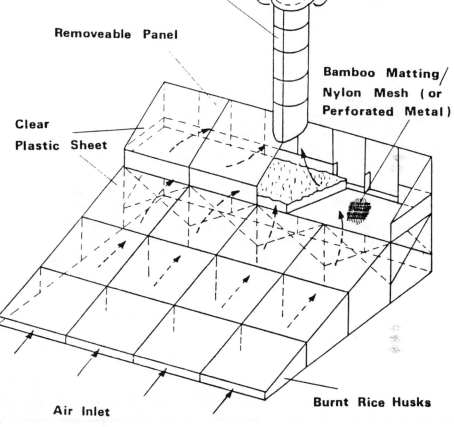

Chimney

Air Outlet

Removeable Panel

Bamboo Matting/ Nylon Mesh (or Perforated Metal)

Clear Plastic Sheet

Air Inlet

Burnt Rice Husks

Figure 9.1   Solar   Chimney   Dryer

(Exell , 1980)

A simpler and smaller version of the 'chimney' dryer, as shown in Figure 9.2, has been developed by the same researchers in Thailand (Exell and Kornsakoo (1979).) It is built over an inclined mound of earth and the collector is a layer of burnt rice husks covered by a clear plastic cover. The collector entrance faces the prevailing wind. The drying chamber has a base of mosquito netting supported by a wooden lattice. As with the chimney dryer, all the sides of the drying chamber are of clear plastic but more importantly the roof is of black plastic to avoid overheating the uppermost layers of paddy thus reducing the tendency for cracking.

9.2   Other Applications

This type of dryer has created some interest in the USA, (Williams (1980), Van Dresser (1979)). A design produced in New Mexico in the USA (Anon (1978)) is shown in Figure 9.3. The collector is made of black corrugated metal, a very common absorber material, under a sheet of clear fibreglass. In contrast with other dryers of this type, only the front of the drying chamber is of fibreglass and the sides and the back are of wooden construction. The drying chamber contains a tier of perforated trays. Fruit, vegetables, herbs, fruit purees and even meat have been successfully dried in this dryer.

Other applications of this type of dryer have been reported; Cheema and Riberio (1978) on bananas in Brazil, Gutierrez et al (1979) on grapes (raisins) in Chile; Ismail et al (1982) on marine products in Malaysia; Martosudirjo et al, (1979) on onions in Indonesia; Moy, et al (1980) on taro in the USA, and Pablo (1980) on fruit and fish in the Philippines.

Key:

Air Flow ———▶

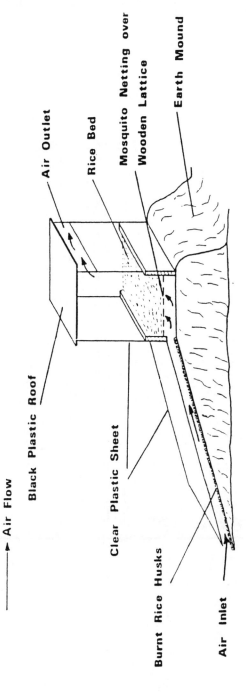

Air Outlet

Rice Bed

Mosquito Netting over
Wooden Lattice

Earth Mound

Black Plastic Roof

Clear Plastic Sheet

Burnt Rice Husks

Air Inlet

Figure 9.2   Solar Paddy Dryer
(Exell & Kornsakoo, 1978)

Key:

 Air Flow

Vent

Air Out

Plywood used for
Body of Dryer

Do

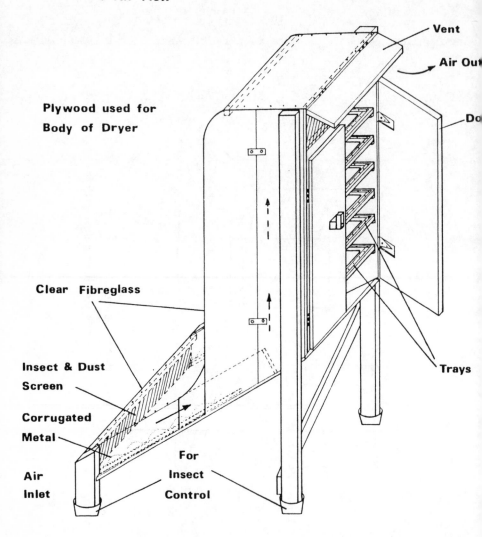

Clear Fibreglass

Insect & Dust
Screen

Corrugated
Metal

Air
Inlet

For

Insect

Control

Trays

Figure 9.3   (New Mexico Solar Energy Association
1978)

10. INDIRECT DRYERS EMPLOYING FORCED CONVECTION WITH SEPARATE COLLECTOR AND DRYING CHAMBER

10.1   Modification of Existing Dryers and Stores

This design of dryer can be considered simply as a solar collector, usually of a flat plate type, and a drying chamber, with a fan moving air from the collector to the drying chamber. It has been used primarily for the drying of grain, particularly in the cool but dry autumns of the grain-growing areas in North America but also in the warm but humid climate of Asia. Compared with the more basic natural convection systems this type of dryer is more capital intensive, particularly attributable to the fan, and tends to be more suitable for larger throughputs.

Results from the work carried out in North America are not directly applicable to most situations in Africa, but the principles of operation are common to both areas. In North America the solar dryer was made by modifying an existing grain storage silo or (ambient air) drying buildings by adapting the walls or roof as a solar collector. As well as the work by Buelow (1961), leading to a dryer as shown in Figure 10.1, studies reported by Davis and Lipper (1961), Foster and Peart (1976), Peterson (1973) and Wrubleski and Catania (1978) are of general interest.

10.2   Use of Plastic Collectors

An interesting development of this type of dryer is the substitution of a metal/wood collector with one of plastic as reported by Foster and Peart (1976) and Williams et al (1976). In the simplest form, the collector consists of a clear polythene cover on a triangular wire frame with black polyethylene film forming the floor and acting as the solar absorber. Air is drawn through the collector by a fan mounted next to the drying bin. A second version has an inflated black plastic absorber inside a semi-cylindrical plastic film enclosure. A third plastic collector employs two inflated tubes: a black absorber tube inside a slightly larger diameter clear plastic tube. The tubes are inflated by blowing the air through the collector, using a fan at the end of the tubes furthest from the drying bin. Bolin et al (1980) have also reported on the use of such a system for drying apricots, raisins and prunes. A 24m long collector of 1m diameter was used to dry 36 kg of fresh grapes with an air flow of 2.2m^{3}s^{-1}, over 80% of which was recirculated. A 0.75 kW fan was used. Prunes were almost dry after 3 days, and raisins were dried in 5 days compared with up to 14 days for conventional sun drying.

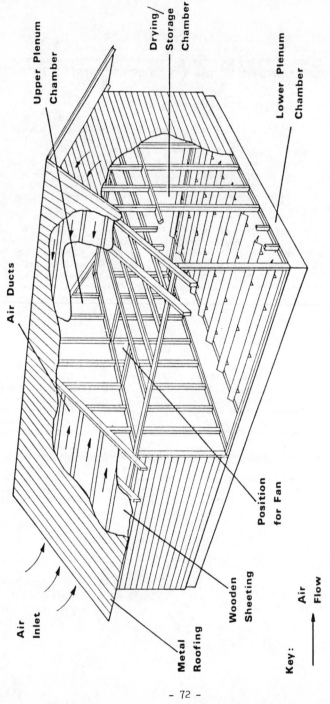

Figure 10.1   Solar Grain Dryer (Buelow, 1961)

Upper Plenum Chamber

Drying/Storage Chamber

Lower Plenum Chamber

Air Ducts

Position for Fan

Air Inlet

Wooden Sheeting

Metal Roofing

Key: Air Flow

10.3 Application in the Tropics

Figure 10.2 shows schematically a typical form of dryer developed for grain in the tropics. Described by Birewar (1978), such a system was used in India to dry 650 kg of grain from 18% to 12% moisture in 10-14 hours using an air flow of 0.3 m^3s^{-1} provided by a 0.75 kW fan. A basically similar dryer was developed by Chakraborty (1976), also in India, for the drying of fish in a time half that of fish dried in the sun. Roa and Macedo (1976) in Brazil dried 600 kg batches of beans using a collector of 8 m^2.

Dryers for the tropics that incorporate the solar collector into the roof of the drying bin or building have also been investigated. An example of this is the development of a rice dryer in India (Muthvererappan et al (1978)), capable of drying one tonne of parboiled rice per day in 2 batches with a glass-covered collector of area 37m^2. It was estimated that 30 litres per day of fuel oil would be saved. Other examples of solar rice dryers of this type have been reported by Mendoza (1979) in the Philippines and Thongprasert (1978) in Thailand. Williams et al (1969) in Malaysia, used collectors made from back-to-back corrugated metal sheets for drying tapioca (cassava).

In Korea an all-plastic dryer of this type was developed (Trim & Ko (1982)). It consisted of a double-skinned plastic tent fastened on a bamboo framework and cross-section as shown in Figure 10.3. On the sun-facing side air was drawn by a fan in through the inlet ports into the annular space between the outer clear plastic skin and the inner black plastic skin and became heated. It then flowed into the drying chamber within the inner skin. Such a dryer 4.3m long and 2m wide could dry 300 kg of red peppers in 4-5 days which is a reduction of about 60% compared with sun drying.

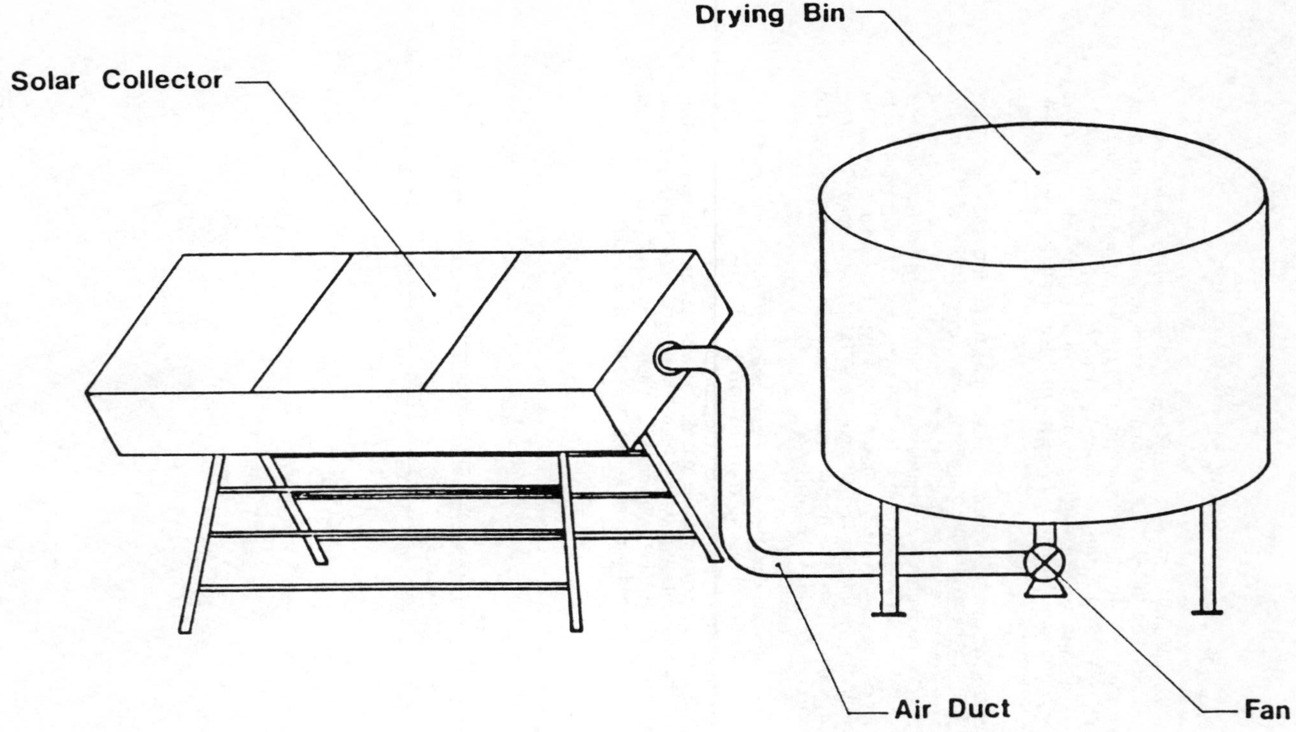

Drying Bin

Fan

Air Duct

Solar Collector

Figure 10.2   Schematic Diagram of a Solar Grain Dryer

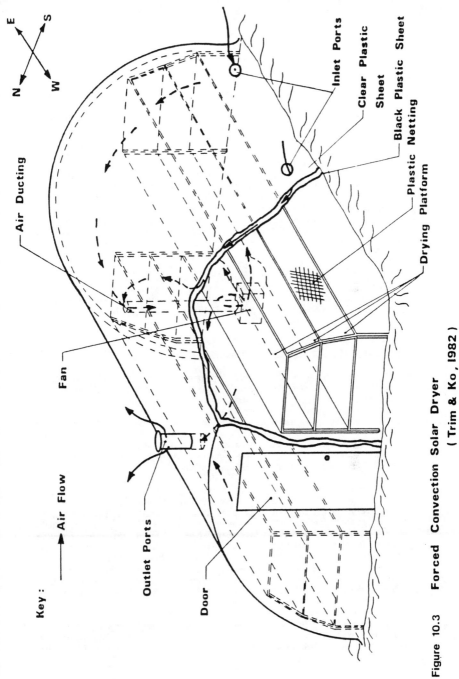

Key:

→ Air Flow

Figure 10.3   Forced Convection Solar Dryer
(Trim & Ko , 1982)

- 75 -

11. HYBRID DRYERS

11.1 Purpose-Designed Dryers

In concept this type of dryer is identical to that described in Chapter 10 but with another means of heating the air incorporated into the system. An example is a coffee dryer developed for co-operative factories in Kenya, (Trim et al (1984), Trim & Kamau (1984)) and shown in Figures 11.1 and 11.2. This system capable of drying 3 tonnes of parchment coffee per day employed a bare plate collector as the roof of the dryer building with a collection area of over $200m^2$ capable of imparting nearly 2000 MJ per day to the air. Air was moved through the system at a rate of $8m^3s^{-1}$ by a diesel powered fan unit designed such that the heat produced by the engine of the fan unit was used to provide additional heat to the air at a rate of 100 MJ per hour. If the same amount of energy was supplied by other methods, for example electricity, a 50 kW electrical heater would be required or about 120 litres per day of diesel oil if a burner system was employed.

Another example of the use of solar heating for drying coffee is that described by Phillips (1965) in Puerto Rico. As with the previous dryer the solar collector was incorporated into the roof of the building. The additional costs of building the collector were recouped from reduced electricity consumption in less than 2 years.

11.2 Modification of Existing Buildings

Hybrid dryers have been extensively developed in North America, (Petersen (1973), Foster and Peart (1976)), with storage silos being modified by the incorporation of solar collectors into the walls and/or roof. Baker and Shove (1977) have summarised the performance of such modifications; savings of 40% or more in energy costs have been recorded. It should be noted that financial appraisal of solar dryers is very dependent upon the cost of the conventional fuel solar heating it is replacing; compared with North America such costs in African countries are likely to be greater. In Zimbabwe there have been several cases reported of the modification of the roofs of crop drying buildings into solar collectors (Johnstone 1979). The basic modification consisted, as in many other cases, of fitting a 'ceiling' beneath the existing roof, thus forming a bare plate collector by drawing air between the 'ceiling' and the roof. In one case with a roof of $570m^2$ modified to a solar collector, the savings in fuel costs were estimated at 30% for the drying of maize. On another farm with a similarly sized collector, solar heating has totally replaced coal-fired heating in the drying of maize albeit with an increase in the drying time. Collection efficiencies of over 30% have been recorded. On a third farm a collector has been assembled using clear and black plastic sheets with dried grass as the insulation below the absorber. Even with such a rudimentary system, a collection efficiency of 20% and a considerable reduction in coal consumption in the drying of coffee have been obtained. In Australia a more elaborate system has been reported (Bowrey et al (1980)) in which the roof of a banana drying plant was successfully modified to a collector working in the single back pass mode. One interesting feature of the collector was the need to fit wire mesh over the glass over as a protection against hailstones. With an air flow of $0.01m^3s^{-1}$ per square metre of collector

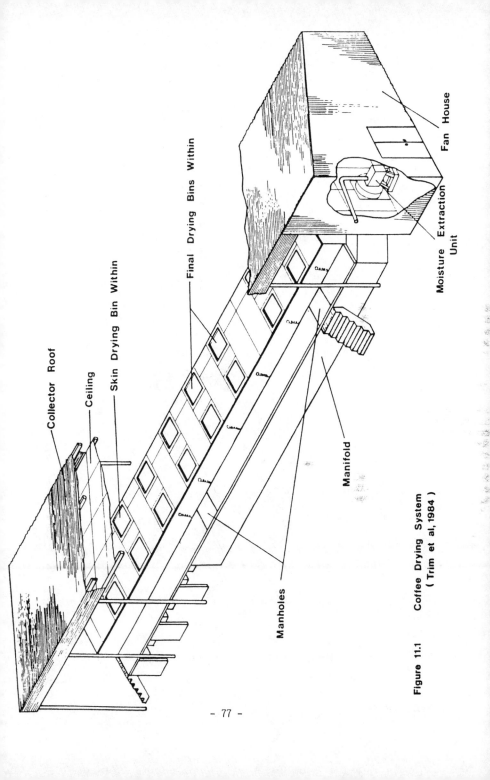

Figure 11.1   Coffee Drying System (Trim et al, 1984)

Collector Roof

Ceiling

Skin Drying Bin Within

Final Drying Bins Within

Fan House

Moisture Extraction Unit

Manifold

Manholes

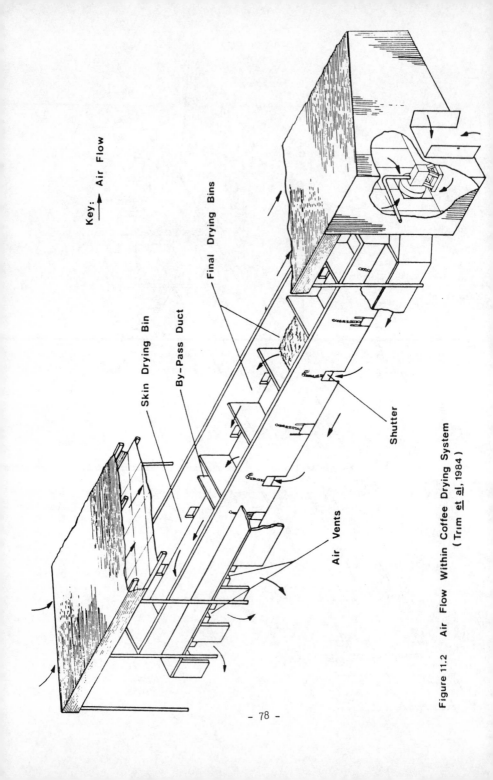

Key: → Air Flow

Skin Drying Bin

By-Pass Duct

Final Drying Bins

Shutter

Air Vents

Figure 11.2   Air Flow Within Coffee Drying System
(Trim et al, 1984)

area collection efficiencies ranging from 40% to 70% were obtained with temperature elevations of up to $40°C$. The higher collection efficiencies were obtained at the lower insolation levels but the temperature rise was less with correspondingly lower heat losses.

The use of supplementary solar heat in the drying (curing) of tobacco has received appreciable interest in recent years (Bose (1980), Chang (1978) and Cundiff (1980)). The curing of tobacco to produce the best quality is a relatively complex process in which moisture is removed from the leaves by careful control of air flow, temperature and humidity over the curing time. For a system developed in India, Bose (1980) reported that the curing and subsequent cooling times were significantly less than those of conventional barns. As a result each barn can cure 50% more tobacco per season. Although capital costs were increased by the incorporation of a double glass covered collector into the barn roof, operating costs were reduced by at least 25%.

12. ANCILLARY EQUIPMENT AND RECENT DEVELOPMENTS

12.1 Fans

In solar drying the rate and distribution of air flow, both through the solar collector and through or across the drying chamber, is of vital importance. The result of insufficient air flow is undesirably long drying times, and with irregular air flow distribution unevenly dried product can result. In natural convection dryers use is made of the buoyancy of warm air (relative to cooler ambient air) to promote the necessary air flow. This can work well in situations where low air flow rates are tolerable and there is no great resistance to the flow of air; however when a high air flow is desired or when there is considerable resistance to the flow of air as in deep beds of grain the use of fans may be necessary.

Table 12.1 provides a summary of the principal fan types and their suitability for various applications. When faced with the problem of selecting a fan for a specific application, the most practical approach for those who are not well versed in the theory of fan design is probably to specify the required air flow and the expected pressure drop through the dryer to reputable agents of fan manufacturers. In most African countries suitable fans, usually of the simpler type such as axial flow or centrifugal, can be obtained in the larger towns without undue trouble. It is considered outside the scope of this Chapter to provide additional information concerning fan theory, except to state that the air temperature, particularly if high (greater than 50°C), may be of importance in fan specification.

The air flow rate required of the fan will be determined from the specifications of the dryer, ie in most cases the air flow required to dry a certain quantity of a commodity in a certain time will be known at least in general terms. The pressure drop produced by the flow of air through a solar dryer can be usually considered in two parts:

(i)   that encountered in the drying chamber;

(ii)   that produced in the solar collector and connecting air ducts.

The pressure drop through the drying chamber, particularly for air flow through a deep bed, will usually be much greater than that through the collector and ducts; indeed the latter can be relatively insignificant. However if the fan is to be positioned between the collector and the drying chamber, the pressure drop through the former, although much less, can be of equal importance as the latter. This is because most simple fans are not designed to function efficiently when there is an appreciable pressure drop, say 100-200 Pa, on their suction side.

The pressure drop across a bed can be calculated from the following equation:

$$v \quad = \quad a \, (\Delta P / h_b)^b \tag{12.1}$$

where v   =   (superficial) velocity (m s^{-1}) ie volumetric air flow divided by the cross sectional area of the bed,

ΔP =   pressure drop across the bed (Pa),

Table 12.1   Types of Fan
(Institution of Heating & Ventilating Engineers (1972))

Fan type	Fan static efficiency	Advantages	Disadvantages	Applications
1. Axial-flow (without guide vanes).	60–65%	Very compact, straight-through flow. Suitable for installing in any position in run of ducting.	High tip speed. Relatively high sound level comparable with 5. Low pressure development.	All low pressure atmospheric air applications.
2. Axial-flow (with guide vanes).	70–75%	Straight-through flow. Eminently suitable for vertical axis.	Same as 1 but to less extent.	As for 1 and large ventilation schemes such as tunnel ventilation.
3. Forward-curved or multivane centrifugal.	50–60%	Operates with low peripheral speed. Quiet and compact.	Severely rising power characteristic requires large motor margin.	All low and medium pressure atmospheric air and ventilation plants.
4. Straight or paddle-bladed centrifugal.	45–55%	Strong simple impeller, least clogging, easily cleaned and repaired.	Inefficiency. Rising power characteristic.	Material transport systems and any application where dust burden is high.
5. Backwards-curved or backwards-inclined blade centrifugal.	70–75%	Good efficiency. Non-overloading power characteristic.	High tip speed. Relatively high sound level compared with 3.	Medium and high pressure applications such as high velocity ventilation schemes.
6. Aerofoil-bladed centrifugal.	80–85%	Highest efficiency of all fans. Non-overloading power characteristic.	Same as 5.	Same as 5 but higher efficiency justifies its use for higher power applications.
7. Propeller.	Less than 40%	First cost and ease of installation.	Low efficiency and very low pressure development.	Mainly non-ducted low pressure atmospheric air applications. Pressure development can be increased by diaphragm mounting.
8. Mixed-flow.	70–75%	Straight through flow. Suitable for installing in any position in a run of ducting. Can be used for higher pressure duties than 2. Lower blade speeds than 1 or 2 hence reduced noise.	Stator vanes are generally highly loaded due to higher pressure ratios. Maximum casing diameter is greater than either inlet or outlet diameters.	Large ventilation schemes where the somewhat higher pressures developed and lower noise levels give an advantage over 2.
9. Cross-flow or tangential-flow.	40–50%	Straight across flow. Long, narrow discharge.	Low efficiency. Very low pressure development.	Fan-coil units. Room conditioners. Domestic heaters.

Fan Static Efficiency $= \dfrac{\text{Static Air Power}}{\text{Shaft Power}} \times 100\ \%$

$= \dfrac{\text{Static Pressure} \times \text{Volumetric Air Flow}}{\text{Shaft Power}} \times 100\ \%$

h_b = bed depth (m)

a, b = empirically determined constants specific for each commodity.

Equation 12.1 can be rewritten as:

$$\ln v = \ln a + b \ln (\Delta P/h_b) \tag{12.2}$$

If empirical results of air flow and pressure drop are plotted according to Equation 12.2, then the constants a and b can be determined from the graph from the intercept and gradient respectively. Figure 12.1 (McCloy, personal communication) shows data for a wide range of commodities likely to be dried in deep beds.

The pressure drop for the flow of air in ducts can be calculated from the equation:

$$\Delta P = \frac{f \cdot L \cdot G_d}{2 \cdot \rho \cdot R_h} \tag{12.3}$$

where f = Fanning friction factor,

L = duct length (m),

G_d = mass flow rate of air per unit cross-sectional area of duct, (kg s^{-1} m^{-2}),

ρ = air density (kg m^{-3}),

R_h = hydraulic radius (m),

For a rectangular duct of width w and height s the hydraulic radius is given by the formula:

$$R_h = \frac{w \cdot s}{2 (w + s)} \tag{12.4}$$

and for a circular duct of diameter, d:

$$R_h = d/4 \tag{12.5}$$

The fanning friction factor can be obtained from Figure 12.2 where Re_h (Reynolds Number) is calculated from the formula:

$$Re_h = \frac{4 \cdot \rho \cdot v \cdot R_h}{\mu} \tag{12.6}$$

where v = air velocity (m s^{-1}),

μ = air viscosity (kg m^{-1} s^{-1}),

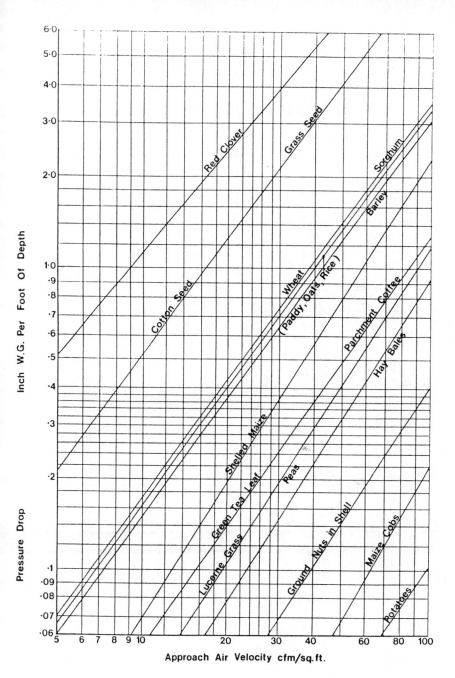

Figure 12·1   Air Pressure Drop Through Grain And Crops

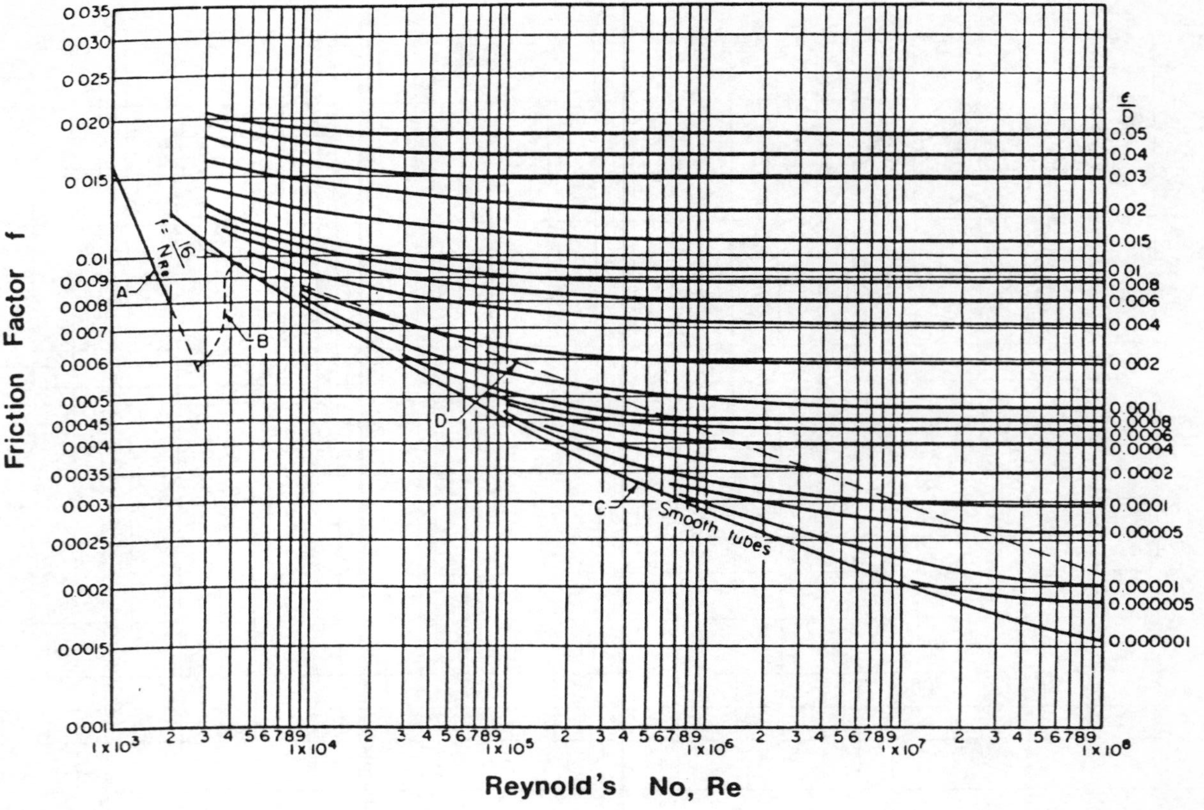

Figure 12.2   Fanning Friction Factors (Perry & Chilton , 1973)

Practical examples of the calculation of pressure drop are given in Appendices 9 and 13.

The solar collector can be considered as a duct for the calculation of pressure drop. The total pressure drop over the dryer is obtained simply by adding together the respective pressure drops for the collector, air ducts and drying chamber.

12.2   Solar Energy Storage

In some drying operations it is advantageous to have a period during which drying can take place longer than is possible with the types of solar drier so far discussed. If solar radiation is the only form of energy available to provide conditions suitable for drying, then some means of solar energy storage are required.

Some possible methods of storing solar energy are:

(i)   as sensible heat, eg in a bed of rocks or a water tank,

(ii)   as latent heat in a material which changes phase, eg Glaubers salt,

(iii)   as "drying potential" in a regenerated desiccant; as a result of removing moisture from the air there is also an increase in air temperature. The heat generated is approximately equivalent to the latent heat of vaporization of the moisture removed.

For drying purposes, sensible heat storage is the simplest of the above methods. In the case of rock storage the only requirement is a container of rocks through which air is passed. The rocks can be heated either by direct insolation or by passing solar heated air through the bed of rocks. It should be noted that the use of storage media in solar drying does not increase the amount of energy available from a given collector; it merely makes the energy available at times when solar energy is not directly available. For example, where a rock bed is used as part of a drying system, positioned between the solar collector and the drying chamber, the drying period may be extended in the evening, but at the expense of slowing down the rate at which the system warms up in the morning. It would appear doubtful that such a system has any advantage over conventional solar dryers except for those few commodities, such as tobacco, where drying has to continue round the clock.

The equipment required to store and exchange heat from water means that the use of sensible heat storage tanks of water is not generally practical for solar drying. This is also the case for phase change materials.

The amount of energy which can be stored by a desiccant is greater (per unit weight) than that which can be stored in rock storage. Desiccants also have the advantage that they can store the energy for a greater time, and need no thermal insulation although a vapour barrier is necessary. Table 12.2 shows the energy which can be stored by various media. Further information on solar energy storage can be found in articles by Choda & Read (1970), Close & Dunkle (1970) and Boisdet & Peube (1979).

- 85 -

Table 12.2   Storage of Solar Energy

Temperature Change of Storage Media °C	Storage Potential MJ m^{-3}			
	Calcium Chloride	Water	Rock	Silica gel
32 – 39	256	12.5	4.4	–
35 – 25	271	42	14.7	–
35 – 20	282	–	–	
As Desiccant	2000**	–	–	330***

Notes:

* Calcium chloride changes phase from solid to liquid at temperatures between 29 and 32°C (the exact temperature is dependent upon the purity) and thus the latent heat stored in the liquid salt can only be absorbed by the air if the latter is at a lower temperature. The use of calcium chloride as a desiccant is limited due to its deliquiescence properties.

** Based upon 50% w/w absorption of moisture

*** Based upon 15% w/w absorption of moisture

12.3   Drying using Solar Regenerated Desiccants

The term desiccant drying is used to describe the process in which air is first de-humidified and then used for drying. The process of air de-humidification using a desiccant can, in many ways, be considered as the reverse of the usual drying process. During air de-humidification, moisture passes from the air to a substance which has previously been dried (regenerated) to a state in which its equilibrium relative humidity is below that of the air. In common with the drying process, heat transfer, as well as moisture transfer, occurs. In the case of silica gel the gain in temperature of air de-humidified in this manner can be quite significant (greater than 10°C for ambient air de-humidified to virtual dryness). Drying or "regeneration" of some desiccants is possible using solar radiation.

Although it is not envisaged that desiccant drying will be used as widely as other solar drying technologies, desiccant drying does, for certain situations, offer some advantages. Some instances where desiccant drying may be attractive are listed below:

(i)   where it is desirable, for reasons of product quality to dry at a temperature little greater than ambient. This may be the case where elevated temperatures, as well as increasing the rate of drying, will also lead to loss of other volatile components,

(ii)   when the final stage of drying is very slow; recirculating air through both commodity and desiccant is likely to be more energy efficient than the more usual method of passing heated air over the commodity. Furthermore, if solar radiation is the only source of energy then use of a desiccant would extend the time during which drying could take place,

(iii)   where it is important that drying is continuous, changing from "normal" solar drying during the day to using desiccant dried air at night will give more continuous operation,

(iv)   desiccants can also be used as an energy storage medium. Desiccants which can be regenerated in solar dryers could be regenerated at periods when the dryers were not being otherwise used.

Both solid and liquid desiccants can be used to de-humidify air, with the result that the air has a greater capacity to absorb moisture from a drying commodity. Examples of solid desiccants are silica gel, activated alumina, molecular sieves and anhydrous salts as calcium sulphate. Liquid desiccants include glycerine, glycol, sulpheric acid and aqueous solutions of various salts. Solid desiccants, in the form of granules, are generally easier to handle than liquid desiccants, are more stable than liquids such as glycerine and glycol, and generally pose no corrosion or safety problems, as would liquids such as sulphuric acid. Further comments will therefore be limited to the use of solid dessicants.

Desirable properties for solid desiccants are as follows:

(i)   a capacity to absorb large amounts of moisture from air at typical ambient conditions,

(ii)   stability, ie the desiccant may be regenerated a large number of times without any significant loss of its properties,

(iii)   regeneration at temperatures which can readily and efficiently be achieved in solar collectors,

(iv)   mechanical integrity, so that the particles of desiccant are not broken during movement of the desiccant, and also so that there is no creation of dust particles which could contaminate the product,

(v)   desiccants should, ideally, be non-toxic and non-corrosive, otherwise the precautions which need to be taken may outweigh any benefits from desiccant drying,

(vi)   low cost.

The previously mentioned solid desiccants, ie silica gel, activated alumina, molecular sieves and calcium sulphate vary quite considerably in their properties. Of these four only silica gel and activated alumina can be successfully regenerated at temperatures below 75°C. Silica gel has a higher moisture absorption capacity than activated alumina (30% by weight compared to 12% at 20°C, 95% RH). Silica gel can also be utilized more efficiently than activated alumina (Miller and Bowman (1978)).

12.4 Photovoltaics

Photovoltaics, ie devices for the conversion of light to electricity, have been available for several years, but only during the past five years have they been practically applied to agriculture, primarily in conjunction with irrigation pumps.

(i)   What are photovoltaics?

Familiar terms such as transistor, semi-conductor diode etc are used to describe the components of radios and cassette recorders; photovoltaics belong to the same family. In a calculator a 'light emitting diode' (LED) is used to give a numerical output, ie conversion of electricity into light. By altering the internal physical/chemical structure of the semi-conductor, the diode can be made to reproduce electricity when light shines on it, ie a solar cell. Essentially, a single solar cell will provide about half a volt and generate a current dependent upon the cell size and the amount of insolation. Typically a 100 mm diameter cell could generate 2 amp at 450mV in bright sunlight.

Since most load systems require voltages greater than that produced by a single cell, cells are combined in series or parallel to give modules of convenient power. For example, 36 cells in series would give about 16V. However, to overcome fluctuation due to changes in sunlight level a battery, similar to that found in motor vehicles, is frequently included in the circuit and arranged such that the solar array charges the battery and the battery powers the load. Various combinations of module can be arranged to give specific power ratings, as shown in Figure 12.3.

(ii)   Peak Power

The most common measure of output of a photovoltaic array is the peak power, which is the maximum power that can be delivered at 1000 $W.m^{-2}$ and 25°C. A point to note is that the correct system voltage is generated at relatively low light intensity but the current output increases proportionally with insolation. In general, therefore, over a realistic operating range, the voltage is constant, but the current and hence the power increase with increasing insolation. It should also be noted that elevated temperatures decrease the power output of an array.

(iii)   Sizing of Photovoltaic Arrays

An array may consist of a number of modules connected in series and parallel. The more modules in series the higher the voltage; the more in parallel the higher the current. Generally, the number of modules in series is calculated by dividing the system voltage by the nominal module output. For example, a 24V system requires two 12V modules in series. The number of modules in parallel is calculated by dividing the daily load in ampere hours/day by the daily module output. For example, if a 12V system needs 28 ampere hours/day in a location of 4 peak hours of sunshine, four 2 amp, 12V modules would be used in parallel $(28/(2 \times 4) = 3.5)$.

A photovoltaic system that could be used in relation to solar dryers is currently under test by TDRI, as shown in Figure 12.4. It should be noted however that no batteries are included.

It consists of photovoltaic panels providing electricity via a controller to fans which are moving air through a solar collector to heat up the air prior to drying. Two 12V, 2.6 amp panels are connected in series to give a nominal 24V system. The controller regulates power to six 11W fans, nominally running at 24V; each fan is capable of delivering $0.05 \text{ m}^3\text{s}^{-1}$ of air at 50 Pa. The collector has been designed to give a temperature rise of about 6°C. A degree of air temperature control is obtained with the system, since when insolation falls power output from the panels falls and the control switches fans out of circuit progressively to match the power generated by the panels and hence the air flow through the collector falls. Since the amount of insolation incident upon the collector is reduced, roughly in the same proportion, drastic changes in air temperature are avoided.

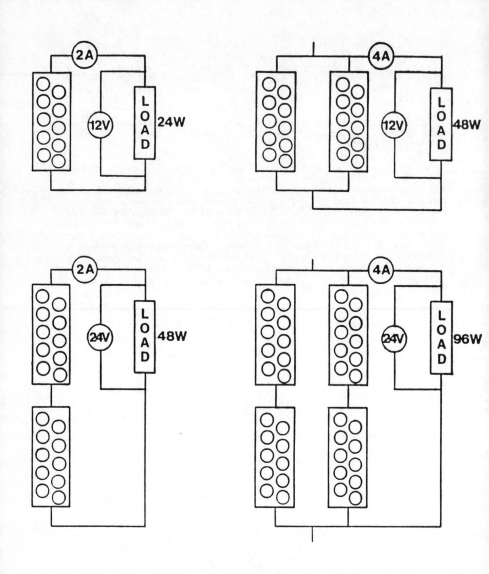

Figure 12.3   Typical Arrangements of Photovoltaic Modules

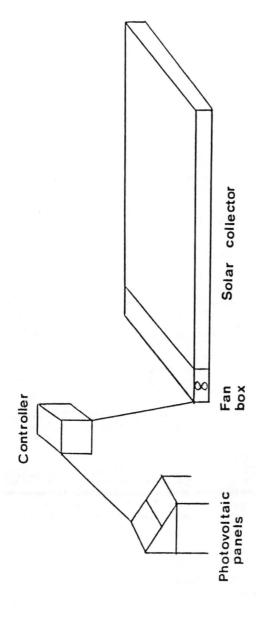

Controller

Solar collector

Photovoltaic panels

Fan box

Figure 12.4   Experimental   Photovoltaic   System

13. QUALITY CHANGES DURING DRYING

The action of applying heat to a material in order to dry it does not merely remove the moisture but can also affect the quality of the dried product. These effects are many and varied; only those phenomena commonly encountered will be described herein.

13.1 Browning

Discolouration of the material during drying, commonly termed browning, can be caused by either physical processes or chemical reactions.

Physical discolouration, evidenced as charring or scorching, can be generally attributed to the thermal breakdown of complex molecules into simpler chemical structures. An example is the caramelization process whereby sugars are broken down into furfurals; however this mechanism only normally occurs at temperatures in excess of $100^\circ C$ - somewhat higher than those normally associated with solar dryers.

Discolouration by chemical reaction can be further categorised as either enzymic or non-enzymic reactions. A common example of a non-enzymic reaction is the Maillard type of reaction in which carbonyl groups, present in some sugars, react with amino groups present in amino acids or proteins. A complex chain of reactions leads initially to pink or red colourations and then to insoluble brown polymers. Perhaps the textbook example of Maillard reactions is the browning of bread during baking and the resultant crust formation. Enzymic reactions are those brought about by the action of naturally occurring enzymes in the drying material which are released as the plant tissue breaks down. An obvious example is the browning of fruit slices such as apples and bananas when the freshly cut fruit is exposed to the atmosphere.

The rate of most browning reactions is greatly dependent upon the combined effects of time and temperature and on the moisture content of the drying material. The Maillard reactions involved proceed slowly in dilute solutions commensurate with very moist foods and crops. As the solutions are concentrated during the drying process the reactions proceed more rapidly. Water is, however, essential for the reactions to occur.

As described previously, the rate of drying increases with increase in temperature and therefore an optimum has to be reached between the highest drying rate and an unacceptable degree of browning. In general this optimum can only be determined by empirical means. Some browning reactions can be counteracted by exposure of the material to sulphur dioxide prior to drying (Chapter 3).

13.2 Migration of Soluble Constituents

As moisture migrates from the interior to the surface soluble constituents present as solutes in the moisture can also move towards the surface. The rate of movement is specific to each constituent and dependent upon its ability to diffuse through the cell walls. As the solution nears the surface water evaporates leaving behind an increasing concentration in the layers nearest the surface. This situation will terminate in a gradient in concentration of soluble constituent from the interior to the surface.

However, the situation is not that simple. As the concentration of soluble constituents increases in the surface layers a (back) diffusion tends to occur of at least the more soluble constituents from the more concentrated layers (at the surface) to the dilute interior. This will continue for as long as the water concentration remains sufficiently high. Both of these physical mechanisms occur in any drying process but depending on the actual drying conditions and the nature of the material concerned one or the other would predominate. In easily controllable mechanical dryers conditions can be varied such that the required properties of the dried product are achieved.

13.3   Case Hardening

This phenomena can perhaps be regarded as a particular example of the effects of the migration of soluble constituents to the surface layers during drying. It is characterised by the material surface becoming dry and relatively impermeable to further flow of moisture but with the interior remaining at a somewhat higher moisture content. Van Arsdel et al (1973) noted that this phenomena had proved troublesome with the drying of whole fruit, soap, meat, fish and leather. The usual reaction to this has been to control the drying conditions in the early stages such that too steep a moisture gradient will not be set up between interior and surface.

Conversely, with the drying of most vegetable and fruit slices (or pieces) case hardening is not commonly observed. Drying of these commodities can be carried out in the early stages under very extreme conditions, eg high temperature, low air humidity and high air flow. Due to the physical structure of these commodities the high initial rates of drying result in the formation of internal cracks caused by shrinkage. This increase in 'porosity' greatly facilitates the migration of moisture through the material in the later stages of drying and the avoidance of case hardening.

Similar phenomena can occur in the drying of grain. If the rate of drying is too high internal stresses are set up which may cause the kernels to crack. This is of particular importance in the case of rice where the grains are consumed in the whole form.

13.4   Loss of Volatile Constituents

In the evaporation of moisture from a commodity the water vapour invariably carries with it traces of every other volatile constituent present in the commodity. This results in an unwanted and ordinarily irreversible loss of flavour characteristics of that commodity in the dried or rehydrated product.

Unfortunately, this is a field of research that has not been greatly investigated though some work has been reported by Menting et al (1970). It is a complex subject; the concentration of a volatile constituent in the water vapour depends on its vapour pressure, the temperature of the food, and also its solubility, and those of other volatile constituents, in water. However, it is an area of great importance, particularly so for spices, herbs and crops such as pyrethrum, and must be given great consideration in an experimental programme when evaluating product quality.

13.5 Rehydration

The rehydration of a dried food product is another important factor particularly in terms of consumer acceptance. It must not be thought that rehydration is a complete reversal of the dehydration process. Some of the changes produced by drying are irreversible. The outer layers of the dried food, crushed and deformed during drying, are unable to return completely to their original size and shape. Soluble constituents in the dried foods leach out into the rehydration water contributing to a loss in nutrients and also a probable loss in flavour and aroma.

The drying conditions employed can also cause problems with rehydratability. The swelling power of starch gel and the elasticity of cell walls, both important rehydration factors, are reduced by heat treatment. With some products, eg dried fish, rehydration in terms of producing a rehydrated product similar in appearance to the original form is not so important as the dried product is utilised in soups or stews by adding directly to the cook pot.

14. QUALITY ASSESSMENT

14.1 Quality

Quality of a foodstuff is assessed on the basis of balancing specific characteristics, each of which has significance in determining the acceptability of the product thus determining overall quality. Each of these characteristics should be measured and controlled independently.

Quality is commonly thought of as degree of excellence. It may be considered as a specification or set of specifications which are to be met within given tolerances or limits. Therefore the level of the excellence of the product may be considered as the average or mean level of quality required in the market place, and not necessarily the highest quality that is obtainable regardless of cost. The uniformity of the product may be described in terms of minimum limits, or a tolerance between the upper and lower control limits.

The above definition refers to the product, but quality must also be controlled for raw materials and supplies, labour, machines, transportation, and selling.

14.2 Standards

An important aspect of quality control is the utilization of reliable methods of measurement in establishing standards or specifications of quality, and grading procedures to control the quality of raw materials as well as the processing operations and the finished product.

Standards of quality have been developed over many years by trade and consumer groups, and government organizations. Their main uses are to ensure that a product is safe for consumption or utilization and provide uniformity of products within a country and between countries. They may be mandatory, such as the Federal Food, Drug and Cosmetic Act of 1938 (Anon (1938)) governing products in America, or the Preservatives in Food Regulations of 1979 governing EEC countries (Anon (1979)), or they may be voluntary, such as those developed by the Codex Alimentarius Commission (FAO (1984)) or by Departments of Agriculture of specific countries.

The food regulations under the American Act of 1938 mentioned above, which is typical of mandatory government legislation can be summarized as follows (Kramer & Twigg (1966)):

(i)   establishment of reasonable standards of identity, quality, and fill of container for any food, conformance to these standards of identity at all times, and label declaration of substandard quality or fill in the event that the food falls below these standards,

(ii)   condemnation of any food (a) that has been manufactured or stored under unsanitary conditions whereby it may have been contaminated with filth or rendered injurious to health, (b) that is unfit for human consumption, (c) that contains a natural or added poisonous or deterious substance which may render it dangerous to health, (d) that contains a coal-tar colour which has not been certified as harmless, (e) that has a deceptive composition, and (f) condemnation of any food container that has a poisonous or damaging composition which may render the contents injurious to health,

(iii) prohibition of any imitation food unless it is so labelled, and any food offered for sale under the name of another food,

(iv) requirement that any food label shall not be false or misleading in any respect, and prohibition of any food container that is so made or formed or filled as to be misleading,

(v) requirement that any packaged food shall bear a label containing the name and address of its manufacturer or distributor, and a statement of its net weight or measure or numerical count; that a food without identity standard shall be labelled with its own name and if consisting of two or more ingredients, with the name of each ingredient. Except for a few specific cases any food containing artificial colouring or any chemical preservative is required to be labelled to show that fact.

14.3 Objective Versus Subjective Methods

Subjective, or sensory, evaluation is made by human judgement using human senses. It suffers from being influenced by environmental conditions, mood and health of the individual, lack of an absolute reference point, tendency for comparative rather than absolute evaluations, and above all, personal bias which may enter the evaluation consciously or subconsciously.

Objective evaluation, that is, use of a calibrated instrument to measure a physical or chemical component is less dependent on the human element. However, unless correctly conducted it can lead to greater errors than subjective evaluation. In addition, human evaluation is the ultimate criterion of the accuracy of any objective method.

If a subjective evaluation is possible, it is generally used in preference to an objective evaluation, eg, Table 14.1 shows a specification for dried onions issued by a typical industrial food processing company.

14.4 Classification of Quality Attributes

Quality attributes can be classified as either sensory or hidden. Sensory characteristics are those which can be detected with human senses, that is, sight, touch, taste and smell, whereas hidden characteristics are those which cannot be evaluated with senses but are of importance to health. Table 14.2 summarizes the quality attributes important in food quality.

Table 14.1   Dried Onion Specification

Raw material	Sound onions of a variety suitable for dehydration, free from disease and mechanical damage.
	Prior to dehydration, the onions should be peeled and trimmed, the base and core removed, and the whole onion sliced into 3 mm slices.
	Where reconstituted product is being examined, 50 grammes should be covered with cold water; allowed to soak for twenty minutes and strained.
Culinary	
Colour	White to cream - not grey or brown
Flavour	Strong and clean, free from bitterness
Texture	Firm and crisp; free from tough pieces which cannot easily be bitten through
Blemish	
Obvious	Maximum two per 50 gramme dry sample (obvious blemish is regarded as those discoloured pieces, etc, which should reasonably be removed during inspection after drying).
Total	Maximum fifteen per 50 gramme dry sample after reconstitution. (Total blemish includes all discoloured, scorched, and diseased pieces, skin and other matter originating in the onion which should have been removed at the trimming stage).
Foreign bodies	Absent
Extraneous vegetable matter	Not more than one piece per kilogramme. (This includes material not originating in the onion, i.e. weeds, etc).
Screening	Not more than 5% through 8 mesh BS Screen
Moisture	
Target	Maximum 7%
Maximum	8%
Yield	On reconstitution 4:1 maximum.

Table 14.2   Classification of Quality Attributes

Sensory

Sight – Appearance	Touch – Kinesthetic (texture)	Flavour
Colour and gloss Size and shape Defects	Finger and mouth feel	Odour Taste
Hidden Nutritive value Adulterants Toxicity		

14.5   Appearance

Factors of quality included in appearance are those evaluated with the eye and are hence the first noticed by the consumer. It is often on its appearance that the product is accepted or rejected, and therefore good appearance is most important.

Colour is an appearance property attributable to the spectral distribution of light. Glossiness and transparency are properties attributable to the geometric manner in which light is reflected and transmitted.

Some of the instruments available for colour measurement will be briefly described. The light source is most important whichever method is used, in particular it should be consistent. Daylight, utilizing a bench under a north facing window (south facing in the Southern hemisphere) is adequate, or if artificial lighting is required standard illuminants are available (Kramer & Twigg (1966)).

Some of the physical and sensory terms used to denote colour attributes are summarized below:

Physical measurement	Sensory term equivalent
Radiant energy	Light
Reflectance	Lightness, value
Dominant wavelength	Hue, colour
Purity	Chroma, intensity, strength
Directional reflectance	Gloss, sheen

The most complex and expensive instrument used for colour measurement is the spectrophotometer which measures the amount of light reflected from the surface of an object at each wavelength in the range of approximately 380 to 770μm.

A quicker and cheaper method is the Munsell system. This uses 3 or 4 colour discs, each of which is calibrated in terms of hue (red, green, etc.), value (lightness or darkness), and chroma (strength of the colour); each of these is expressed on a scale. The discs are overlapped so that the proportion of each disc which is exposed may be adjusted until the blend of colour, obtained by spinning the discs, matches the object whoe colour is being measured. The percentage of each disc exposed, and the disc notations are converted to Munsell notations using tables and charts.

The other main colour instrument is the Hunter colour difference meter. It is less expensive than the spectrophotometer but more costly than the Munsell system. It measures the value (as in the Munsell method), the amount of redness/greenness and the amount of yellowness/blueness, ie, Hunter values, which can be converted to Munsell notations.

Size and shape are such obvious factors of quality that they can be overlooked. Having uniform size and shape facilitates packing and will give a more attractive package and hence increased sales potential. If grading has been correctly carried out prior to drying then the dried product should be fairly uniform. However, visual examination before packing will eliminate any grossly oversized, undersized or misshapen pieces. For industrial operations size and shape can be controlled by weight, volume and length, width and diameter measurements.

Defects are another factor of quality largely evaluated by the consumer's eye. Many products of high quality in all other respects may be downgraded because of defects. Therefore it is an important quality factor to consider. Defects may be classified into the categories (i) genetic-physiological, (ii) entomological, (iii) pathological, (iv) mechanical, and (v) extraneous or foreign matter.

Genetic-physiological defects occur as a result of hereditary abnormalities of the raw material or as the effects of unfavourable environmental conditions during the growth and maturation of the crop. Normal functions of metabolism of the plants may be distributed by extremes of temperature, water supply, nutrition, or genetic aberrations. Most pieces with this type of defect should have been eliminated during sorting, but for example cauliflower with hollow stem, (a common defect with cauliflower (USDA, (1951)), would not be detected until after drying.

Entomological defects are caused by insect attack and are a major source of defects in fruits, vegetables, fish and grain. The damage may be direct, as a result of the insect's own activities such as feeding, oviposition, and stings, or indirect, caused by a disease organism introduced into the commodity by the insect (Ross (1948)). These defects can be minimized by the correct pre-drying processing operations and by fumigation after drying and during storage.

Pathological defects occur as a result of the action of bacteria, fungi, mould, or virus prior to drying. The crop may only suffer in quality but frequently a reduction in quantity occurs (Heald (1933)); the crop becomes disfigured or deformed. Pieces with these defects should again have been eliminated during sorting but a visual examination is adequate after drying to separate any deformed pieces from the good ones.

Mechanical defects arise from damage to the product of a physical nature. Although it may be impossible to eliminate such defects, the degree of severity of such damage can be reduced by care in handling and by proper adjustment of equipment. Bruising of tissue, which results in discolouration, is the most common mechanical defect; the consequences of bruising have already been explained under pre-drying processing operations, (Chapter 3). Care in handling is the most effective way to prevent mechanical defects.

Extraneous or foreign material defects may be harmless such as leaves or harmful such as stones. Again, correct sorting should eliminate such defects but a final check prior to packing removes any strays.

14.6 Texture

Kinesthetic or texture characteristics deal with the sense of feel, that is, finger and mouth feel. For dried products the texture of the reconstituted product is of importance and therefore should be assessed and regularly checked. Incorrect pre-drying operations and incorrect drying procedures can drastically affect the texture of the reconstituted product. For finger feel the main sensory characteristics are firmness, softness and juiciness, and for mouth feel, stickiness and oiliness.

The best way to assess texture is by taste panelling as described later. There are instruments available to quantify texture which use compression, shearing, cutting, tensile strength and shear-pressure as principles of measurement. Details of these can be found in the literature (Kramer & Twigg (1966)).

14.7 Flavour

Flavour attributes of quality are those the consumer evaluates mainly with the senses of taste and smell although the sense of feel in the form of touch, warmth and cold may also be involved (Beidler (1957)). Flavour is most conveniently and usually judged by taste panelling, but gas chromatography is also used industrially.

14.8 Nutritive Value

Nutritive value is not usually considered in the market place, even in an industrial scale although some mandatory regulations are applied for some products. Table 14.1 shows that in an industrial specification for dried onions no mention is made of the nutritive value. However, in countries where food is scarce or not very nutritious, resulting in manlnutrition and ill-health, attention should be paid to such an important issue.

Table 14.3 shows the nutritive value of raw, dried and canned foods. It can be seen that during drying, minerals and, in particular, vitamins are lost. This also occurs in canned foods but can be easily compensated for by the addition of nutrients to the can before sealing. Only small amounts of vitamins are necessary to maintain good health, and every effort should be made to preserve them. Vitamins are degraded by light, heat, the presence of oxygen or exidizing substances, and extremes of pH as well as enzymes and minute amounts of metals, (Lee (1983)). Thiamin (vitamin B1) is unstable in oxygen and heat and in neutral or alkaline conditions. Ascorbic acid (vitamin C) is unstable in neutral or alkaline conditions as well as to light, heat, and to air. Riboflavin (vitamin B2) is unstable to light. Several things can be done to minimize the loss of vitamins, that is, keeping blanching times to a minimum, sulphuring, and, if possible drying in the shade. Chemical tests can be performed to assess vitamin contents, (Appendix 2).

In the case of fish, protein can become denatured during drying. Protein, as well as fat and sugar content may be assessed by the standard tests also described in Appendix 2.

14.9 Adulterants and Toxicity

Moulds or bacteria are undesirable since under favourable conditions rapid growth could occur with detrimental effects to health. The excessive use of additives in foodstuffs can be harmful and government standards (as already described) provide legal limits for dosage. These standards should be consulted and the tests typical of those in Appendix 2 used to determine the amount present.

Whilst not a food "additive", insecticides are used to combat insect infestation in dried commodities particularly with fish and grain. Some insecticide is inevitably absorbed and is present in the dried product and therefore the use of insecticides must also be strictly controlled.

14.10 Taste Panelling

Taste panelling otherwise known as sensory analysis is an important aspect of quality assessment and should be carried out correctly. It is therefore worthy of further details. It must be stressed that before taste panelling is attempted, the food should be checked to determine whether it is fit for human consumption.

Sensory analysis is used in:

(i)   Quality control,
(ii)   Evaluation of new processes,
(iii)   Formulation and introduction of new products.

In order to make correct decisions, information is required on the appearance, flavour and mouth-feel of the products because those properties will largely determine the consumer's reaction to the product.

Table 14.3   **Nutritive Value of Selected Raw, Dried and Canned Commodities**
(all values are per 100g bone dry material)

Food		Calories	Water (g)	Protein (g)	Carbohydrate (g)	Minerals Calcium (mg)	Iron (mg)	Vitamins C (mg)	B1 (mg)
Coconut Kernels	– Raw	–	85	7	13-27			trace	trace
	– Dried	–	2	7	6		2	trace	trace
Apricots	– Raw	215	669	6	52	132	8	54	0.31
	– Dried	347	33	6	89	89	7	16	0.01
Peaches	– Raw	264	614	4	65	84	14	57	0.14
	– Dried	349	33	4	91	64	8	24	0.01
	– Canned	330	400	2	86	18	10	20	0.05
Cabbage	– Raw	278	1,011	3	42	803	14	667	0.67
	– Dried	202	5	2	33	537	5	368	0
Carrots	– Raw	211	1,011	8	48	410	4	44	0.56
	– Dried	243	5	8	48	352	4	24	0.42
	– Canned	211	1,011	8	48	296	14	33	0.44
Potatoes	– Raw	363	317	9	87	32	3	125	0.46
	– Dried	276	5	7	63	29	2	27	0
Tomatoes	– Raw	233	1,567	15	47	222	7	333	1.00
	– Dried	152	5	13	25	158	5	211	0.53

Some important properties can be determined by instruments or by chemical analysis but such measurements must be related to consumers' preferences by sensory evaluation. Direct sensory evaluation is often the only practicable method, especially when the combined effect of several different properties is concerned.

In sensory evaluation the reactions of a selected group of people testing the product under controlled conditions are used to predict the ultimate acceptability of the product. Useful information will only be obtained if the right questions are asked of the right people. It is necessary first of all to define the exact information required, eg, if the process for an established product is to be changed, it will be necessary to know whether the product has changed and if so whether it is for better or worse. A worse product might still be acceptable if its price is low enough to off-set any inferiority compared with the traditional product. In the case of a new product, it may be necessary to discover what consumers like and dislike about products of this type and then to compare the new product with any other products that might compete with it.

These are just a few of the factors that a sensory evaluation specialist will have to consider in order to choose a satisfactory test procedure. Depending on the type of product being tested different assessors are required.

(i)   Expert assessors

Expert assessors know a great deal about the production, uses and marketing of a commodity. They can describe all the attributes of a sample in detail and can usually indicate the causes of any defects. Their training is a long and expensive process and they are usually to be found working in the product development departments of large food manufacturing companies or in consultancies and specialist commodity dealers. Tea tasters and perfumers are typical examples of expert assessors. They usually work alone or in small groups and can assess anything from one to fifty samples in a session. Frequently, they are full-time assessors.

(ii)   Experienced assessors

These are people selected for their ability to recognize, describe and quantify basic characteristics of foods and to detect small differences between samples. They may or may not specialize in one commodity. Experienced assessors are usually employees of the company who spend only part of their time as assessors. They work in panels of 10 to 15 members. Most quality control and product development work is done with assessors of this type.

(iii)   Untrained assessors

Untrained assessors are selected to be as typical as possible of the consumers or potential consumers of the product concerned. They work in panels of 15 to 30 usually assessing acceptability and preference before consumer trials are begun.

(iv)   Consumers

Consumer panels are large untrained groups of at least 100 members. They are selected at random from the section of the population at whom the product is aimed and usually concerned with preference and acceptability. If it is impossible for practical reasons to obtain a random sample of the population, all of the company's employees in suitable grades, the member of a local social club or the children in a local school may be used.

Untrained assessors are selected only for:

(i)   availability   They must be willing and able to take part in as many tests as is necessary.

(ii)   interest   They must be interested in the product and in taking part in the tests. They should normally be consuming the traditional or similar product or commodity themselves at home.

(iii)   consistency   They must be consistent in their assessments. If they are presented with the same samples several times they will express the same preference in a significant proportion of these tests.

Experienced assessors will also be able:

(i)   to detect small differences between samples,

(ii)   to use separate scales for each attribute of a product in addition to the simple hedonic scale,

(iii)   to give brief, clear reasons for their assessments,

It is best to select assessors on the basis of the results of practice sessions using the product to be tested. Preliminary screening tests are sometimes advocated for use in the selection of assessors but they are usually irrelevant. Tasting sessions in which assessors learn to recognize and describe the basic tastes and the more common flavour notes are useful as training, but the use of such tests for selection purposes sometimes eliminates useful assessors who have initial difficulties in understanding what is required of them, in finding the right words or perhaps in finding the confidence to make a judgement.

Whatever preliminary screening tests or training procedures are used, the assessors must be selected on the basis of their performance with the commodity under test because some assessors are extremely good on some commodities and very bad on others.

Except for consumer tests, which are carried out as far as possible in the place where the consumer uses or buys the product, all tests are carried out in a controlled environment. The essential requirements are:

(i)   an area where the assessors can work that is free from outside distractions such as noise, laboratory or cooking smells or people coming and going. There must be some means of stopping assessors distracting each other; this is usually achieved by using booths which may be permanent, in a special taste-panel room, or temporary, made from wood and erected on a bench or desk as needed;

(ii)   plain dishes or bowls in which samples can be served. These should be ceramic, metal or good quality plastic so that samples can be served in a standard but appetising way that will not bias the assessment;

(iii)   when part-time assessors are used, it is essential that the importance of this work is explained to their managers and general approval for their staff to take part obtained. If this is not done, managers are likely to pressure their staff into missing sessions and hurrying over their work;

(iv)   assessors must be comfortable. They must have stools of the right height to sit on, a supply of drinking water to rinse their mouths with, enough space to work in and somewhere to spit samples they do not want to swallow;

(v)   good natural or artificial lighting is sufficient for most purposes. It is sometimes necessary to use coloured lights to disguise differences in appearance that might bias assessors and lamps that can be fitted with colour filters are desirable.

Unless there is a specified control sample, all samples are identified only by a code, usually a three digit random number, so that the assessor has no idea which sample is which. Only expert assessors work knowing the identity of the sample they are testing.

The order in which an assessor tests the samples can affect his assessment. Consequently the order of presentation is either arranged so that every possible order is tested by each assessor or the order is completely random.

Each sample must be treated in the same way. If the assessor wishes to rinse his mouth out between samples, he must do so between all samples and before the first sample. Similarly, he should swallow all samples or spit out all samples. Samples so unpalatable that the assessor has to spit them out should be avoided. The number of samples provided to the assessor should not be so many that he becomes too full.

Samples should be big enough to enable the assessor to get their full flavour. Each assessor should take at least one normal mouthful of each.

Depending on the product, assessors can test up to five samples per session. The blander the product and the more experienced the assessors the more samples can be handled. Assessors must rest briefly between samples. They can rinse their mouths at this time if they wish or if it is necessary for that product.

Once the assessors have tested all the samples it is usually permissible for them to retest but they must avoid jumping about from sample to sample and retesting several times. If they do this they will tire their palates or noses in a taste or smell test and will no longer be able to discriminate.

There are several different types of tests.

(i)   Difference tests.

     (a)   Paired comparison triangle test, where the assessors are asked "Is one sample different from one or more other samples?"

            In triangle tests all possible combinations must be used, i.e. two of sample A and one of B, or two of B and one of A, and with the odd sample varied to all positions in each case.

     (b)   Paired comparison duo-trio test, where the assessors are asked "Is the sample different from a given control sample?"

            The duo-trio test is related to the triangle test. In this test the assessor is given a sample then two more samples and has to decide which of the second two is the same as the first sample (or the most like it if all three are slightly different).

            Triangle and duo-trio tests are useful when it is not possible to obtain homogeneous samples. If, for example the product is fruit, each piece of fruit is different although they all come from the same variety or treatment. If one asked in a triangle test, which is different, the answer would be that they were all different. It is possible however, to ask which is most different and this should pick out any difference that might exist between varieties or treatments. In paired comparison tests the question is whether the pair are the same or different. The assessors must expect to find as many identical pairs as different pairs in a series of tests or they will start to automatically answer 'different' each time.

     (c)   The difference can be simple difference or it can be difference in one aspect or direction i.e. which sample, if any, is sweeter?

            These tests are very widely used in both development work and quality control.

(ii)   Preference tests

     In these tests assessors, usually untrained, or consumers say which of two samples they prefer or occasionally which of a larger number they prefer. The procedure is the same as for the directional difference test.

(iii)   Ranking test

     Sometimes it is necessary to compare several samples at once. In this case the assessors rank the samples in order of preference of sweetness strength or whatever the criterion is. This type of test is easier for the less experienced assessors than a similar scoring test would be.

(iv)   Scoring tests

These tests require that the assessors have had some training, unless the
test procedure is very simple.

In all these tests the assessors score along some kind of scale. It may be a
'structured' scale, that is one with points that are described. An example of this
is the commonly used hedonic scales, one running from 1 to 9, and the other from
-4 to +4 centred around 0.

Like extremely	9 or 4
Like very much	8 or 3
Like moderately	7 or 2
Like slightly	6 or 1
Neither like nor dislike	5 or 0
Dislike slightly	4 or -1
Dislike moderately	3 or -2
Dislike very much	2 or -3
Dislike extremely	1 or -4

This is the basic type but different scales can be used for different commodities.
The scale can be shortened to 5 or 6 points either symetrically or by dropping
some of the lower points (after all, if your assessors dislike the product more
than moderately all it proves is that the product is not ready for panel testing).
It may be necessary to alter the scale when translating it into another language.

A similar scale can be used for intensity of some aspect of the product, softness
or mealiness for example. The scale may have only the end points described,
with or without the intermediate points being marked and the points may be
given numbers on the questionnaire or these may be added later for purposes of
calculation. In some types of scale, such as magnitude estimation, the assessor
determines which numerical value the different scale points will have. Hedonic
scales are used mainly with untrained assessors although, if a large, trained panel
is typical of the consumer group it is often used.

Special scales related to the product are designed for quality control and in this
case experienced or expert assessors are used. Table 14.4 shows a typical score
sheet which could be used.

If at all possible, only one kind of test should be used at a time; a difference test
should not be combined with a preference or scoring test nor should too many
questions be asked at one time. In practice, however, it may be necessary to
combine tests and occasionally it is possible to do this in a single test as in the
type of scale that relates the intensity of a particular characteristic to the
assessor's personal preference. There is no one type of test that will answer all
questions.

Tables and simple calculation formulae are published in many of the standard
reference books for difference tests and ranking tests (Amerine et al (1965),
Kramer & Twigg (1966), Larmand (1977)). The scores from tests using scales can
be analysed by the statistical methods used for other types of measurement and
many reference books give details of how to apply t-tests, analysis of variance,
and correlation or regression analysis to taste panel results.

Table 14.4:   Score Sheet for Sensory Analysis

Judges:

Please evaluate the samples for their qualities as _____
_____. Do not base your scores on a personal like or
dislike for the product in general. Please do not communicate with anyone while
scoring the sample.

Use numerical scores from the following score card. Enter your score under the
sample numbers in the scoring chart below. Please accompany all scores with
comments when requested.

Score Card

Range	Class	Score
Unacceptable	Very poor	1 or 2
	Poor	3 or 4
Barely acceptable	Fair	5 or 6
Acceptable	Good	7 or 8
Highly Acceptable	Unusually good	9 or 10

Scoring Chart

Qualities Tested		Sample
Colour	Score	
	Comment	
Texture	Score	
	Comment	
Flavour	Score	
	Comment	

14.11 Filth Detection

In addition to moulds, yeasts and bacteria, other contaminants such as insects, insect fragments, rodents and dirt, commonly known as filth, are important in quality assessment and quality control. Such contamination does not in all cases cause spoilage but will downgrade the quality causing it to become devalued. Infestation not only occurs in the dried product but can occur in any of the processing operations, therefore quality control procedures should be enforced right from receipt of the raw material to despatch of the product.

Miscroscopic examination of the finished product is especially important for food products which have been comminuted, such as herbs and spices. In such products filth which may have been visible on the raw product becomes scattered throughout the mass in the form of tiny particles which become undetectable without the aid of a microscope. In some cases, i.e. fruit and nuts, extraction and microscopic procedures may not be necessary since contamination is readily indentified using the naked eye or with the aid of a magnifying glass.

Although visual examination plays an important role, other simple tests such as smelling may be just as important and should precede a more complicated examination, since changes in odour of the dried product can occur as a result of contamination.

Microscopic methods involve the separation of the filth elements from the food material, and the isolation and concentration of this filth or evidence of decomposition so that it may be examined, counted and identified. The major methods for isolation procedures use the principles of sedimentation, solution dispersion, filtration, oil flotation and the Wildman Trap Flask, and surface active and sequestering agents as described by Kramer & Twigg (1966). Microanalytical techniques and the identification of filth can only be performed expertly after competent instruction and much practical experience. Careless analysis by an incompetent analyst can lead to erroneous decisions.

Identification of insects by their whole bodies and especially by only body fragments is a very difficult task. However it is an important part of the microanalysis, since proper identification may be necessary to determine the source of contamination and the proper control methods. Classification and keys to insect identification can be found in most entomology textbooks.

The interpretation of insect count data may cause some difficulty, especially with insect fragments. One insect may break into several pieces, thus contaminating the food with many fragments. Qualitatively, any fragment, regardless of its size or nature, is an indication of contamination and should be a signal for initiating or expanding preventative control measures.

Rats and mice live on or in practically every food material used by man and are found in fields, storage areas, or any place where food is located. They eat or otherwise destroy vast quantities of food material, damage non-food items such as containers and buildings, transport filth on their tails, feet, and fur, and are carriers of many diseases such as Salmonella food poisoning.

There are various methods for isolating and detecting the different types of filth deposited by rodents and other animals. Gross rodent infestation can be readily discovered by the presence of burrows for nests, dark oil and dirt stains on rodent runways, odour of mice, filth deposition, and physical damage to dried food, i.e. teethmarks and holes. Rodent excreta can be detected visually around food processing areas. Rodent hairs and small quantities of excreta may require isolation and detection by the microanalytical methods already described. The identification of rodent filth is less of a problem than insect matter; usually the combination of the size, shape and colour are unique for a specific animal.

In general, contamination of the product by insects, insect fragments or excreta is possible only where an infestation is present. Thus, a preventative rather than a curative control programme is preferable.

14.12 Other Contaminants

At harvest, catch or slaughter all produce contains a mixed population of micro-organisms and this is likely to increase and to be further diversified by contamination during post-harvest handling. Some micro-organisms may cause spoilage of produce, lowering its quality and consumer acceptibility; others may render it poisonous to a lesser or greater degree. Food microbiology is a highly specialised subject; for present purposes attention is confined to a brief description of the three main types of food-borne organisms - bacteria, moulds and yeasts.

Bacteria are the smallest of the micro-organisms associated with food spoilage, and also the most primitive. Single cells, or collections of single cells, they grow, as do all spoilage micro-organisms, at the expense of the food on which or in which they live, by absorbing nutrients through their cell walls. This process involves some degradation, and hence spoilage, of the food's constituents. Bacterial reproduction is by simple vegetative cell division or for a few bacteria by sporulation.

Moulds, thought of typically as fluffy or hairy growths, are structurally more complex. Their filamentous growth habit, where long, branching cells or chains of cells (hyphae) form the vegetative part of the organism (mycelium), is quite different in form from that of the bacteria. Reproduction is also more complicated. Sexual spores are formed after the fusion of two colony cells in some species. Asexual spores (formed without previous cell fusion) are produced by most mould species, either within enlarged cells, or in chains. All types of spores are important for the continuation of the mould's life cycle since they are, in general, more resistant to climatic extremes than the mycelium itself, and can be borne away from their parent plant by wind or water to other food sources, where in suitable conditions they can germinate and so repeat the cycle. Only two groups of moulds are of major importance in food spoilage, the Pin Moulds (Class Phycomycetes, Sub-Class Zygomycetes, Order Mucorales), which have asexual spores, and the Fungi Imperfecti, a group of moulds usually lacking sexual spore formation.

Yeasts differs from moulds in their reduced and simplified life forms, although they are both members of the same group of organisms, the Fungi. More like bacteria in external appearance they often form colonies which are aggregates of single cells. Multiplication is by budding, a method not unlike the method of cell division found in the bacteria. One group of yeasts, however, form sexual spores in the same way as that class of moulds known as the Ascomycetes, and hence their classification as Fungi and not bacteria.

Both the growth and activity of micro-organisms and the types present are variable for different commodities and in different drying regimes. Regardless of the reason for their presence, a preventative control programme should be set up for all stages in the processing in collaboration with a microbiologist of other suitable specialist, and needless to say, good housekeeping is the first step in achieving this.

Food may be rendered poisonous by micro-organisms in two ways. The organism may be pathogenic to humans, and cause infection on ingestion. Salmonella poisoning falls under this heading. In other instances, the organism produces a toxin in the course of its growth within the food, and poisoning results directly from ingestion of the toxin. Of particular importance in this category, for produce drying, are the mycotoxins which are produced in foods by some moulds -for example the aflatoxins which are produced by Aspergillus flavus in damp produce. Aflatoxins are amongst the most poisonous substances now known.

14.13 Quality Factors for Specific Commodities

The previous discussions on quality assessment have been of a general nature and apply to all commodities and all processing operations. The principles should be considered thoroughly since if the quality for a particular market is not maintained selling prices will fall, markets may disappear, and health may suffer. This is not to say that all dried products must be produced to the official standards. If, for instance, unsulphured apricots which dry brown rather than orange are an acceptable product for a particular market, then there is no need to spend the extra money on sulphuring them.

The details below categorize different groups of crops and quality considerations which are of particular importance to these crops. Appendix 2 details suitable analytical methods for the most common factors.

(i)   Cereals.

Good quality in cereals implies the absence of imperfect grains and extraneous matter, absence of sprouting, severe weathering, mould, infestation, unpleasant aroma or flavour, and requires the grain to be sound in colour and appearance. Physical characteristics, such as grain shape and size, "1,000 grain" weight and hectolitre weight are also of importance industrially. The colour, sensory and microanalytical methods previously described are suitable for cereals.

For good milling, the grain must yield a flour having good colour and low ash content. The moisture content fo the grain should not exceed 15% for short-term storage, or 13% for long-term storage.

High drying temperatures, i.e. in excess of 66°C (Kent (1982)) should be avoided to prevent protein damage (which affects baking quality), germination capacity, and kernel cracking. The Codex Alimentarius standard (FAO (1980)) for cereals and cereal products should be consulted if further details on quality assessment are required.

(ii)   Fruit and vegetables.

The main considerations in the quality of fruits and vegetables are colour, appearance and in particular uniformity, taste, and freedom from infestation. All these can be measured and analysed using the methods already described.

If preservatives or other additives have been used in the production of the dried product, their level should be determined. Obviously moisture content is also an important factor to determine.

(iii)   Fish.

The major quality attributes important for fish are appearance, odour, flavour, and texture; the methods of assessment having already been discussed. Moisture and salt contents are the most important chemical analyses to conduct, but others which may be of use are:

-     ash and acid-insoluble ash for measuring bone and grit contents,

-     fat and protein content,

-     total volatile bases (TVB) as an index of (microbial) spoilage,

-     thiobarbituric acid assay (TBA) as an index of rancidity.

(iv)   Spices, tobacco and other cash crops

This group of crops is usually produced on an industrial scale and the buyer usually provides the quality specifications. If the specific test is not detailed in Appendix 2 of the AOAC literature (AOAC (1970)) should be consulted.

14.14 Water Activity and Dryness of Products

So far in the quality assessment, the question "How dry do we want a product?" has not been fully answered. This depends on a number of factors, which include the market requirement, the ability of the dryer to reach a certain moisture content, storage conditions, additives used, and crop composition and maturity. In all these cases, <u>water activity</u> is most important.

Water is essential for growth of micro-organisms and for the germination of spores. Within a micro-environment the availability of water for growth and other vital functions is determined by its relative vapour pressure or water activity rather than by its concentration. Water activity (a_w) is defined as the ratio of water vapour pressure (P_w) of the system to the vapour pressure of pure water (P_o) at the same temperature:

$$a_w = \frac{P_w}{P_0} \qquad (14.1)$$

Likewise, when the water within a system is in equilibrium with its vapour, the relative humidity (RH) of the system, expressed as a percentage, bears a simple relationship to water activity:

$$a_w = \frac{RH}{100} \qquad (14.2)$$

Since the responses of P_w and P_0 to temperature are nearly proportional, a_w is only slightly influenced by temperature over the growth range characteristic of mesophilic micro-organisms.

The relationship between a_w, or RH at equilibrium, and moisture content are described by moisture sorption isotherms, such as shown in Figure 14.1. Each commodity has its own unique set of isotherms generally of a similar shape to those shown in Figure 14.1. Sorption isotherms are useful to determine the lowest moisture content attainable under specified drying conditions, and how moisture content will be affected by different storage conditions.

The microbiological stability of dried foods results from an interruption of vital processes essential to microbial growth or spore germination which is mediated by depressed water activity. Every micro-organism has an optimum and a minimum water activity for growth. Any level below the optimum reduces the growth rate, but the total significance of water activity is also dependent on such factors as temperature, concentration of nutrients, pH and oxygen. As would be expected micro-organisms differ widely in their response to inhibition by depressed water activity, as indicated in Table 14.5 below.

Prevention of spoilage is usually achieved in dried products when the water activity is 0.8 or below. Table 14.6 shows moisture contents of various foods with water activities of 0.80. As it can be seen, commodities all have different water activity properties. It should be noted that water activity can be adjusted by the use of additives such as salt, sugar and glycerol.

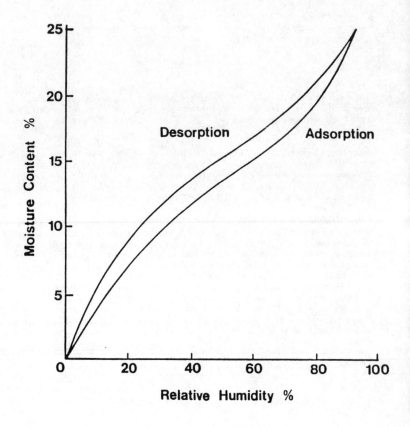

Figure 14.1   **Typical Sorption Isotherms**

Table 14.5   **Minimum Water Activities for Microbial Growth or Spore Germination** (Van Arsdel et al, (1973))

0.98	Organisms producing slime on meat
0.97	Pseudomonas, Bacillus cereus spores
0.96	Achromobacter, Escherichia coli
0.95	Bacillus subtilis, Clostridium botulinum spores
0.94	Bacillus cereus, Aerobactor aerogenes
0.93	Clostridium botulinum, Salmonella
0.92	Sarcina
0.91	Most bacteria
0.90	Staphylococcus aureus (anaerobic)
0.88	Most yeasts
0.86	Staphylococcus aureus (aerobic)
0.85	Aspergillus niger
0.83	Alternaria citri
0.80	Most moulds
0.75	Halophilic bacteria
0.65	Xerophilic fungi
0.62	Osmophilic yeasts

Table 14.6   **Moisture contents for Various Foods at Water Activities of 0.80** (Van Arsdel et al, (1973))

Food	Moisture content % (dry basis)
Apples	41.9
Apricots	37.2
Prunes	35.9
Wheat	15.3
Corn	14.7

15. PACKAGING AND STORAGE OF DRIED FOODSTUFFS

15.1 Principles of Packaging

With the exception of cereal grains, which are well suited to handling and storage in bulk, dried foodstuffs are normally packaged in some way for storage and marketing. Whether the package is a large one, perhaps for distribution to an industrial or trade customer, or a small package for sale to a household consumer, three basic functions of the package can be recognized.

(i) Containment of the foodstuff, enabling the chosen quantity to be handled as one unit without loss, throughout the hazards of transport and storage. This function is a necessary pre-condition for effective performance of the remaining functions.

(ii) Protection of the foodstuff against the hazards of transport and storage, and preserve its required attributes through a planned shelf life.

(iii) Communication of information about the foodstuff such as its nature, origin, method of use, quantity etc. or its destination or ownership.

Containment aspects of packaging involve consideration of the strength of the package, the mechanical hazards of transport, and the physical properties of the contents. They are not specific to dried foodstuffs and will not therefore be considered further here, but it must be exphasized that it is vital that a package withstand the hazards of transport without losing its contents if it is to protect them effectively. Communication aspects of packaging are of marketing rather than technical interest and will also not be discussed further. For effective planning of packaging for dried food products, it is therefore necessary to have good information about the following topics:

(i)	the product	–	Susceptibilities, modes of deterioration, moisture sorption isotherm,
(ii)	the market	–	types of outlet, consumer characteristics and requirements, shelf life,
(iii)	distribution	–	journey and storage conditions,
(iv)	production	–	demands of labour and machinery,
(v)	regulations	–	any legal requirements, especially of importing countries,
(vi)	packaging materials and packages	–	properties and performance

15.2 The Need for Protection

The protection which the package is required to provide against the hazards of distribution and storage is dependent on the particular susceptibility of the foodstuff. The product may be assessed in relation to the various groups of hazards.

The mechanical hazards, i.e. shock, vibration and compression, are usually of minor importance in relation to dried foodstuffs, although breakdown of friable particles may occasionally be a potential problem which can be taken into account in package selection.

Climatic hazards are much more relevant. Moisture is of primary importance and is frequently the principal consideration in protective packaging. High temperature may have adverse effects on foods but packaging cannot provide direct protection except in the very short term. Oxygen is a significant factor in deterioration of many foods, especially those containing fats or oils, and this should be taken into account in the packaging system. Light may have similar effects to oxidation or may promote oxidation, and the package can be selected to exclude light from the food. Although not strictly climatic hazards, the questions of tainting of the food by foreign odours and retention of preservative (sulphur dioxide) in the package are conveniently considered at the time since they also involve the permeability characteristics of the package.

Biological hazards to dried foods need attention throughout production and distribution, although they are usually a secondary consideration in relation to selection of a package. Bacterial spoilage will not be a problem in a dried food, and the action of a package is simply to exclude contamination, thereby preventing any increase in the bacterial load. Fungal spoilage can occur if any part of a product reaches an equilibrium relative humidity (erh) of about 70% or higher, and with foodstuffs for which this is a significant risk, for example dried fish, packaging must be selected to reduce the chance of such conditions arising. Infestation by mites or insects is a potential problem with most dried foods; packaging has a part to play in control, but will only be effective if combined with other measures. Protection against mammals (especially rodents) and birds cannot be provided economically through packaging, although good packaging practice will assist through minimizing spillage. These pests must be excluded from food stores by appropriate store design and management procedures.

Consideration of the protection requirements of a product, together with production and marketing factors, is the first step in choosing packaging for a product.

For any particular product a profile of the required protection can be developed; some examples are given in Table 15.1.

Table 15.1   Protection Requirements of Products

	Moisture	Oxygen	Light	Mould	Insects
Dehydrated carrots	x		x		x
Dried fruits	x			x	x
Dried fish	x	x		x	x

15.3 Protection against Moisture

Dried foods are made by removing water from natural foods and they will tend to absorb water again during storage. The tendency to pick up water, as water vapour, is determined by the equilibrium relative humidity of the storage atmosphere, not merely by the moisture content of the food. With some foods, e.g. potato crisps, moisture content relates directly to a critical quality attribute (crispness), and in conditions where the food gains moisture during storage the shelf life is simply the time taken to reach a "critical" moisture content. With many other foods the moisture content influences the rate of deterioration in quality through chemical and biochemical reactions or through microbiological spoilage and with a moisture content changing in storage there is a more complex relationship between moisture content and storage life. However, if a required shelf life is defined at specific storage conditions then a suitable water activity and corresponding moisture content can be selected. Using the moisture sorption isotherm for the product the suitable humidity for storage can be determined. The moisture content corresponding to any given e.r.h. depends on the nature of the commodity. Table 15.2 shows how some food products are classified depending on their moisture content and water activity.

Table 15.2   Classification of Foods by Moisture Content

Group	Moisture Content % (wb)	As produced water activity	Examples
1	2 - 8	0.1 - 0.3	Most dried vegetables
2	6 - 30	0.5 - 0.7	Cereals, nuts, most dried fruits, fish
3	25 - 40	0.8	"High moisture" dried fruits (eg prunes)

Group 1 requires packaging giving good protection against moisture uptake; group 2 requires little protection under most climatic conditions, while group 3 needs protection against moisture loss combined with some treatment (hot fill or preservative) to prevent microbiological spoilage.

15.4   Protection against Oxygen

In general, a package contains air in addition to the product, and therefore oxygen is available for oxidative reactions. The quantity of oxygen needed to develop off-flavours may be quite small, and with products of low bulk density sufficient can be contained within the bulk; in such instances the package may be irrelevant to protection against oxidation. If oxygen is removed from the product by evacuation or flushing with an inert gas, a package with a high resistance to oxygen transmission is needed to maintain the desired condition. The packaging material and processing costs make vacuum packaging expensive and only relevant where the dried product has a high market value.

15.5 Transmission of Vapours and Gases through Packaging Materials

All flexible packaging materials to some extent allow transmission of water vapour, oxygen and other gases. Standard test methods are available for measuring transmission rates or permeability constants, and these show values ranging over 2 or 3 orders of magnitude between different flexible packaging materials. For homogeneous films, transmission rates are inversely proportional to film thickness. While there is a reasonable amount of data on the permeabilities of common packaging films to water vapour, oxygen, carbon dioxide and nitrogen, there is little quantitative data on transmission of other gases or of volatile organic compounds typical of flavour components. It is usually assumed that materials which are good oxygen barriers also show low permeability to these other agents.

A packaging material which resists water vapour and/or gas transmission will only display the same properties in the package if it can be adequately sealed, so that transmission through the seals is not greater than that through intact material. For small flexible packages this is normally achieved by heat sealing. It is also necessary that the sealed pack will resist normal handling during transport and that it will resist puncturing by the product.

The rate of passage of water vapour through a package is proportional to its area. The effect on the product of a quantity of water vapour will be proportional to its mass and hence to its volume. Therefore the effects of permeating moisture will be more marked in packages with a high surface to volume ration, i.e. more evident in small rather than large packages. Hence, to maintain a specified shelf life, small packages must be made of material with better barrier properties than large packages. Similar considerations apply in respect of oxygen and other gases and vapours.

15.6 Shelf Life Estimation

Where the shelf life of a product is determined by changes in moisture content it is possible to make some estimate of the shelf life with a given barrier material, or the barrier properties required for a particular shelf life. Packaging textbooks should be consulted for the appropriate method (Cairns et al (1974), Pain (1981), Sacharow (1976)).

15.7 General Packaging Materials

Traditional packaging materials used for long established products such as dried fruit and dried fish include baskets, bales, jute sacks, wooden boxes and cardboard boxes. These can only be used for packaging dried products which do not require water vapour or oxygen barriers under the prevailing climatic conditions, and are appropriate for commodities which are transported in large packages to a central marketing point and then sold loose. These packages can often be used several times and are usually cheap; the need for good hygiene must be emphasized. Inclusion of a low density polyethylene film lining in a "traditional" package can add substantial protection against uptake of water vapour.

A wide range of protective packaging materials have been used for dried foodstuffs including metal cans, glass jars and rigid moulded plastic containers as well as the more commonly found flexible packs. Rigid packages may be assumed to have negligible permeation rates for water vapour and gases, if they are properly sealed, but they are relatively expensive and will not be considered further here. The principal relevant flexible materials are paper, aluminium foil, moisture-proof cellulose film, and plastic films (low and high density polyethylene, polypropylene, polyester and nylon) together with laminates incorporating two or more of these. Each of these materials is discussed separately below.

Flexible materials may be used as the sole component of a small package or as a barrier component in a package. A transport package is also required, in each instance; this could comprise a basket, a fibreboard or wooden box, a paper wrap, or a textile or paper sack. In practice, therefore, the complete package system should be planned as a whole. It should be noted that in many circumstances the choice of packaging materials is limited, and it may be a case of utilizing whatever material is available.

15.8   Flexible Packaging Materials

(i)   Paper.

Despite newer materials, paper remains an important packaging component. Paper is both hygroscopic and highly permeable to water vapour, and it is normally porous and therefore highly permeable to gases. The valuable properties of paper in packaging are high strength combined with low extensibility, good printability and cheapness. Paper alone is used for bags for packaging foods of low moisture sensitivity, e.g. flour, in appropriate climates. When barrier properties are required, paper may be coated with a less permeable material, e.g. polyethylene, or incorporated into a laminate; alternatively a package may have separate layers of paper and a barrier material, e.g. paper sacks with an inner ply of aluminium foil laminated to paper.

For consumer packs of particulate foods, paper is best used as block bottom bags (sos style). Two ply bags can also be made with the inner ply of a different material, either a paper such as grease-proof, or a film or laminate.

(ii)   Aluminium Foil.

Aluminium foil is the only metal foil used in substantial quantities in packaging. Lamination is essential to strengthen aluminium foil for almost all packaging operations. In most instances a sealed pack will be required, and some provision for heat sealing (or cold sealing) must normally also be made. A coating or lamination of low density polyethylene is by far the commonest heat sealing medium. Heat seal lacquers and wax/tissue combinations have also been used.

Aluminium foil is incorporated in flexible packaging materials mainly because of the excellent barrier to transmission of light, water vapour, gases and odours that it affords. It is however an expensive material, and is increasingly being replaced by alternative materials in all but the most demanding applications.

(iii)   Cellulose Films.

Cellulose films used for protective packaging comprise a base sheet of regenerated cellulose with polymeric coatings which impart heat sealability and moisture-proofness. The barrier properties of cellulose films are mainly determined by the coatings and are therefore unaffected by film thickness. The range of thicknesses normally used for packaging films is from $19\mu m$ to $30\mu m$. Strength does increase with thickness; cellulose films show rather low extensibility and are quite resistant to a simple tensile stress. However, if a tear is initiated, the resistance to its propagation is very low, and therefore cellulose films can be easily damaged. They are not very suitable for hard sharp products, such as dried cauliflower.

Cellulose films may be used alone in small bags, and laminated to polyethylene where greater package integrity is required. Their appearance and printability are good, they are relatively stiff and have wide tolerance of heat sealing conditions. A major disadvantage in tropical countries is the sensitivity of the films themselves to moisture; the recommended storage conditions for reeled film are $18-20°C$, 35-50%r.h. Cellulose films tend to be more expensive than plastic films, and in many applications cellulose films have been replaced by alternatives.

(iv)   Polyethylene Films.

Polyethylene is commonly described as either low density (LDPE) or high density (HDPE), but in fact three density ranges are usually recognized: 0.910 - 0.925, 0.926 - 0.940 and 0.941 to 0.965 g cm^{-3}. Density is a more important property because it is an indicator of the degree of crystallinity of the plastic, which influences in particular the stiffness and the permeability of a film.

LDPE film can be produced as thin as $9\mu m$, but this is very weak indeed and is only used for garment wrapping; film used for bags for consumer packs of dry foodstuffs is likely to be in the range $38-76\mu m$ thick. LDPE is a reasonably good barrier to water vapour. However it is a rather poor barrier to gases such as oxygen, and also to many organic vapours.

HDPE film is very much stiffer than LDPE and most HDPE film packages are $2-38\mu m$ thick. HDPE has water vapour and gas transmission rates around half those of LDPE. Both LDPE and HDPE can be printed if they are pretreated and are widely used as pre-made bags. End-weld bags are made direct from lay flat tube, whereas side weld bags are made from flat film. The former have a more reliable seal, and are often preferred for packaging, especially of particulate products. Sealing of polyethylene films results in welding of the two sides, unlike the surface sealing of cellulose films; a good seal should be as strong as the film. It is essential to avoid stressing the melted plastic.

LDPE bags and film are probably more widely available than any other flexible packaging material, and provide excellent general purpose packaging. Often LDPE is used for consumer packs for products where its good water vapour resistance is not necessary; the choice is made because of the film's adequate strength and transparency, good sealability and convenience of use. The water vapour transmission rate, WVTR, can be reduced to almost any desired value by increasing the film thickness, so LDPE could be used for the most hygroscopic products. The disadvantages of LDPE are its high gas permeability and poor resistance to transmission of organic materials. The better barrier properties of HDPE can make this a more economical choice when a particular WVTR is required.

(v)   Polypropylene Films.

Polypropylene is produced at only one density (around 0.90 g cm^{-3}), but several different types of film are produced from it. Cast polypropylene and heat sealable orientated polypropylene (OPP) are the most common.

Cast polypropylene is a very clear film, more rigid than LDPE of the same thickness, and with barrier properties comparable to those of HDPE. Cast polypropylene can be heat sealed, but there is sometimes a tendency for the film to be embrittled along the edge of the seal. As pre-made bags, cast polypropylene can be used for almost any purpose for which polyethylene would be suitable.

For packaging purposes OPP film thickness is in the range 18-40μm. OPP films are surface-sealable and they require the same type of sealers as cellulose films, but temperature control must be good so that the polypropylene itself does not melt or shrink. Heat sealable OPP films are now the most widely used group of materials for packaging of dry food products in small consumer packs.

The WVTR of OPP is similar to that of HDPE and gas barrier properties are either similar to HDPE or substantially better depending on the make-up of the film. OPP films are also important in laminates, with 2-ply OPP and OPP/LDPE especially widely used.

(vi)   Polyester Films.

Polyester film is made from polyethylene terephthalate, the polymer also used for textiles. It is not heat sealable, and it is always used laminated to other materials. The usual thickness of film for lamination is 12μm. Polyester is a very strong film, with good barrier properties, high tensile and tear strenth, high transparency and a softening point above 200°C.

(vii)   Polyamide (nylon) Films

There are several nylons, all fairly tough films. They are somewhat hygroscopic, and therefore most of their properties are dependent on the ambient humidity. The water vapour transmission rate is fairly high; gas transmission rates are low at low humidities but increase as the relative humidity is raised. Nylon films are mostly used in laminates with LDPE to provide mechanical strength and an oxygen barrier. These laminates are commonly used for vacuum packaging.

15.9 Composite Flexible Packaging

(i)   Coatings.

Major applications are in the manufacture of cellulose, polypropylene and other films, but various functional coatings are also applied by packaging material converters, sometimes over print. Important products of coating processes include PVDC/paper, LDPE/paper and PVDC/LDPE/paper. These materials can be handled like paper, but have useful water vapour barrier properties.

(ii)   Metallization.

By using vacuum deposition techniques a thin coating of aluminium can be applied to suitably prepared films to give a bright metallic layer. This is very thin, of the order of $0.025\mu m$ thick. Metallization gives a marked improvement in the barrier properties, for polyester, polypropylene and cellulose films.

Although the manufacturing process is highly specialized, metallized films are cheaper than aluminium foils, and for many applications have sufficiently good barrier properties to be used as foil replacements. The metallized films are either incorporated in laminates or coated to protect the thin metallic layer.

(iii)   Laminates.

Laminates are used in order to combine the desirable properties of different materials and an almost infinite number of possible constructions can be made. Film/film laminates are usually chosen to optimize barrier properties and performance in packaging machines. An increasing number of similar composite plastic materials are being produced by coextrusion processes and may be described as coextrusions rather than as laminates; the most interestng materials have three layers, e.g. LDPE/PVDC/LDPE.   Laminates incorporating aluminium foil are usually three layer (e.g. paper/foil/LDPE, polyester/foil/LPDE) or four layer (e.g. paper/LDPE/foil/LDPE).

One benefit from the use of laminates is that they can permit the use of "sandwich" printing. In this technique, print is applied to the back of a transparent film which is then laminated to another material; print with a high gloss which is protected both from the foodstuff and from external damage is obtained.   A example of such a laminate is OPP/print/metallizing/OPP, both OPP films being heat sealable.

15.10 Selection of Packaging Materials

The factors in selecting a packaging material are likely to be:

(i)   Permeability characteristics required for product protection,

(ii)   Mechanical characteristics required for product protection under the storage and distribution conditions,

(iii)   Marketing requirements, including graphics,

(iv)   Filling and closing system to be used,

(v)   Prospective demand,

(vi)   Availability and cost.

Because conditions vary, there is never a universal best package specification for a foodstuff; while the practice of other products may provide a useful guide, it should only be used as a starting point in developing or selecting an appropriate package. For dried foods sold at rural level the properties required from the package are simple, but for urban marketing and export the demands placed on the package are greater and therefore more attention to the specification of the package is needed.

15.11 Storage Considerations

During storage of dried foodstuffs, deterioration can be caused by heat, moisture, moulds, insects, mites, rodents and birds.

Deterioration by heat can be minimized by storing in the shade in a well ventilated area. If a storage building is used, excessive heat gain can be prevented by reflection of solar radiation, correct orientation, shading of walls, insulation and controlled ventilation.

Moisture uptake can be greatly reduced by particular packaging materials, such as polyethylene films. Whatever the packaging material and whatever its size, the package should be stored under cover with complete protection from rain. In storage buildings the roof, walls, doors and ventilation openings should exclude wind-blown rain. If water absorption from the ground below is a problem, the floor must be supplied with a damp-proof course or the packaged goods should be stacked on pallets, boards or poles, giving 100 mm floor clearance or on moisture-proof sheets.

Rodents and birds can be excluded from buildings by sealing all unnecessary openings, screening the ventilation openings and minimizing gaps around doors. Poisoned baits can be used to eliminate rodents but should be used very carefully, preferably by experienced persons.

Insects and mites can be killed by effective fumigation with a suitable gas, like phosphine or methyl bromide. Stacked produce can be fumigated under gas-proof sheets if these are properly used. Fumigation of the building itself can also kill pests throughout the interior of the building but it is not always easily and effectively achieved. Insects and mites can also be controlled by treatment with contact pesticides, especially where these can be admixed with produce, like cereal grain and pulses, for which there are approved and acceptable dosage rates. Only those pesticides recommended for such purposes should be used.

Detailed methods for rodent elimination and fumigation can be found in storage textbooks (FAO (1970)). In general, storage areas and surroundings should be kept clean and tidy and free from any contaminants. Although good housekeeping goes a long way towards keeping away most pests, it must be recognized that supplementary pest control measures will almost certainly be needed, especially in tropical climates.

Cereal grains and cereal products can be packed in jute or cotton sacks or in bulk storage containers. Sacks should be stacked tidily and methodically so that the stacks can be kept clear of walls without collapsing. Attention to good housekeeping, proper inspection procedures, adequate sampling and testing to check the moisture content, temperature, and the presence of insects are all important. When insect infestation is discovered, appropriate action should be taken immediately to determine the extent and significance of the infestation and to make arrangements for suitable disinfestation treatment, if necessary, to prevent further damage.

These same principles apply also to rural storage situations but, where modern pesticides are not available or cannot be safely used, there is need to make best possible use of locally traditional methods such as airtight storage or the admixture of wood ash, abrasive dusts or suitable vegetable oils, many of which give some protection to stored pulses in particular.

16. DRYER SELECTION AND DESIGN

Subsequent to establishing that solar drying of a particular commodity is potentially viable and gaining an appreciation of the different types of solar dryers and their respective advantages and disadvantages, the next step is the selection and design of the most suitable type of dryer. This should be considered in two stages, technical and socio-economic.

16.1 Technical Criteria

The following design factors must be established:

- the throughput of the dryer over the productive season,

- the size of batch to be dried,

- the drying period(s) under stated conditions,

- the initial and desired final moisture content of the commodity,

- the drying characteristics of the commodity such as maximum drying termperature, effect on sunlight upon the product, quality, etc,

- climatic conditions during the drying season, i.e. insolation intensity and duration, air temperature and humidity and wind speed (such data may be available from local meteorological stations),

- availability and reliability of electrical power,

- the availability, quality, durability and price of potential construction materials, such as:

   glazing materials; glass, plastic sheet or film,
   wood, prepared or unprepared,
   nails, screws, bolts, etc.,
   metal sheet; flat or corrugated,
   angle iron,
   bricks (burnt or mud), concrete blocks, stones, cement, sand, etc.,
   roofing thatch,
   metal mesh, wire netting, etc.,
   mosquito netting, muslin, etc.,
   bamboo or fibre weave,
   black paint, other blackening materials,
   insulation materials; sawdust etc.,
   fossil fuels (to power engines to drive fans if electricity is not available),

- the type of labour available to build and operate the dryer.

In any one situation there may well be other technical factors that need to be considered.

16.2 Socio-Economic Criteria

From the initial considerations, estimates of the capital costs of the dryer, the price of the commodity to be dried, the likely selling price of the dried product will have been made. Other factors that need to be considered are the following:

- who will own the dryer?

- is the dryer to be constructed by the end-user (with or without advice from extension agencies), local contractors or other organizations?

- who will operate and maintain it?

- how can the drying operation be incorporated into current pre-drying and post-drying operations?

- the availability of clean water at the site for preparation of the commodity prior to drying?

- sources of finance from local authorities, extension agencies etc.

Obviously there are many other socio-economic factors, particularly those of a local nature, which must be taken into account. It cannot be stressed too highly that if such factors are not taken into account and evaluated then there is every chance that an inappropriate dryer design will result. Equal emphasis must be placed on both technical and socio-economic factors.

16.3 Design Procedure

Having obtained technical and socio-economic data the type of solar dryer can be selected.

The design of the dryer will involve the specification and/or calculation of the following:

- batch size,

- quantity of moisture to be removed,

- drying time,

- typical ambient conditions, particularly insolation and air temperature and humidity,

- drying temperature,

- air flow through the dryer,

- area of collector,

- drying chamber configuration, bed depth etc.,

- pressure drop through the dryer,

- fan duty.

17. EXPERIMENTAL METHODOLOGY

17.1 Planning of Experimental Programmes

Only once the proposed objectives of the research programme have been clearly defined can a decision be made on what experiments or series of experiments should be undertaken. In doing so, it is important that they are carefully planned taking into consideration the overall objectives of the programme, the time available, the availability of equipment and expertise. During this planning stage it is often worthwhile asking the question 'if the results were available now (a) what use would be made of them and/or (b) what would be the next step?' All too often the answer to (a) is 'nothing' and the answer to (b) 'I don't know'. More importantly on the basis that it is better to execute a limited programme successfully than an extensive one badly, having considered the individual experiments in detail it may be necessary to modify the overall objectives such that they are commensurate with the expertise and equipment available.

17.2 Recording of Data

It cannot be emphasized too strongly that in carrying out any experimental programme the researcher must be as methodical as possible and the keeping of a logbook with all the experimental details meticulously recorded is of paramount importance; many a good experiment has been spoilt because a set of results was recorded on a piece of paper which was later lost. From practical experience accumulated over a number of years the authors have found the following methodology to be of great value.

(i)   For a sub-set of trials a brief descriptions of the particular dryer configuration should be included with the trial records. It may be found useful to include sketches of particular features, lists and costs of materials and components, and construction and labour requirements. Clearly it is important that the positioning of the dryer, relative to the North-South axis, is recorded.

(ii)   Full records should be kept of the commodity handling and processing stages between procurement (from farmer, market place etc.) and the commencement of actual drying trials. These will vary for each trial due to factors outside the control of the researcher. Knowledge of the history of the commodity prior to drying is of particular importance with respect to produce quality.

(iii)   A daily log should be kept of the operation of the dryer. Besides the start-up and shut-down times any interruptions to normal operation should be recorded. It is recommended that the duration and timing of dryer operation should follow closely that likely to be carried out by the end-user.

(iv)   Appendix 5 is included as a guide in drawing up a Trial Logsheet.

(v)   When monitoring performance it is always helpful to plot out a rough copy of, for example, moisture content versus time curves, as the experiment proceeds rather than 'a few days later'. In this way any obvious errors in measurement are soon detected and can quickly be corrected.

17.3 Use of Instrumentation

It is essential that the researcher is fully aware of the capability of the instrumentation available to him and the correct methods to be used when setting up and using instruments. Instrumentation can be as simple or as complex as one wants or the budget allows. Generally speaking, for field work the simpler the equipment the better.

Instrumenting a solar dryer to determine its operating characteristics is not difficult and the parameters are easy to measure provided the correct procedures are followed. For most studies the following parameters are monitored.

- air temperature,

    (a) ambient,
    (b) leaving the collector/entering the drying chamber,
    (c) leaving the drying chamber,

- air humidity,

- air flow rate,

- pressure drop,

- insolation,

- weight

With the exception of insolation all these parameters are common to many experimental programmes and the testing of most types of dryer. Most of the necessary equipment will be available in laboratories. For the measurement of temperature the most obvious and basic instrument to use is liquid-in-glass thermometers but taking sophistication to the extreme, high precision, platinum resistance thermometers (PRT) telemetered over large distances, with multi-pen chart recorders could be used. In the discussion that follows the basic principles are outlined which are applicable to instrumentation in general regardless of their degree of sophistication.

17.4 Temperature Measurement

For liquid-in-glass thermometers the points below should be noted.

(i) Before use all thermometers should be checked for accuracy. This can be done simply for putting them together in the shade and leaving for at least 30 minutes. Upon inspection any thermometer that reads more than a quarter of a degree different than the rest should be marked accordingly. Such a check can also be carried out with thermocouples and platinum resistance thermometers.

(ii)   When measuring temperatures the thermometer must be shaded from the direct rays of the sun.

(iii)   The thermometer bulb should be placed well into the air stream to ensure a true reading of the air temperature.

(iv)   The temperature of the air leaving the collector or the drying chamber should be monitored at several points and the average used for purposes of calculation.

(v)   The thermometers should be placed where they can be read easily and do not need to be removed from the dryer in order to take a reading. In this respect thermocouples or PRTs have an obvious advantage over thermometers.

17.5   Humidity Measurement

Perhaps the most commonly used and simplest instrument is the whirling arm hygrometer. It is normally supplied with full operating instructions, nevertheless the following points should be borne in mind.

(i)   The wicks should be kept clean and free of dust and the water in the reservoir changed regularly.

(ii)   To take a reading the hygrometer should be swung for at least 15 seconds. The wet bulb temperature should then be read immediately.

(iii)   When 'whirling' the hygrometer it is good practice to remain stationary to avoid the instrument hitting obstacles and the thermometers getting broken.

(iv)   If the wet bulb thermometer does get broken, and no replacement is readily available, then the dry bulb thermometer can be substituted and the dry bulb temperature taken using a liquid in glass thermometer placed nearby.

(v)   If a whirling hygrometer is placed in a duct the velocity of air across the bulb must be at least 5 m s^{-1}.

17.6   Air Flow Measurement

Although upon first consideration air flow is easy to measure it is, in fact, somewhat more difficult, principally because the flow of air in both natural and forced convection dryers is generally uneven. Because the velocities are very low, frequently less than 10 mm s^{-1}, the measurement of air flow caused by natural convection is extremely difficult, if not impossible, unless very specialized and accurate equipment is available. In a duct the air flow can be described as either turbulent or laminar. In turbulent flow (Re greater than about 3000) there is considerable mixing of particles within the air stream. In laminar flow (Re less than about 2000) there is little disturbance; the air stream maintaining an essentially uniform distribution. The mixing of particles in turbulent flow renders it more effective in heat transfer applications. The velocity profiles (pipe flow) are shown schematically in Figure 17.1.

The following points should be noted when measuring air flow.

(i)   As many readings as possible should be taken commensurate with the respective sizes of the duct and the measuring instrument(s). It may be a good idea to divide the cross section of the duct into a number of rectangular or square "cells" and place the instrument at the centre of each cell each time; in this way consistency between successive measurements is easily achieved.

(ii)   If a vane anemometer is used, i.e. an instrument that 'counts' air flow, it must be compensated for low air velocities. It must be ensured also that the vanes are aligned at right angles to the direction of flow. Similarly when using a tubular hot-wire anemometer it is important that the parallel section of the sensing head is held directly in line with the direction of flow.

(iii)   When measuring the airflow it is essential that the air temperature (at the point) is measured simultaneously and the air flow reading adjusted to a common temperature ($0°C$ or $25°C$).

(iv)   Since volumetric air flow is the product of air velocity and area of cross-section, it is essential that the latter is accurately known.

(v)   Great care should be taken when measuring the air velocity that the act of measurement does not in any way affect the normal functioning of the dryer or alter the normal pattern of air flow. To achieve an even air flow it is often a good idea to put a slight restriction to flow across the cross-section of the duct. Material such as sacking is sufficient; mosquito netting does not present adequate resistance to air flow at the velocities normally encountered.

17.7   Pressure Drop Measurement

The pressure drop is not a measurement frequently required but is sometimes necessary to determine the size of fan required for the dryer. Static pressure, i.e. the pressure exerted on any plane parallel to the direction of flow is the factor of interest rather than the dynamic pressure which is a function of the velocity of the air. The easiest way to measure the static pressure is to drill a hole in the side of the duct or chamber and attach a manometer tube as shown in Figure 17.2.

Laminar Flow

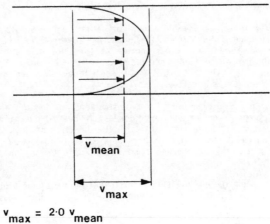

$$v_{max} = 2 \cdot 0 \; v_{mean}$$

Turbulent Flow

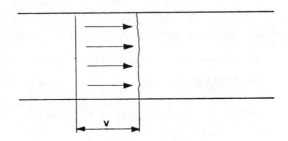

Velocity Constant Across Cross-section

Figure 17.1   Velocity Profiles for Air Flow in Pipes

Figure 17.2   Pressure Tapping

For greater sensitivity the
manometer tube can be inclined
and paraffin used for the manometer
fluid. Should separate pieces
of tubing be used for the
two legs care must be taken
that the diameter of both pieces
is exactly the same.

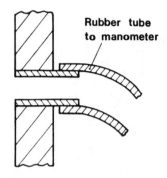

**Rubber tube
to manometer**

Tapping to be small diameter
and flush with duct.

17.8   Insolation Measurement

Experience in the field gained by TDRI has shown that simple dome solarimeters
are perfectly adequate for experimental purposes.   Such instruments are
extremely easy to use and once calibrated retain their accuracy for long periods.
It is necessary though to ensure that the instrument is set up exactly in the
horizontal plane using the two spirit levels incorporated. Methods of calculation
of the amount of insolation incident upon a sloping surface relative to that
measured on a horizontal surface has been given in Chapter 6 (Equation 6.8). It
should be noted that the angle of the clear collector cover is immaterial and the
angle of the absorber surface is the one to be used in Equation 6.8.

Insolation data is also required for design purposes.   Rather than use data
collected during the experimental programme it is likely to be far more accurate
to use data from a nearby meteorological station, since this will have been
accumulated over many years rather than a few weeks.

17.9   Weighing Procedures

Weight is an important parameter because in the determination of drying
characteristics the commodity will need to be weighed at frequent intervals.
The method of weighing in the field will generally be with a spring balance or a
beam balance.   These types of balance whilst eminently suitable, do have
associated with them the errors or fixed errors. For best use of these balances
the appropriate size commensurate with the size of sample should be chosen, eg
for a sample which initially is 8 kg when wet and 1-2 kg when dry a balance with
a full-scale reading of about 50 kgs would not be suitable. It is not good practice
to use two balances, since the errors associated with the two instruments would

be different. It is often a good idea to decide the sample size based on what balance is available and arrange that the sample size is commensurate with the mid range of the balance. If possible having to make two or more additive weighings should be avoided since individual errors would be compounded.

Weighing the trial batch at intervals over the trial period is probably the most practical method of monitoring the drying rate. However, if large batches are being used, then this is impractical and direct measurement of moisture content is the only effective method. With this method great care should be taken to ensure a typical sample; sub-samples should be taken from several locations within the drying chamber and particularly large, small or otherwise unusual pieces should be excluded from the sample. Moisture content measurements should be made at least in duplicate. The recommended method of moisture analysis should be used if possible.

NB If a sample of X g of 'wet' commodity is dried in a moisture determination test to Y g when bone dry then:

$$\frac{X - Y}{Y}$$ is the moisture content expressed on the dry basis (db), and

$$\frac{X - Y}{Y}$$ is the moisture content expressed on the wet basis (wb).

Confusion can easily occur and therefore the basis of measurement should always be stated within the text, ie. 'a'%(wb) or 'b'%(db).

17.10 Electronic Instrumentation

Whilst the previous comments concern simple instruments most Centres will have access to mains or battery operated instrumentation. A few words on the relative merits of these particular devices are relevant. A point, often forgotten, when using an electronic technique, is that just because it gives an answer it does not necessarily mean that the answer is correct. When setting up apparatus it is always worthwhile to check the readings given by say, thermocouple and platinum resistance thermometers etc. with mercury-in-glass thermometers. Similarly readings given with hot wire anemometers should be checked with hand-held vane anomometers and those given by pneumatic transducers for measuring pressures should be checked with a manometer. In this way once the readings that the electronic instruments are outputting are deemed reasonable, and only then, can purely electronic output be relied upon. Another point to be wary of is that it is very easy to attach numerous thermocouples (for example) to the device and have transducers everywhere. When it comes to the analysis of these results, one page of the graph plotter becomes so congested that it is very difficult to make any meaningful sense from the data.

On the question of battery or mains operation there are several options available to power instrumentation; a battery, a battery/mains combination with automatic change-over, a battery/mains combination with manual change-over, and power derived from a battery which itself is completely recharged at all times by the mains. Of these options the last is the best; it can be compared to a motor car battery which is recharged while the engine is running, but even when the engine switches off one can still draw power from the battery. With this system, whether the mains fail or not, there is no disruption in supply to the instrument. The second arrangement is perhaps the next best, i.e. a battery that in the event of mains failure automatically changes over. One potential hazard with this is that the electrical shock in the change over from mains to battery can frequently upset instrumentation, particularly pulse counting circuits. The use of dry batteries is a very safe option, but it can be very expensive, particularly with recorders, etc. If rechargeable cells are available it is better, but it is necessary then to ensure that these are then topped up and charged on a daily basis.

The use of instrumentation dependent upon mains only is not to be recommended for extended field trials since the power invariably fails during the most crucial part of an experiment!

17.11 Control Batches

A small batch of the commodity should be dried as a control at the same time as that being solar dried. In most cases the control batch should be dried by the method solar drying is hoped to replace. This will usually be sun drying. The importance of a control batch is twofold; it enables a direct comparison of drying rate between solar drying and the other method and it also facilitates a direct comparison of the quality of the dried commodity produced by the two methods.

18. FROM THEORY INTO PRACTICE

In previous Chapters the subjects of solar collector and solar dryer selection and design have been considered largely from a theoretical viewpoint. This Chapter considers the practical aspects of constructing solar collectors and dryers which may result in designs differing slightly from those predicted from a purely theoretical basis. Before the design of a collector or dryer for a specific application is undertaken it is useful to consider the more general aspects of moving from theory into practice since special care must be taken in transforming the information obtained from the design equations into a practical working system.

18.1 From Design Equations into Practice

Information on the construction of collectors is not as readily available as that for solar dryers and greater care is needed before working drawings are prepared.

The design equations and recommendations on air flow conditions given in Chapter 6 enable the designer to determine values for collector area and duct depth. The equations do not however take into account all the practical aspects necessary for the design of the collector. The most obvious example in this case is that supports for the absorber plate may, if the duct depth is small, form a considerable obstruction to the air flow through the collector. This in turn will affect both the heat transfer characteristics and the pressure drop characteristics of the solar collector. The diameter of the inlet or outlet duct to the fan is likely to be of the order of 100 - 500 mm, whereas the collector duct may be several metres in width. If air enters a wide duct from a narrow opening abruptly the distribution of air flow across the duct is likely to be uneven leading to poor collector performance. An effective solution to this problem in many cases is to introduce some resistance to the air flow at the entry to the collector. However care must be exercised to prevent excessive loading on the fan and subsequent reduction in air flow. Sacking may be suitable in many cases. Figure 18.1(a) shows the flow path of air in such arrangments. The distribution of air flow across the collector assumes more importance as the ratio of duct width to length increases. Conversely, if air is drawn through the collector to the fan a tapering section helps maintain good flow conditions as shown in Figure 18.1(b).

In many cases the roof of a building forms an integral part of a solar collector and this dual purpose may impose rigid constraints on the design regarding the dimensions and orientation of the collector, especially where the concept of using the roof as a solar collector has only been considered after the building has been erected. The limitations imposed by an existing structure will in most cases lead to a down-grading of collector performance and this should be taken into consideration in the design. Equations are often based upon certain assumptions which are only applicable under certain conditions of operation and therefore if the dryer or collector is intended for widespread use some caution must be exercised. Typically an equation derived from experimental work relating to air velocities of 1 - 10 m s^{-1} should not be applied for velocities as low as 0.1 m s^{-1}.

Key: Air Flow ⟶

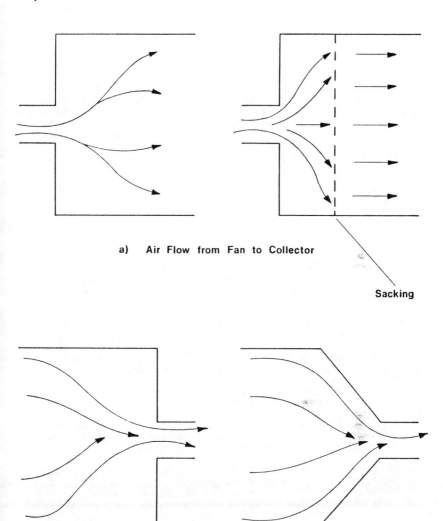

a)   Air Flow from Fan to Collector

Sacking

b)   Air Flow from Collector to Fan

Figure 18.1.   Air Flow in Collectors and Ducts

Variation in climatic conditions from site to site will affect collector performance over which the designer has no control which, together with the (daily) unpredictability of the weather requires that a decision be made as to whether it is desirable to size the solar collector or dryer based upon maximum or mean insolation levels. Clearly local knowledge here is invaluable. How safety factors are applied will clearly depend on what is being designed. In the case of a collector, a safety factor may be applied simply by increasing the area of the collector obtained from the design equations by say 10%, or perhaps by using a value for insolation in the design equations which is lower than expected. In the case of a dryer a safety factor can be applied by designing for a larger batch size or a shorter drying time. A more specific example is in the use of a chimney to promote natural convection; if the theoretical equation, as discussed in Appendix 11, suggests a chimney height of 2.5m, a chimney height of 3 m is likely to ensure that the air flow through the dryer will be adequate in most circumstances. It may well be that as a result of this, the dryer or collector is somewhat more expensive but this must be balanced against a design which does not meet its requirements.

18.2   Collector Scale-up

It will often be the case that the size of the dryer or collector required by the end-user is quite different to that tested in the experimental stage of the project. Some guidelines are given below as to how best to allow for changes in the scale of operation.

It may, for some reason or another, be necessary to increase the air flow or the temperature elevation (or both) or restraints may be imposed by external physical factors. To scale-up a collector for instance, it would appear reasonable at first sight to increase the collection area and the air flow proportionally. However an increase in area will affect collector performance in terms of pressure drop and heat transfer characteristics. It is instructive therefore to consider what happens during scale-up by looking closely at a typical problem. Consider the case where a collector of given dimensions has been developed and operates effectively under certain conditions of air flow, insolation and temperature elevation. A farmer requests a design for a solar collector with a four-fold increase in air flow but similar temperature elevation. How can the tested collector be scaled up for use by the farmer?

The dimensions of the tested collector are as shown in Figure 18.2. On the basis that the air velocity must remain at least equal to v to maintain heat transfer requirements, Table 18.1 shows some possible arrangements by which an area of 4A can be obtained and how the various configurations affect the air velocity, the pressure drop through the collector and the fan power required. Some simplifying assumptions have been made in determining the pressure drop and the fan power. The pressure drop across a duct is proportional to the length of the duct and to the square of the air velocity. Fan power is proportional to the pressure drop and to the volumetric air flow.

Consideration of the pressure drop and fan power columns of Table 18.1 shows how far reaching the effect of increasing the dimensions of the collector can be. Consider now the various individual options in more detail.

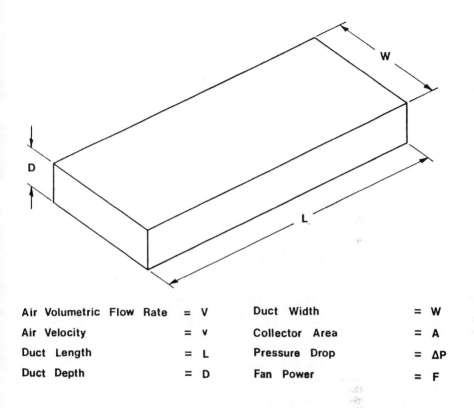

Air Volumetric Flow Rate	= V	Duct Width	= W
Air Velocity	= v	Collector Area	= A
Duct Length	= L	Pressure Drop	= ΔP
Duct Depth	= D	Fan Power	= F

Figure 18.2
Schematic Diagram of a Solar Collector

Table 18.1 Effect of Collector Dimensions

Collector	Volumetric flow rate	Collector width	Collector depth	Collector length	Collector Area	Air Velocity	Pressure Drop Across	Fan Power Rating
A (tested collector)	V	W	D	L	A	v	ΔP	F
B	4V	W	D	4L	4A	4v	64P	256F
C	4V	4W	D	L	4A	v	P	4F
D	4V	2W	D	2L	4A	2v	8P	32F
E	4V	W	2D	4L	4A	2v	16P	61F
F	4V	W	4D	4L	4A	v	4P	16F
G	4V	2W	2D	2L	4A	v	2P	8F

Collector B - it is probable that due to the higher air velocity a collector built to these dimensions would be more effective in heating the air passing through it; however a considerable price is paid in the increased pressure drop and fan power required.

Collector C - this configuration can be considered as four separate units of the tested collector. One likely drawback is the high width to length ratio which may cause difficulties in obtaining an even air flow distribution.

Collector D - the ratio of width to length for this collector is the same as for the tested collector and the higher velocity will give better heat transfer. As for collector B the increased velocity leads to increased pressure drop and power requirement.

In collectors E, F and G the duct depth has been increased to lessen the increase in velocity caused by the increase in volumetric flow rate. Changing the depth of the duct is a more fundamental change in the collector design than changing its length or width, possibly requiring some redesign of the support for the upper cover of the duct. Other changes due to the increased duct depth can be seen from Table 18.1.

Clearly there is a very large number of configurations which will give the desired collector area, some are obviously better than others but nevertheless the choice is not as simple as may have been assumed initially.

The final choice of collector dimensions will also be influenced by the capital and operating costs for the fans, the availability and price of materials for the collector structure, and any restrictions placed on the location where the collector is to be built, especially if it is to be part of another structure.

If a significant change in air temperature elevation is required relative to the tested design then this cannot be achieved by a similar scale-up procedure and will necessitate a basic re-design since the relationship between temperature elevation and air velocity is complex.

Constraints on the desired design may also occur where the collector is to be part of an existing roof; these might include roof area and dimensions, orientation, slope and materials of construction. There is no clear-cut design methodology which can be applied in such situations. For example, if the (existing) roof is of corrugated iron, a material of good thermal conductivity, then a bare plate collector (with the air ducted beneath the absorber) is possible. If the roof is of, say, asbestos, a material of poor thermal conductivity, then a covered plate collector (with the air ducted above the absorber) is more suitable. In addition there may be other constraints, such as the position of rafters and joists which impede air flow, all of which affect performance and for which due allowance should be made.

It should be recalled that in most situations the major pressure drop in a dryer is attributable to the flow of air through the loaded drying chamber rather than that through the collector.

18.3 Dryer Sizing

Before sizing a solar dryer it is important to be fully aware of the quantity of crop to be dried over the season, the pattern of harvesting, the relationship between batch size and drying time, and the effect of drying time on product quality. Once this information has been obtained, the dryer size, the number of dryers, batch size, and expected drying time can be determined. It should be noted here that a reduction in drying time will not necessarily be of financial benefit to the user. For example, a farmer who harvests his crop once a week has little to gain by reducing the drying time for his crop from four days to three days, unless of course there is the improvement in quality gained by drying more rapidly or an appreciable reduction in labour.

A point which is sometimes overlooked in deciding on the size of the dryer, especially in the case of natural convection dryers for use at a rural level, is that it is not necessarily beneficial or desirable that a dryer be designed to handle all of a farmer's or co-operative's production. Dryer design should be based upon the drying load and not the total crop harvested.

The dryer developed by the research worker will, if it has been carefully considered, be such that it can be easily constructed from materials readily and cheaply available to the end-user using locally available skills. Furthermore, with proper consideration given at the development stage, the dryer should permit ease of operation, e.g. easy loading and unloading. Increasing the size of the dryer may necessitate the use of stronger, and hence more expensive, materials of construction. For example, for a large dryer incorporating a collector made from plastic sheeting, the collector cover may be made up from individual smaller plastic sheets. Joining one sheet to another can be difficult and may give rise to air leaks and areas where tears may be initiated. For these reasons it may be more sensible, when using natural convection dryers, to build and operate a number of small units. Additionally, should one dryer become non-operational for any reason, then drying using the remaining dryers can continue, albeit on a reduced scale. However, for forced convection dryers, there may be some economies of the scale by increasing the size of the dryer. The main economy of scale in this case is that attributable to the fan and motor required; a fan of double the output of another will in all probability cost considerably less than twice the price of the smaller fan. Two factors counteract this advantage. Firstly, as previously shown with the scale-up of collectors, increase in collector size in some cases leads to a proportionally much larger fan. Secondly, where harvesting, and therefore drying, varies throughout the season a single large dryer will, at times, be using more fuel than would two or more smaller dryers.

18.4 Construction Methods and Materials

Construction methods and available materials may vary considerably from location to location and it is not within the scope of this manual to discuss individual local circumstances. Some general guidelines regarding factors which must be considered can however be given:

(i)   Dimensions of "standard" materials. Where possible designs should take account of the sizes of materials locally available. For example, it would be poor design to specify the width of a corrugated iron collector as 1.1 m if the standard width of corrugated iron sheet is 1.0 m. Before finalizing a design, the commercial availability of materials must be ascertained.

(ii)   Use of "rural" materials. The cost to the end-user of building a solar dryer can be minimized if he is able to use wood cut straight from the forest rather than prepared timber. Careful design in the development stage of a dryer can often facilitate the use of such cheaper materials. Difficulties caused by these materials are in joining pieces of the structure, in sealing the structures against air leaks and attaching the plastic sheet to the (wooden) frame, but there is obvious scope for designs which use prepared timber at strategic places and unprepared at others.

(iii)   Use of plastic sheet. For many solar dryers the clear plastic sheet used is the major capital cost to the farmer and therefore the choice of the type of plastic is important. A choice must be made between a relatively cheap plastic such as ordinary polyethylene which will last, at best, for one season due to photo-degradation and wear and tear, a more expensive, better quality plastic less prone to photo-degradation or even glass or a rigid plastic.

Attaching plastic sheet to the framework structure, so as to minimize the likelihood of tears in the plastic being initiated at the join is perhaps the greatest difficulty in building a dryer. Listed below are some general points which should be followed to prolong the useful lifetime of plastic sheet on a solar dryer.

(i)   When attaching plastic sheet to the framework, care should be taken that there is no stretching of the plastic at the points of attachment, nor should the plastic be so loose that it will flap about in the wind.

(ii)   Rather than merely stapling or nailing the plastic directly to the framework, it is preferable to "sandwich" the plastic between the framework and a batten. This may not be practical when unprepared wood or other materials are being used.

(iii)   No sharp edges should come in contact with the plastic sheet since these will initiate tears.

(iv)   The plastic should be folded at the point of attachment to the frame, so that there are two or more layers of plastic, to help prevent tear initiation.

(v)   When fixing the sheet over the framework, sags and hollows in which water can collect should be avoided wherever possible.

(vi)   The dryer should be handled as carefully and as seldom as possible both during operation and when not in use.

18.5   Fan Power and Motor Sizing

Appendix 12 shows how the theoretical fan power can be determined from a knowledge of system pressure drops and volumetric air flow rate. As for other components of a solar drying system it is wise to use a safety factor when specifying a fan and motor size. Given a choice of fans or motors, selection of those with higher capabilities than required generally results in lower maintenance costs and longer working life.

18.6   Conclusions

It must be realized that design is an iterative process. It is started by setting up initial ideas and as it progresses it is altered by consideration of external factors ever present in real life. It is doubtful whether two people given the same information would arrive at the same final design. Neither would be necessarily right or wrong; different people place emphasis on different aspects. Good design evolves by balancing the often conflicting requirements demanded of it to produce an acceptable working solution.

19. ECONOMICS

19.1 Framework for Investment Decisions

All Economic Appraisal decisions are about choices among possible courses of action in the future. Since virtually all such decisions involve the alternative use of often scarce resources, their commitment to one course of action prevents their utilisation for another purpose. The choice that must be made is the extent to which a given course of action meets the stated economic improvement objective(s) of the decision maker(s).

Economic appraisal decisions range from the individual working alone and having access to minimal resources, to combinations of individuals and resources as companies or even governments. Whatever the case is, the decisions are essentially the same, and are concerned with the optimum organisation and utilisation of resources to produce the best outcome at the best time and place. However, what, at first hand, appears to be an apparently simple action is beset by a very real problem; that of uncertainty about the future and imperfect knowledge of the present.

In a situation of constantly changing economic environment, such as persists in many developing countries, it is often impossible to accurately assess the degree of achievement, especially after the event. Furthermore, the use of the phrase "best" to describe outcome, time, place and price presupposes a general consensus as to the criteria for the determination of "best". Whilst it may be difficult to ascribe a single measure to what constitutes the "economic best" choice, it is still reasonable to suppose that most people, whether operating as individuals or part of a large organisation or country, would wish to apply resources as economically as possible.

The foregoing discussion raises the question of "What is Economic?" A simple conceptual approach to defining the term economic would be one that seeks to minimise input (cost) for a given output (benefit); or put another way, to maximise the output (benefit) from a given input (cost). The relative scarcity of the resources, in relation to the demand for them, would make them more likely to be expensive and thus increase the pressures to utilise them more economically (efficiently). The combination of efficiency of resource application with the belief that self-interest is the greatest motivator for most people, provide a framework for what has been described as 'economic rationality' (Freear, (1980)); according to which each decision is taken on the basis of the course of action that maximises the decision maker(s) wealth.

The types of economic decisions concerned with the optimum utilisation of resources are commonly known as "investment decisions". In most appraisals, these decisions are presented under assumptions of perfect markets and certainty about future outcomes. This is done so as to establish their nature and relationships with financing and consumption decisions. Once the assumptions of perfect markets and certainty are removed, investment decisions become more complex and less susceptible to simple approaches.

In a normal free enterprise business situation there is an implicit belief that each person, by acting in their own economic self-interest, will ensure, through market forces, that economic resources are used with optimum efficiency to produce desirable goods at desirable prices. Thus the investment that will be made to transform inputs into outputs will depend on the price or value that the consumer is prepared to assign to particular goods and services. Resources are therefore best used to meet the consumers' desires, as expressed by their 'monetary valuation' in the market place.

For example, the price or economic value which a small scale rural farmer would ascribe to a novel solar dryer would be based on the major criterion of its potential to increase his/her wealth, and not necessarily on the improved efficiency of energy use and performance that is promised.

The judgement might be influenced by the answers to the following questions.

(i)   Will the solar dryer increase the farmer's outputs for the same inputs, e.g. reduce post-harvest losses through more efficient drying?

(ii)   If the inputs have to be increased in order to obtain greater outputs from the novel solar dryer, would the increased returns cover the additional inputs; i.e. can the farmer find markets for the extra produce that will be generated?

(iii)   If the farmer is already deriving optimum benefits from his enterprise, could an additional investment in the solar dryer increase his wealth further by opening up new opportunities; e.g. could the improved rate of drying enable him to utilise the time saved to sell drying space to other producers, or to increase his own production? And if so, would the outputs (benefits) be greater than the additional inputs (costs) required to increase the production?

The essence of all of the above is that the farmer's perception of the solar dryer's worth is not necessarily set in a context of its energy conservation or import substitution potential. It is based primarily on the opportunities for personal wealth maximisation that the novel technology offers. The energy improvement options only become relevant in a situation where the new technology is substituting directly for a less efficient alternative (both in terms of cost and performance). Of course the measure of efficiency need not be just technical, it could come from an overall improvement in benefits from the assured energy supply of the solar option. In most cases, an inability to obtain energy security will be the only way in which the individual entrepreneur will perceive a national 'energy crisis'.

The above discussion is based on the underlying assumption that each society or groupings of people can make their preferences known through the use of monetary valuation. This excludes from consideration those who may have real needs but cannot express them in the form of money. Nor can such a system deal effectively with 'externalities' (indirect or spill-over effects). In the small economies of most developing countries the indirect effects of a project could assume particular importance, especially if the project is large relative to the economy as a whole or uses a large proportion of available resources of finance and skilled labour. For example, the use of solar crop dryers could improve the supply and quality of food to the poorest sectors of the society, even though they may not be able to afford the investments for the new technologies. However, the society as a whole may well take the view that it should itself provide the new investments as this would lead to an improvement in the collective wealth of the society.

In a different set of circumstances, a developing country may well have to choose one option out of several alternative renewable energy technologies which have the potential to optimise its socio-economic development. For although research and development has proliferated in recent years, the practical application of each technology does require massive financial or material investments. For example, should a country opt for the promotion of solar crop dryers to poor farmers, or should the emphasis be on solar water heaters which can find a ready market amongst the rich urban people, and therefore generate immediate monetary returns? The dilemma may well lead to improvements in overall energy efficiency and thus reduce the society's reliance on external energy resources.

Not surprisingly, all the dilemmas and investment liquidity problems have brought about increasing government intervention in economic appraisal decisions. In fact in most developing countries, the government takes the dominant role in shaping economic objectives and activity.

Economic decisions involving individuals or business are usually made on the basis of a **Financial Appraisal**, in which all inputs (costs) and outputs (benefits) can be forecast in direct monetary terms over the entire life time of a project. In a Financial Appraisal, it is possible to estimate the profitability of projects and to evaluate the likely benefits to the investor. Where group interests are involved, a financial appraisal may not give reliable estimates of a project's value and a full **Economic Appraisal** is normally considered desirable. In general there are said to be three situations where this may occur **(Anon (1982)):**

(i) those taking account of indirect costs or benefits: normally uncontroversial and possible to set in financial terms;

(ii) those where apparently profitable projects are a consequence of protective measures, usually in the tariff structure: here one needs to take account of equivalent international costs and benefits;

(iii) those incorporating other objectives, usually socio-welfare; this is the most complex and contentious, involving value judgements and an implied consensus within the society as the overall perception of wealth maximisation.

The last of the three situations is the most controversial and impinges on political ideologies and philosophies. Not surpisingly, there is great controversy and much academic debate as to the best appraisal methods for such situations (De.V. Graat (1957), Mishan (1971)).

Several techniques have been developed for expressing socio-welfare objectives in monetary terms (Eckstein (1961), Little & Mirlees (1974), UNIDO (1978), though the quantification of moral issues continues to present severe problems of value judgement and monetary accountability (Foster (1966), Wereko-Brobby (1983)).

In practice most project appraisals will be taken from the business perspective, whether as individuals or companies. In this situation a straightforward financial appraisal will be applied.

The Government's influence will in general be indirect, and will be in the form of fiscal and monetary policies, which will have an impact on the firm's wealth maximisation capabilities. Even where the Government exerts a direct influence in determining value maximisation objectives, the essential first step in the Economic Appraisal of a project is a systematic forecasting of all costs and benefits over the project's lifetime, i.e. a Financial Appraisal.

In practice most appraisals will only be concerned with the financial evaluation. Thus the following sections will deal only with approaches employed in Financial Appraisals.

19.2   Cash Flow Statement

The main elements of an investment decision are the amount and timings of "cash flows" and the "discount rate(s)" relevant to the decision. The calculation of cash flow is fundamental to the whole notion of economically rational investment decisions. A Cash Flow Statement sets out all the income and expenditure over the lifetime of the project at current market prices. Table 19.1 gives an example of a Cash Flow Statement for a project in which a solar dryer is to be used to dry 1,000 kg per year of maize over a 10 year period. The year 0 depicts the costs incurred in the construction and commissioning of the dryer prior to its operation.

In the years of operation, revenue (benefits) will begin to accrue, as will costs, though these will in general be smaller than for the pre-operational period. The difference between the benefits and the costs in the operating years give the Net Benefits or Net Cash Flow. The three most important constituents are costs, benefits and project life; and it is important to have a clear understanding of each and their role in the financial appraisal of projects.

19.3   Costs

A cost is defined as a sacrifice or giving up of resources for a particular purpose. In Financial Appraisals, it represents the monetary value that must be paid for goods and services. There are several cost-accounting systems which vary in their complexity, with the degree of detail increasing with the desired accuracy of data for decision making (Horngren, (1981)). For most project appraisals, it is sufficient to establish the Capital and Operating Costs. Capital Costs are usually incurred in the pre-operational period of the project (i.e. Year 0 in Table 19.1). Operating Costs are those for operating and maintaining the project. In general, the elements of these costs will be as set out in Table 19.1, though there may be variations from project to project. In many evaluations a contingency allowance of 5-10% is added.

Capital costs for items such as land, dryer construction materials and storage units are known as Fixed Capital.

- 148 -

Table 19.1 Solar Dryer Project: Cash Flow Statement
Constant Prices: $

Years	0	1	2	3	4	5	6	7	8	9	10
CAPITAL COSTS:											
Land	500										
Solar Dryer	7,000										
Storage Unit	2,000										
Instrumentation	500										
Working Capital		1,000	500	400	200	–	–	200	–	–	(2,300)
Salvage Value											–
1. TOTAL CAPITAL COSTS ($)	10,000	1,000	500	400	200	–	–	200	–	–	(2,300)
OPERATING COSTS:											
Material		1,000	1,000	1,000	1,000	1,000	1,000	1,000	1,000	1,000	1,000
Labour		330	360	390	420	450	450	450	450	450	450
Maintenance		100	100	100	100	100	100	100	100	100	100
Overheads		100	100	150	150	150	150	150	150	150	150
2. TOTAL OPERATING COSTS ($)		2,000	1,530	1,560	1,640	1,670	1,700	1,700	1,700	1,700	1,700
3. TOTAL COSTS (1+2)		3,000	2,030	1,960	1,840	1,670	1,700	1,900	1,700	1,700	(600)
4. REVENUE	–	2,000	2,500	3,000	3,000	3,400	3,400	3,650	3,650	3,650	3,650
5. NET CASH FLOW (4–3) ($)	(10,000)	(1,000)	470	1,040	1,160	1,730	1,700	1,750	1,950	1,950	4,250

Capital costs for stocks, spares and to operate the business prior to receiving revenues constitute the <u>Working</u> (or Operational) <u>Capital</u>. In a Cash Flow Statement, it is only in the first year of operation that the net Working Capital required is entered in full. In subsequent years, only the requirements over and above those of the previous year are included. In Table 19.1, working capital is shown as the penultimate item in the Capital Cost section.

19.4 Benefits

The Cash Flow Statement sets out the benefits to be derived from the Project. Benefits can take several forms; the easiest being a situation where all of the products are sold through well established markets. In this case, the valuation of benefits is simply an estimate of the sales value of the products. Where all the produce is not sold, there may be some problems with quantifying benefits. For example, if the farmer in Table 19.1 consumes 100 kg of the annual output, this must be valued and included in the estimation of benefits. In the same vein, should the use of the solar dryer lead to an improvement in the quality of the final product, this may well be reflected by better prices for the product. The benefits will then be estimated from the net value of price increases. Again, if the use of a solar dryer reduces post-harvest losses, resulting in an increase of the annual marketable volume from 1,000 kg to 1,200 kg, the benefits from the dryer include the additional sales value of the extra 200 kg of produce.

19.5 Project Life

In Cash Flow analysis, the project life is determined primarily by two factors; the life of the main asset, in this case the solar dryer, and the appraisal technique employed. There is a distinction between the physical life and the economic life of the main asset. For example, the solar dryer may need to have its collector cover changed every so often, due to breakage of glass or deterioration of plastic sheet after long exposure to the sun. Once the cover is replaced, the dryer becomes fully operational again. The cost of this and other similar exercises to sustain the operational capability of the dryer constitute the maintenance costs. However, there may come a time, when the maintenance costs become so high that it is no longer economic to operate the dryer. The period from the start of the operation (Year 1) up to the point of uneconomic operation constitutes the economic life of the asset.

If at the end of the economic life of the dryer, the owner manages to obtain some benefits from the sale of the whole or bits of it, then the monetary gains represent the Salvage Value of the asset. By convention, this is shown in the Cash Flow Statement as an additional benefit in the last operational year (last item under the Capital Costs column of Table 19.1).

19.6 Appraisal Methods and Techniques

Having established the expected costs and benefits over the economic life of the solar dryer, the next step is to appraise the whole project.

As already stated, the primary objective of all appraisals is to ascertain whether or not the expected benefits justify the costs of establishment and operation. Also it is to ascribe priority when faced with a choice of alternative projects.

There are some very simple methods used in project appraisal which quite often lead to misleading conclusions about project feasibility. This is particularly true in a situation of constantly changing economic climates; especially when operating in a high inflationary situation. These methods, though not recommended, are often employed by decision-makers.

Two of the most common examples are discussed below, to provide for familiarisation and to provide early warning of the potential dangers. The two methods are Payback and the Accounting Rate of Return.

19.7 Payback

Payback (also known as Payoff or Payout), is the measure of time it takes to recoup, in the form of operational cash inflow, the Capital Cost of the project. Table 19.2 sets out a Payback analysis for the solar dryer project. The method simply measures how quickly investment capital may be recouped. From Table 19.2 it can be seen that at the end of the seventh year the cumulative net profit of $11,190 exceeds the capital cost of $10,000. The method does not measure profitability and this is a major weakness since a shorter payback period for one project does not necessarily mean that it should be preferred to another. For example, it could well be that a simpler design of solar dryer, costing $8,000 instead of $10,000 could dry the same 1,000 kg of maize per year. Assuming that the average annual Net Cash Flow is $1,500 for the 1,000 kg of maize, the expected payback will be:

For the first dryer:

$$P_1 \quad = \quad \frac{10,000}{1,500} \quad = \quad 6.67 \text{ years}$$

For the second dryer:

$$P_2 \quad = \quad \frac{8,000}{1,500} \quad = \quad 5.33 \text{ years}$$

The Payback appraisal indicates the cheaper model of dryer to be more desirable. However there is a hidden snag in respect of the cheaper dryer because its useful economic life is only 5 years. Ignoring the impact of compound interest for the moment, it is obvious that the cheaper dryer results in no benefit as it comes to the end of its economic life before the capital has been recouped, whilst the $10,000 dryer continues to generate cash flows for another 3.33 years beyond its payback period.

The point needs to be reinforced that the main objective in investing is profit, not the recouping of the initial capital cost.

Table 19.2   Solar Dryer Project - Payback Calculation

End of Year	Capital ($)	Annual Profit ($)	Cumulative Profit ($)
0	10,000	–	–
1		0	0
2		970	970
3		1,440	2,410
4		1,360	3,770
5		1,730	7,540
6		1,700	9,240
7		1,950	11,190

Profit includes working capital.

19.8   Accounting Rate of Return

The Accounting Rate of Return (also known as rate-of-return on assets) is defined as the rate of increase in future average net cash flows to the initial increase in required investment. In the appraisal of the new project as a whole, the initial increase in required investment is equivalent to the Total Capital employed, i.e. all expenditure in the pre-operational year as well as the working capital. The general equation for the accounting rate of return is:

$$R_a = \frac{0 - D_a}{I} \qquad (19.1)$$

where: R_a is the average annual return on initial additional investment,
0 is the average annual incremented cash flow,
D_a is the average annual depreciation, and
I is the initial incremental amount invested.

With the solar dryer of Table 19.1, the revenue minus the operational cost would give the profit on which the accounting rate of return can be calculated. Assuming that the dryer's economic life is 10 years, the annual average depreciation in its value would be $10,000/10 = $1,000, the net cash flow averages $1,500 per year and the initial capital employed is $10,000.

Substitute these values in equation (19.1):

$$R_a = \frac{1,500 - 1,000}{10,000} = 5.0\%$$

If another variation of the method is used (Table 19.3), the accounting rate of return is 12.2%, compared to the 5.0% above.

A further complication with the technique relates to the question of whether the return should be calculated before or after tax and allowances. A major difficulty of the technique therefore, is that it can produce a wide variety of

Table 19.3 Solar Dryer Project – Rate of Return on Total Assets

Year	(1) Fixed Capital	(2) Working Capital	(3) Total Capital (1) + (2)	(4) Revenue	(5) Operating Costs	(6) Net Profit (4) – (5)
0	10,000		10,000			0
1		1,000	1,000	2,000	2,000	970
2		500	500	2,500	1,530	1,440
3		400	400	3,000	1,550	1,360
4		200	200	3,000	1,640	1,700
5		–	–	3,400	1,670	1,730
6		–	–	3,400	1,700	1,950
7		200	200	3,650	1,700	1,950
8		–	–	3,650	1,700	1,950
9		–	–	3,650	1,700	1,950
10		(2,300)	–	3,650	1,700	1,950
			12,300	31,900		15,000

Average Profit = $\dfrac{15,000}{10}$ = \$1,500

Rate of Return on Total Capital = $\dfrac{1,500}{12,300}$ = 12.2%

rates of return from the same basic data. This is because the figures used are derived from the application of arbitrary accounting conventions, such as those dealing with depreciation. The accounting rate of return is said to be essentially unreliable because it neither recognises the importance of cash flows ('It is money that buys things, not figures of profit'), nor the time value of money. Also, it is not always clear, nor obvious, what has been the criteria used to arrive at a particular rate of return.

19.9 Discounting Techniques

Given the choice of receiving $100 today and $150 in five years' time, what would be your decision? The answer is of course "It depends". However, whatever one's personal situation is today, there is the old problem of "uncertainty" about the future to contend with. Will you still be around in 5 years' time to receive the windfall, and even if you were, will the money still be worth $150 in real terms? The old adage that 'a bird in hand is worth two in the bush' underpins the appraisal techniques which take account of the time value of money.

The **Discounted Cash Flow** (DCF) model explicitly and systematically weighs the time value of money. It is therefore recommended as the best method to use for long-range decisions. Another inherent advantage of the method is that it focuses on cash inflows and outflows, rather than on net income.

There are two main techniques of the DCF method: (a) **Net Present Value (NPV)** and (b) **Internal Rate of Return** (IRR). Two assumptions are made with the DCF method. First, there is certainty that the predicted cash flows will occur at the times specified. Second, the original amount invested (capital cost) is regarded as being either borrowed or loaned at some specified interest rate.

For example if one was to accept the $100 offered today (Year 0) and invested it in a fixed deposit account which paid 10% per annum, then the nominal value of the money would grow as follows:

Table 19.4   Fixed Deposit Returns on Investment

Time	Interest ($)	Total Value ($)
End of Year 1	10.00	110.00
End of Year 2	11.00	121.00
End of Year 3	12.10	133.10
End of Year 4	13.31	146.41
End of Year 5	14.64	161.05

Thus at the end of Year 5 today's $100 invested at 10% annual interest would be worth $161.05, which is $11.05 more than the $150 promised in 5 years' time. By the same token, a sum of $161.05 five years' hence is equivalent to $100 today if the average interest rate stays at 10% over the period.

It is the same principle that is applied to a project's Net Cash Flow such as shown in Table 19.1. Indeed it is for the very purpose of being able to discount the Net Cash Flow that the statement is set out as in the table.

To simplify the otherwise tedious business of calculating the discount factor for each year of operation, Tables of Discount Factors are used (Appendix 14). Each page of the table deals with a particular rate of interest whilst the first column of the table itself gives the number of years being considered. If the Net Cash Flow is the same for each year, the method is simplified further as there is no need to carry out the task for each year. A Table of Annuity Factors (Appendix 15) gives the total value of the sum of all discount factors up to the number of years shown in the Table.

19.10 Net Present Value

The Net Present Value (NPV) technique assumes that there is a minimum desirable rate of return that would make a project acceptable. Thus all the expected future cash flows are discounted to the present, using the minimum desired rate. If the result is positive, the project is acceptable; if it is negative, the project is rejected. Where the choice is between several projects, the one with the largest NPV is deemed the most desirable.

A major problem of the NPV approach is the selection of an appropriate rate of return. A pragmatic solution is usually to take the real rate of interest (inflation-adjusted) at which money can be raised on the money markets. If a project is able to yield returns that more than cover the total costs (capital and operating), as well as the cost of borrowing money, then its net present value would be positive and thus the project is acceptable. A discounted analysis of the Solar Dryer Project shows a net present value of $2,691 at an accrued discount rate of 10% (Table 19.5).

Table 19.6 shows the NPV calculation at 5% discount rate. This gives a present value of $384, which makes the project viable.

19.11 Internal Rate of Return

The Internal Rate of Return (IRR) is defined as "the maximum rate of interest that could be paid for the capital employed over the economic life, without a loss on the project". In effect it is the discount rate that makes the present value of the anticipated cash flows equal to the cost of the project; ie the discount rate that produces a zero net present value. If the IRR is greater than the stipulated interest rate, then the project is viable. On the other hand, if the IRR is less than the stipulated interest rate, then the project is not viable.

The approach to calculating the IRR is similar to that for calculating the NPV, except that no discount rate is given; the analyst takes the annual cost and

Table 19.5   Solar Dryer Project – Net Present Value

Year	Capital Costs (1)	Operating Costs (2)	Total Costs (1) + (2) (3)	Total Benefits (4)	Net Benefits (4) – (3) (5)	Discount Factor at 10% (6)	Present Value (5) x (6) (7)
0	10,000	–	10,000	–	(10,000)	1.000	(10,000)
1	1,000	2,000	3,000	2,000	(1,000)	0.909	(909)
2	500	1,530	2,030	2,500	470	0.826	388.2
3	400	1,560	1,960	3,000	1,040	0.751	781.0
4	200	1,640	1,840	3,000	1,160	0.683	740.1
5	–	1,670	1,670	3,400	1,730	0.621	1,074.3
6	–	1,700	1,700	3,400	1,700	0.564	958.8
7	200	1,700	1,900	3,650	1,750	0.513	897.8
8	–	1,700	1,700	3,650	1,950	0.467	910.7
9	–	1,700	1,700	3,650	1,950	0.424	826.8
10	(2,300)	1,700	(600)	3,650	4,250	0.386	1,640.5
				Net Present Value at 10%			(2,691)

Note: The Net Present Value of ($2,691) means that if the farmer has to borrow $100,000 at 10% discount rate, then the project is not viable.

- 156 -

Table 19.6   Solar Dryer Project – NPV at Discount of 5%

Year	Net Benefits ($)	Discount Factor 5%	Present Worth ($)
0	(10,000)	1.000	(10,000)
1	(1,000)	0.952	(952)
2	470	0.907	426.3
3	1,040	0.864	898.6
4	1,160	0.823	954.7
5	1,730	0.784	1,356.3
6	1,700	0.746	1,268.3
7	1,750	0.711	1,244.3
8	1,950	0.677	1,320.2
9	1,950	0.645	1,257.8
10	4,250	0.614	2,609.5
Net present value ($)			383.9

Table 19.7   Solar Dryer Project – Internal Rate of Return

Net Benefits (1)	Discount Factor at 5% (2)	Present Value (1) x (2) (3)	Discount Factor at 8% (4)	Present Value (1) x (4) (5)
(10,000)	1.000	(10,000)	1.000	(10,000)
(1,000)	0.952	(952)	0.926	(926)
470	0.907	426.3	0.857	402.8
1,040	0.864	989.6	0.794	825.8
1,160	0.823	954.7	0.735	852.6
1,730	0.784	1,356.3	0.681	1,178.1
1,700	0.746	1,268.2	0.630	1,071.0
1,750	0.711	1,244.3	0.584	1,022.0
1,950	0.677	1,320.2	0.540	1,053.0
1,950	0.645	1,257.8	0.500	975
4,250	0.614	2,609.5	0.463	1,967.8
		383.9		(1,577.9)

IRR = Lower Discount Rate + Difference between Discount Rates x

NPV at low rate
Change in NPV between
higher + lower rates

IRR = 5 + 3 $\dfrac{(383.9)}{1,961.8}$ = 5 + 0.59 = <u>5.6%</u>

revenue values and fixes various discount rates until one is reached which makes the NPV equal to zero. A calculation of the IRR for the solar dryer project is shown in Table 19.7.

The IRR method is in many ways preferred to the NPV. This is because it allows comparison between projects on the basis of the most efficient use of capital, as against the NPV which is an absolute measure whose value is very often influenced by the size of the project. It is advisable to calculate both the NPV and IRR in all project appraisals.

19.12 Inflation and Discounted Cash Flow

The persistent and growing problem of inflation (the decline in the general purchasing power of the monetary unit) has prompted a situation, where all appraisals need to take account of its effects if they are to arrive at realistic judgements as to project viability. To cope with the risk of inflation, investors usually increase the discount rate to incorporate the expected rate of inflation. Thus if an inflation rate of 10% per annum is expected over a project's lifetime then a 10% discount rate becomes 20% for appraisal purposes.

Inflation adjustment for DCF methods need to be internally consistent. That is, if the discount rate of say 20% includes an element for expected inflation, the predicted annual cash flows should also be adjusted for inflation. A common error is to adjust only one of the two factors. The adjustment of the annual cash flows is made by either (a) using a general price level index or (b) preferably using a specific index such as a wages or materials index.

19.13 Income Taxes and Project Appraisal

Income taxes are significant costs of business. They are cash disbursements and thus can influence the amount and/or timing of cash flows. Their basic role in investment appraisal is no different from any other cash disbursement (costs). However, taxes tend to narrow the cash differences between projects. The major concern is to assess the effect of income taxes on the choice of depreciation methods and on capital budgeting decisions.

Income tax effects are usually quite prominent when making decisions about new investments and must be considered very carefully where they are relevant to investment appraisal decisions.

A case study illustrating many of the techniques described above is presented as Appendix 16.

20. EXTENSION OF SOLAR CROP DRYING TECHNOLOGY

It has been suggested that the approach of Evaluation, Experimentation and Extension is necessary for the introduction of a new technology such as solar drying. However, whereas the importance of the three E's cannot be overstated, the three stages should not be taken in isolation of each other. A well evaluated and tested technology is the one which is most likely to be widely adopted irrespective of whether there is extensive extension effort. Indeed it can be argued that the level of extension effort required decreases proportionally in relation to how well the first two E's have been undertaken. Problems in extension are often a result of poor evaluation and experimentation, and no amount of extension work will correct poor evaluation and experimentation. Extension cannot therefore be discussed in isolation of evaluation and experimentation.

In this Chapter some of the problems likely to be encountered in efforts to promote the solar drying technology to the rural population will be considered. Suggestions will also be given on methods of overcoming these problems. A note of caution needs to be pointed out here that examples cited may be pertinent only to extension of engineering technology to agriculture, and not necessarily as typical of general extension practices.

20.1 Pre-requisites to Successful Extension of Engineering Technologies in Agriculture

Many extension experts admit that among the most difficult technologies to extend to farmers (especially smallholder farmers) are the so-called "engineering technologies" (Eicher and Baker (1982)). An example often quoted is the adoption of hybrid maize seeds by small scale farmers in East Africa (which succeeded over a 20-year period compared with 50 years in the United States) as compared with the unsuccessful adoption of modern farming tools like oxen-powered cultivation and tractors (where the situation has remained static over the past 50 years throughout East Africa, i.e. 80% of cultivated land is still being cultivated by use of hand tool technology now as was the case in the 1930's) (Mrema (1981, 1983, 1984 a, 1984 b)). In this context engineering technologies are such technologies as improved and modern cultivation implements and machines, and post-harvest processing techniques including solar crop drying, etc. In many cases such engineering technologies 'aim' at optimizing the use of labour inputs as well as the reduction of drudgery. Several reasons have been given for the limited adoption of engineering technologies in agriculture.

(i)   Engineers have tended to design expensive and complicated equipment/implements which are beyond the financial and technological capabilities of the farmers and even the extension workers.

(ii)   These technologies have often aimed at optimizing labour use and hence they are socially conceived as leading to increased unemployment especially in rural areas.

(iii)   These technologies have relied on imported inputs which are difficult to obtain locally.

(iv)   Research and development by engineers has often been done in laboratories without any regard to the situation pertaining in the field.

Some or all of the above reasons may be quite relevant with regard to specific technologies but what is often forgotten is the fact that unlike the traditional agricultural technologies, e.g. improved seeds, fertilizer and pesticide application, engineering technologies demand that the user has to have a certain level of technical knowledge. For whereas introduction of a new hybrid maize seed may involve many years of highly complicated research by geneticists, agronomists, etc., what is eventually extended to the farmer are seeds which he merely has to plant in a particular way. The farmer need not understand the genetic engineering principles behind the new seeds. However for new implements, i.e. a solar dryer, or an improved ox-drawn plough, the farmer needs to have a much higher level of technical appreciation of new technology than in the case of hybrid seeds. Of greater importance is the fact that the frontline extension worker should be technically well informed about the new technology. The poor technical know-how of both the farmer and the extension worker has been one of the most serious handicaps in the extension of engineering technologies to farmers.

For successful extension of engineering technology to the agricultural situation there is therefore a need for:

(i)   proper evaluation and experimentation before extension. In this regard the engineer should understand the whole farming system in which the farmer and extension agent are working in and he should endeavour to develop his technology to suit the local scene rather than expecting that the local scene will adapt itself to his technology,

(ii)   the front line extension worker to be well trained and conversant with the new technology. If the extension agent does not himself understand the new technology it is unlikely that he will extend it effectively and likewise it is unlikely that the farmer will understand and adopt it,

(iii)   the technology to aim at solving a problem which both the farmer and extension agent see as a problem (and not what is conceived by the engineer in his laboratory as a problem) and which the farmer regards as a priority problem among his many other problems. There is no point for example of concentrating on a solar maize dryer when the farmer's principal problem is timely land preparation, planting and weeding to exploit the short rainy season common in his locality. He will certainly not invest in a dryer if he is not even sure of getting the maize to dry,

(iv)   the technology to aim at solving the problem by optimizing the use of labour at a reduced level of human energy expenditure, i.e. the technology must not increase drudgery,

(v)   the technology to aim at relieving those tasks where the main decision maker on the farm is involved first (often in Africa this is the man) before tackling other problems. The fact is that the main decision maker will first invest in a new technology in an area where he himself is directly involved

(vi)   a financial or obvious incentive to adopt the new technology,

(vii)   the technology to be within the financial resources of the farmer in
         addition to being easily and inexpensively repaired if there is any
         breakdown.

These are some of the problems which need to be considered in the extension of
solar drying technologies or any engineering technology in agriculture.   The
important fact however is to understand the farming system in which the farmer
is operating. Both exogenous and endogenous factors, which affect the system
need to be considered. Identification of the main constraints and how they can
be relieved must be made before a decision is made to develop any technology.
This can be achieved by either multi-disciplinary teams, involving economists,
sociologists, agriculturists, engineers and extension experts, or by the engineer
endeavouring to understand and appreciate the relevant aspects of the other
disciplines. Although the former may be the ideal method, manpower constraints
and disciplinary conflicts may create more problems than they solve and hence
the latter approach may result as a more effective means of successfully
developing a new technology.

20.2   Extension Outlets Available

Researchers developing solar drying techniques have several routes through
which their technology can reach the farmer.

(i)   Frontline Extension Workers: these are normally employees of
         Governmental Ministries; of Agriculture for crops, of Livestock for
         livestock products and of Natural Resources for fisheries and forestry.
         They are normally, in most African Commonwealth countries trained to
         'certificate level', i.e. two years' specialized training in either
         Agriculture, Forestry or Fisheries after 'O' Level education. In some cases
         some extension auxiliaries have been promoted after a long working
         experience.   The frontline extension workers' level of understanding of
         engineering principles is usually quite low.   There is typically one
         extension worker per Location/Ward for each Ministry working under a
         Diploma Level Officer at Division level. The latter invariably has some
         subject specialists reporting to him, and he in turn could be supervised by
         a Degree holder at District level together with some subject specialists,
         e.g. Agricultural Engineers, etc.

(ii)   Crop Authorities Extension Agents: in some countries, e.g. Kenya and
         Tanzania, some crop authorities, such as those for coffee and tea, have
         their own extension officers directly in contact with farmers. These tend
         to be specialists in that particular crop and can be effectively utilized to
         extend new technologies like solar crop drying.

(iii)   Extension Departments in Universities/Research Institutes: many
         University Faculties have their own extension departments which carry
         out some extension work.   They are normally staffed by highly trained
         extension experts, usually possessing a Ph.D. One limitation however is a
         tendency to experiment on different extension techniques rather than
         carrying out extension in its own right.

(iv)   Appropriate Technology Centres: in recent years many appropriate technology centres have been established with differing mandates but essentially for the development and adaptation of technologies to local conditions, e.g. the Appropriate Technology Centre at Kenyatta University College in Kenya. Their effectiveness, especially in extension, cannot be evaluated at this time.

(v)   Open Days, Exhibitions, Agricultural Shows: these are other routes through which a researcher can propagate his technology. They are however quite limited in their effect.

(vi)   Commercial Companies: where there is quite an apparent need for a particular item of equipment commercial companies can purchase the patent of a particular technology and commence large-scale production or manufacture under licence.   The marketing departments of these companies are then used to do the extension work.   In such cases commercial companies look for profit and the initial evaluation tends to be thorough. Once a commercial company enters into such an enterprise, it can then be said that the technology stands a very high chance of being extensively adopted.

(vii)   Individual Extension Efforts: in some cases the individual researcher may extend his own research findings to farmers. In such a case he either selects a 'progressive' farmer himself or one is suggested to him by the other extension agencies mentioned above.   This method is however expensive and other than serving a good testing facility it has limited potential for widescale adoption of the technology.

In addition to the above routes, there are other routes of extension through churches, women's groups, local cultural groups, schools, etc. which may be used to popularize the technology and hopefully lead to its wider adoption. The route which is most effective in propagation and hence widespread adoption of the technology is best determined by careful examination of the local situation.

20.3   Extension Techniques

In addition to the route through which the technology reaches the farmer or target group there are also different methods through which the technology can be demonstrated to farmers. Many of these techniques have been developed for agricultural technology - e.g. crop husbandry, livestock husbandry, etc. and how effective they may be for engineering type of tehnologies is difficult to ascertain. The main techniques are four in number.

(i)   Demonstration at market places/meeting places.   In this case the extension officer or researcher takes the technology to a place where the people in that particular area gather in large numbers. This may be a market place, Baraza, a church, etc. He then exhibits his solar dryer (or any technology) to the people providing as much information as possible. Interested farmers can then be identified and these are encouraged to purchase the equipment in question for their own use. In such a case the extension officer must have adequate numbers of the dryer for immediate delivery or sale to the farmer or, in the case where the farmer is to construct the dryer himself, all the inputs required must be readily available on the local market and instructions clearly spelling out the steps to be followed in manufacturing the unit must be provided. However if the farmer encounters any problem in manufacturing or use of the dryer he must approach the extension officer for further advice. In other words there is little follow-up action by the extension officer after the exhibition and the initiative is left entirely to the farmer. This demonstration technique can be a cheap way of effective extension of a technology but owing to the conservative nature of most farmers, few will take the risk of investing in a technology which they have not seen working elsewhere. However, where the risk is low the farmer may afford to take the risk of experimenting with the new technology, such as with improved crop varieties a farmer may buy 0.5kg of seed and plant on a small area of his farm to test them.

(ii)   Progressive Farmer Techniques. In this case a progressive farmer in a particular locality is selected and encouraged to use the new technology (either on loan or subsidized price) and if he is satisfied with its performance he can, through the demonstration effect, encourage other farmers to follow his example. These progressive farmers are usually the more educated and richer members of the community and quite influential. Due to their financial position, they are better able to take risks, which may not be the case for the less progressive and poorer farmers. However if a technology has been well evaluated and the benefits can clearly be seen, then the chances of widescale adoption through this extension technique are great.

(iii)   Focus and Concentrate Technique. In this case farmers are selected using a criteria established by the extension officer according to the technology which is being extended, given the technology (usually free of charge), and the extension officers focus all their efforts on these farmers until the technology is adopted. If it is adopted then neighbouring farmers are likely to copy it. It is an expensive method of extension and in many cases the selection criteria results in the selection of only the progressive and influential farmers. Another disadvantage is that those farmers who are supposed to copy the technology later on will also expect a free initial input as was given to the selected farmers.

(iv)   Training and Visit Technique. This technique, which was first developed in India (Benor (1978)) and has been tried on an experimental basis in several districts of Kenya since 1980, (Akober et al (1983)), involves grouping farmers in groups, of say 10-15 people with a group leader. These farmers then meet in a specified place and are given training on the new technology. This is followed by a programmed visit at specified intervals to the farmers throughout the season where further training is given until the end of this season. It is claimed that this extension technique has been quite successful and has led to increased yields wherever it has been applied (Carr (1983)). However it is quite expensive and it requires significant input in trained manpower resources as well as transport facilities.

Any of the above four techniques could be used to propagate the use of solar crop dryers. The method to be selected will depend on local conditions as well as resources available to the extension officer/research worker.

20.4 Problems of Extension of Solar Dryers and Other Engineering Technologies

By and large on the African continent, with the exception of a few large-scale farms and irrigation projects, the engineering profession has had very little input in the agricultural production system. This is quite apparent especially to the small-scale farmers who form the majority of the farming population in most African countries. Thus the agricultural production systems have been dominated by the agriculturist insofar as technology inputs are concerned. A number of problems exist which affect the extension of engineering technologies in agricultural production systems.

(i)   Professional Conflicts. As noted above, agricultural production systems are dominated by agriculturists. The agriculturist is trained mainly in biological and agricultural sciences e.g. agronomy, soil science, plant breeding, etc., with little training in engineering principles. Conversely most engineering schools produce graduates with very little appreciation of agriculture. Not surprisingly development of engineering technologies is in most cases carried out by such engineers and in many cases it is done without consideration of the agriculture-related aspects of the situation. The engineer is therefore dependent in most cases upon an extension worker, who is usually an agriculturist, to extend his innovation to the farmers. This undoubtedly leads to professional conflicts. There are three solutions to this: use of multi-disciplinary teams, training the agriculturists to have a better appreciation of engineering principles, or training of the engineer to have a better appreciation of agricultural problems. Each of these can be tried depending on prevailing local conditions.

(ii)   Concept of Intermediate Technology. Many of the ideas developed for agriculture in the Third World in the recent years may be described as "intermediate" technology. This in many cases has fallen between the most rudimentary form of technology common in agriculture in most Third World countries and the advanced technologies common in the industrialized countries.

Proponents of this "intermediate" (or "appropriate") technology have often argued that the use of modern technologies common in the advanced countries is undesirable in the Third World countries for a multiplicity of reasons. Both the supporters and opponents of this concept fall into three broad groups:

(a)   those who will repudiate the use of advanced technologies as unsuitable in all situations in the Third World countries. They therefore see the use of these 'intermediate' technologies as a lasting thing,

(b)   the second group comprises those who view the 'intermediate' technology as a transitional stage in development. They therefore advocate the use of technologies which are socially and environmentally acceptable for the well-being of the whole society,

(c)   the third group comprises those who will oppose the use of these intermediate technologies as inefficient and obsolete. They argue that these technologies will not produce the results claimed of them and where the modern technologies have failed this has been mainly as a result of poor management and technical know-how.

Most of the engineering experts found in Africa and presumably elsewhere fall into one of the above groups. They play a very significant role in advising and prejudicing key decision makers (politicians, agriculturists, etc.) on what form of technology should be promoted. This has had significant influence on the support given by the political system on whether to adopt or reject an intermediate technology. Consequently therefore the political systems may view a solar crop dryer from any of the three viewpoints outlined above and the support given will depend on how they view the technology. This support is quite crucial especially when seeking funds for local research and development efforts as well as extension.

(iii)   Cost of the Dryers. The other major problem of introducing engineering technologies to agriculture, such as a solar crop dryer, is that their cost tends to be quite high compared to agricultural technology. Although in many cases this tends to be a capital cost rather than a recurrent one, many farmers will find it quite difficult to raise enough money to buy or construct a dryer.

With the introduction of improved crop varieties a farmer can experiment at little cost with a small quantity of seed. With a solar dryer, or any other item of plant for that matter, there is not an analogous method by which the farmer on his own can test it before making a large financial commitment. This problem can however be alleviated by encouraging co-operative ownership of the equipment where the people are well organized, as well as a pricing mechanism based on quality for the produce being dried.

(iv)   Durability and Ease of Operation. The other important point which needs to be considered during design of the dryer is the durability of the dryer. African farmers have been shown to have strong preference for durable implements or equipment even if they are more expensive. Thus if the dryer is designed in such a way that it appears that it can be damaged quite easily the task of convincing the farmer to purchase or adopt one is made even more difficult. In addition, the ease of operation is an important design factor. The dryer should not increase the demand of labour on the farmer as compared to the traditional methods of drying, e.g. sun drying. It should be remembered that we are dealing with a post harvest operation where the timing of the operation may be as critical as in the pre-harvest operations. In addition the energy demand per unit input of labour should not be greater than in the traditional systems. Although land may be a constraint in some high potential areas, this is an exception rather than the rule to most of Eastern, Southern and Central Africa, and a technology based on higher return per unit labour input is much more likely to be readily and widely adopted than a technology based on a higher return per unit of land.

All the above factors need to be considered during the evaluation and experimentation stages as they are bound to affect the outcome of the extension stage.

20.5   Conclusions

The extension problems likely to be encountered in the promotion of use of engineering technologies to small-scale farmers such as solar crop dryers, have been described above. It would seem that extending such technologies is much more difficult than extending the traditional agricultural technologies. This may, at least in initial stages, necessitate a different approach to ownership of the device; by groups such as co-operatives or crop authorities rather than individual farmers.

REFERENCES

ABU AHMED A T, ULLAH M R, RUBBI F I & MUSLEMUDDIN M (1981)
Investigations on Solar Tent Drying of Rupchanda (Pomfret), Stromateus Sinenas (Bloch) and Shrimp Macrobrochium Dayanus (Hendeson)
Presented at 3rd National Zoological Conference, March 15-17, Dhaka, Bangladesh. 6pp.

AHMED S (1979)
Solar Radiation Characteristics and Potential of Solar Cooking and Solar Drying Fish in Bangladesh
Proceedings of Inter-regional Symposium on Solar Energy for Development, Paper B9, Tokyo, Japan. Tokyo: JSETA

AKYURT M & SELCUK M K (1973)
A Solar Dryer Supplemented with Auxiliary Heating Systems for Continuous Operation
Solar Energy, 14, 313-320.

ALAM A, YADAV D S & GUPTA S K (1978)
'Solar Blower' for Grain Drying and Ventilation
Proceedings of International Solar Energy Society Congress, 'The Sun - Mankind's Future Source of Energy', New Delhi, India. Parkville, Australia: ISES. 2184pp.

ALCOBER D L, CORNELIS J, MEDLAND J, MREMA G C, PRAYAG J & SHARROCK G O (1983)
Agricultural Development and Research Priorities for a Semi-Arid Area in Kenya.
Bulletin No 10, International Centre for Research into Agriculture, Wageningen, Netherlands.

AACC (1976)
Approved Methods of the American Association of Cereal Chemists.
Minnesota, USA: AACC Inc.

ANEDELINA E (1978)
Sub-Project: Inland Fisheries
Proceedings of UNESCO Solar Drying Workshop, Manila, Philippines. Manila: BED.

ANON (1938)
Federal Food, Drug and Cosmetics Act of 1983
Washington, USA: US Government Printing Office.

ANON (1955)
Microanalyses of Food and Drug Products.
Food and Drug Circular No 1. US Government Printing Office, Washington, USA.

ANON (1956)
Report of the Joint FAO/WHO Expert Committee on Food Additives
Rome, Italy: FAO.

ANON (1960)
Microscopic Analytical Methods in Food and Drug Control
Food and Drug Technical Bulletin No 1, US Government Printing Office, Washington, USA.

ANON (1965)
How to make a Solar Cabinet Dryer for Agricultural Produce
Do-it-Yourself Leaflet L6. Brace Research Institute, Sainte Anne de Bellevue, Canada. 9pp.

ANON (1970)
IHVE Guide Book
London, UK: The Institution of Heating and Ventilating Engineers.

ANON (1974)
Construction and Operation of a Simple Tapioca Chipper
Peninsular, Malaysia: Farm Mechanization Branch, Dept of Agriculture. 25pp.

ANON (1975)
Solar Power turns plums into Prunes
New Scientist, 29, May, 507.

ANON (1976)
Drying Fruits and Vegetables at Home
Bulletin No 655, University of Idaho, Moscow, USA 6pp.

ANON (1978 a)
A Simple Solar Dryer
Appropriate Technology, 5, 2, 11.

ANON (1978 b)
Solar Energy Collector used in Coffs Harbour Banana Processing Factory
Banana Bulletin, February, 6-7.

ANON (1978 c)
How to Build a Solar Crop Dryer
Sante Fe, USA: New Mexico Solar Energy Association. 10pp.

ANON (1979)
The Preservative in Food Regulations 1979
Statutory Instruments No 752, European Economic Commission, Brussels, Belgium.

ANON (1980)
Utilisation of Solar Energy in a Fish Dryer
Antofagasta, Chile: University of the North. 5pp.

ANON (1981)
Chilli Drying, Vegetable Seed Drying
Annual Report, Central Institute of Agricultural Engineering, Bhopal, India. 132pp.

ANON (1982)
A Manual on Project Planning for Small Economies
London, UK: Commonwealth Secretariat.

ANSCHUTZ J, LIPPER R, SPILLMAU CK & ROBBINS F V (1970)
Drying Grain with Air from a Solar Heater Designed for Animal Shelters
Manhattan, USA: Kansas State University. 9pp.

AOAC (1970)
Official Methods of Analysis of the Association of Official Analytical Chemists.
(11th Edition)
Washington, USA: AOAC. 1015pp.

BAKER J L & SHOVE G C (1970)
Solar Grain Drying Systems
Paper 77-3009, American Society of Agricultural Engineers, St Joseph, USA.
9pp.

BAILEY P H & WILLIAMSON W F (1965)
Some Experiments on Drying Grain by Solar Radiation
Journal of Agricultural Energy Research, 10, 191-196.

BEDROSIAN K, NELSON A I & STEINBERG M P (1959)
The Effect of Borates and other Inhibitors on Enzymatic Browning in Apple
Tissue
Food Technology, 13, 722-726.

BEIDLER L M (1957)
Facts and Theory on the Mechanism of Taste and Odour Perception
Proceedings of Quartermaster Food and Container Institute's Symposium,
'Chemistry of Natural Food Flavours'. Chicago, USA. Chicago: Quartermaster
Food and Container Institute.

BENOR D (1977)
The T and V Extension Service Report, International Bank for Reconstruction and
Development, Washington, USA.

BESANT R W, SCHOENAU G J & FIGLEY D A (1980)
Solar Air Preheaters
Proceedings of 1980 Annual Meeting of American Sector of ISES, Phoenix, USA.
Newark: ISES.

BHATIA A K & GUPTA S L (1976)
Solar Dryer for Drying Apricots
Research and Industry, 21, 9, 188-191.

BHATTACHARYYA T K & MAZUMDAR S K (1976)
Solar Drying in Thin Layer
Mechanical Engineering Bulletin, 7, 3, 89-94.

BIREWAR B R (1978)
Development of Flat Plate Type Solar Energy Grain Dryer
Bulletin of Grain Technology, 15,2, 108-113.

BISWAS D K & TANDON SK (1978)
Studies on Performance Characteristics of Solar Grain Drying System
Proceedings of ISES Congress, 'The Sun - Mankind's Future Source of Energy',
pp1935-1939, New Delhi, India. Parkville, Australia: ISES. 2184pp.

BLAGA A (1978)
Use of Plastics in Solar Energy Applications
Solar Energy, 21, 331-338.

BOLIN H R, HUXSOLL C C & SULUNKHE D K (1980)
Fruit Drying by Solar Energy
Confructa 25, 3/4, 147-160.

BOOTHUMJINDA S, EXELL R H B, RONGTAWNG S & KAEWNIKOM W (1983)
Field Tests of Solar Rice Dryers in Thailand
Proceedings of ISES Solar World Forum, pp1258-1263, Perth, Australia.
Parkville: ISES.

BOSE S C (1978)
Commercial Solar Energy Dryers - Indian Experience
Proceedings of UNESCO Solar Drying Workshop, Manila, Philippines. Manila:
BED.

BOSE S C (1980)
Tobacco Curing with Solar Energy
Research and Industry, 9, 127-132.

BOWMAN G E (1962)
A Comparison of Greenhouses Covered with Plastic Film and with Glass
Proceedings of 16th International Horticultural Congress, pp 716-725, Brussels,
Belgium. Gembloux: J Ducolot S A.

BOWREY R G, BUCKLE K A, HAMEY I & PAYENAYOTIN P (1980)
Use of Solar Energy for Banana Drying
Food Technology in Australia, 32, 6, 290-291.

BROOME R H (1952)
In the Orchard - Sun Drying of Apricots
Journal of Agriculture (Victoria), December.

BEULOW F H (1961)
Drying Crops with Solar Heated Air
Proceedings of UN Conference on New Sources of Energy, Rome, Italy. Rome:
FAO.

BUELOW F H (1962)
Corrugated Heat Collectors for Crop Drying
Sun at Work, 1962, 8-9.

BUELOW F H & BOYD J S (1957)
Heating Air by Solar Energy
Agricultural Engineering, 381, 28-30.

de BUSSY R P (1981)
Tedlar 400 SE PVF Film for Glazing Solar Collectors - a Cost-effective
Breakthrough
Proceedings of ISES Solar World Forum, Brighton, UK. London: ISES.

CAIRNS J A, OSWIN C R & PAINE F A (1974)
Packaging for Climatic Protection.
London, UK: Newnes - Butterworth.

CALDERWOOD D L (1982)
Solar Assisted Rice Drying in Continuous Flow Dryer
Transactions of ASAE, 1728-1732.

CARNEGIE E J (1977)
Research on the Application of Solar Energy to Industrial Drying Processes
Final Report, Phase 1 - Design, California Polytechnic State University, San Luis
Obispo, USA. 73pp.

CARNEGIE E J (1978)
Research on the Application of Solar Energy to Industrial Drying Processes
Final Report, Phase 2 - Construction, California Polytechnic State University,
San Luis Obispo, USA. 85pp.

CARNEGIE E J (1979)
Research on the Application of Solar Energy to Industrial Drying Processes
Final Report, Phase 3 - Evaluation, California Polytechnic State University, San
Luis Obispo, USA. 57pp.

CARR M (1983)
Personal Communication

CATANIA P, DAVIDSON H & KWON Y (1980)
Comparative Performance and Economics of Solar Drying of Wheat in Canadian
Prairies
Proceedings of American Section ISES Annual Meeting, Phoenix, USA. Newark:
American Section of ISES.

CHAKRABORTY P K (1976)
Solar Dryer for Drying Fish and Fishery Products
Research and Industry, 21, 3, 192-194.

CHAKRABORTY P K (1978)
Technological Development in Artificial and Solar Dehydration of Fish in India
Proceedings of Symposium on Fish Utilisation Technology and Marketing in the
IPFC Region (IPFC/78/SYMP/31), Manila, Philippines. Rome, Italy: FAO.

CHANG H S (1978)
Solar Energy Utilisation in a Greenhouse Solar Drying System
Agricultural Mechanisation in Asia, Winter, 11-16.

CHAU K V & BAIRD C D (1980)
Solar Grain Drying under Hot & Humid Conditions
Proceedings of National Energy Symposium, Kansas City, USA. St Joseph: ASAE.

CHEEMA L S (1978)
Solar Drying of Cassava for Alcohol Production
Proceedings of ISES Congress, 'The Sun - Mankind's Future Source of Energy', pp 1940-1942, New Delhi, India. Parkville, Australia: ISES. 2184pp.

CHEEMA L S & RIBERIO C M C (1978)
Solar Dryers of Cashew, Banana and Pineapple
Proceedings of ISES Conference 'The Sun: Mankind's Future Source of Energy' pp2075-2079, New Delhi, India. Parkville, Australia: ISES. 2184pp.

CHIRIFE J (1971)
Diffusional Process in the Drying of Tapioca Root
Journal of Food Science, 36, 327-333.

CHIRIFE J & CACHERO R A (1970)
Through-circulation Drying of Tapioca Root
Journal of Food Science, 35, 364-368.

CHODA A & READ W R W (1970)
The Performance of Solar a Air Heater and Rockpile Thermal Storage System
Proceedings of 1970 ISES Conference, Melbourne, Australia. Parkville: ISES.

CHRISTIE E A (1970)
Spectrally Selective Blocks for Solar Energy Collection
Proceedings of 1970 ISES Conference, Melbourne, Australia. Parkville: ISES.

CLARK C S (1981)
Solar Food Drying: A Rural Industry
Appropriate Technology, 8, 4, 14-16.

CLARK C S & SAHA H (1982)
Solar Drying of Paddy
Renewable Energy Review Journal, 4, 1, 60-65.

CLOSE D J (1963)
Solar Air Heaters for Low and Moderate Temperature Applications
Solar Energy, 7, 3, 117-124.

CLOSE D J & DUNKLE R V (1970)
Energy Storage using Desiccant Beds
Proceedings of 1970 ISES Conference. Melbourne, Australia. Parkville: ISES.

CLUCAS I J (1981)
Fish Handling, Preservation and Processing in the Tropics, Part I
Report G114, TDRI, London, UK. 144pp.

COULSON J M & RICHARDSON J F (1966)
Chemical Engineering, Vol 1, (3rd Edition)
Oxford, UK: Pergamon Press. 449pp.

COURSEY D G, MARRIOT J, MCFARLANE J H & TRIM D S (1982)
Improvements in Field Handling, Chipping and Drying Cassava
Journal of Root Crops, 8, 1 & 2, 1-15.

CUNDIFF J S (1980)
A Renewable Resources System for Curing Tobacco
Proceedings of National Energy Symposium, Kansas City, USA.   St Joseph:
ASAE.

DARK R (1982)
Dried Fruit - Natural Goodness all the Year Round
Wellingborough, UK: Thomsons Publishers Ltd.

DAVIDSON H R (1980)
A Review of Solar Crop Drying in Western Canada
Proceedings of Solar Crop Drying Workshop, pp51-70, Barbados.   London, UK:
Commonwealth Science Council.

DAVIS C P & LIPPER C I (1961)
Solar Energy Utilisation for Crop Drying
Proceedings of UN Conference on New Sources of Energy, pp273-282, Rome,
Italy. Rome: FAO.

DENG J C, CHAU KC, BAIRD C D, HEINIS J J, PEREZ M & WU L (1979)
Drying Seafood Products with Solar Energy
Proceedings of 2nd International Conference of Energy Use Management,
pp1884-1892, Los Angeles, USA. New York: Pergamon Press.

DIOUF N (1980)
An Attempt to Protect Dried Fish by Pyrethrum and Solar Energy
Presented at FAO Consultants Meeting on Fish Technology in Africa,   February
11-15, Dar-es-Salaam, Tanzania. 5pp.

DOE P E (1979)
A Polythene Tent Fish Dryer - A Progress Report
Proceedings of Conference 'Agricultural Engineering in National Development',
Paper 79-12, Selangor, Malaysia. Selangor: University Pertanian.

DOE P E, BHAT B K & MENARY R C (1979)
Preliminary Studies of a Low Fuel Hop Drying Kiln for Himachal Pradesh, India
Food Technology in Australia, 31, 293-296.

DOE P E, AHMED M, MUSLEMUDDIN M & SACHITHINANTHAN K (1977)
A Polythene Tent Dryer for Improved Sun Drying of Fish
Food Technology in Australia, 29, 437-441.

DUFFIE J A & BECKMAN W A (1980)
Solar Engineering of Thermal Processes
New York, USA: John Wiley and Sons. 762pp.

ECKSTEIN O (1961)
A Survey of the Theory of Public Expenditure Criteria, in Public Finances:
Needs Sources and Utilisation.
Princeton University Press.

EDLIN F E (1958)
Plastic Glazings for Solar Energy Absorption Collectors
Presented at Annual Meeting ASME, December 1-6, New York, USA.

EICHER C L & BAKER D (1982)
Agricultural Research and Development in Sub-Saharan Africa
Critical Evaluation Development Paper No 2, Michigan State University, East Lansing, USA.

ENO B E & FELDERMAN E J (1980)
Supplemental Heat for Grain Drying with a Transportable Solar Heater
Transactions of ASAE, 959-963.

EXELL R H B (1980)
Basic Design Theory for a Simple Solar Rice Dryer
Renewable Energy Review Journal, 1, 2, 1-14.

EXELL R H B & KORNSAKOO S (1978)
A Low Cost Solar Rice Dryer
Appropriate Technology, 5, 1, 23-24.

EXELL R H B & KORNSAKOO S (1979)
Solar Rice Dryer
Sunworld, 3, 3, 5.

EXELL R H B & KORNSAKOO S & THIRATRAKOOLCHAI S (1979)
A Low Cost Solar Rice Dryer for Farmers in South East Asia
Agricultural Mechanisation in Asia, Autumn, 75-78.

EZEKWE C I (1981)
Crop Drying with Solar Air Heaters in Tropical Nigeria
Proceedings of ISES Solar World Forum, Brighton, UK. London: ISES.

FARINATI L E & SUAREZ C (1984)
Technical Note: A Note on the Drying Behaviour of Cottonseed
Journal of Food Technology 19, 739-744.

FAO (1970)
Food Storage Manual, FAO, Rome, Italy. 799pp.

FAO (1980)
Review of Cereals and Cereal Products
Codex Alimentarius Commission Report, FAO, Rome, Italy.

FAO (1981)
The Prevention of Losses in Cured Fish
Fisheries Technical Paper 219, FAO, Rome, Italy. 87pp.

FAO (1984)
Codex Alimentarius. FAO, Rome, Italy.

FILINO HARAHAP & MUSTADJAB (1978)
Some Data on Simple Solar Drying
Proceedings of UNESCO Solar Drying Workshop, Manila, Philippines. Manila: BED.

FOSTER C.P. (1966)
Social Welfare Functions in Cost Benefit Analysis in Operational Research as the Social Sciences
Tavistock Publications, London.

FOSTER G H & PEART R M (1976)
Solar Grain Drying - Progress and Potential
Agriculture Information Bulletin No 401, USDA, Washington, USA. 14pp.

FREEAR J (1980)
(In) Fundamental Aspects of the Dehydration of Foodstuffs, pp42-53. London, UK: Society of Chemical Industry.

GHOSH B N (1973)
A New Glass-roof Dryer for Cocoa Beans and Other Crops
Proceedings of International Congress 'The Sun in the Service of Mankind'. Paris, France. Paris: UNESCO.

GOMEZ M I (1982)
Effect of Drying on the Nutritive Value of Foods in Kenya
(In) Food Drying: IDRC-195e. (Ed) Yaciuk G. Ottawa, Canada: IDRC. 104pp.

De V GRAFF J (1957)
Theoretical Welfare Economics
Cambridge, UK: Cambridge University Press.

GRAINGER W, OTHIENO H & TWIDDELL J W (1981)
Small Scale Solar Crop Dryers for Tropical Village Use - Theory and Practical Experience.
Proceedings of ISES Solar World Forum, Brighton, UK. London: ISES.

GUTIERREZ, H H, ALVARADO S & PUYOL E (1979)
Construction and Experimental Tests of a Radiative/Convective Type of Solar Dryer
Simiente Investigaciones, 49, 3-4, 51-37.

HARIGOPAL U & TONAPI K V (1980)
Technology for Villages - Solar Dryer
Indian Food Packer, 34, 2, 48-49.

HELLICKSON M A (1981)
Design & Performance of a 'SeiTes' System for Livestock Building Heating and Crop Drying
Brookings, USA: South Dakota State University. 6pp.

HOPE G W & VITALE D G (1972)
Osmotic Dehydration - A Cheap and Simple Method of Preserving Mangoes, Bananas and Plantains
Report IDRC-004 el. IDRC, Ottawa, Canada. 13pp.

HORNGREN C T (1981)
Introduction to Management Accounting
Prentice Hall International.

HOWARTH S (1978)
Solar Dryer
Technical Paper No 34, Pakhribas Agricultural Centre, Dhankuta, Nepal. 3pp.

HSIEH R C & CHANG H S (1979)
Application of Solar Energy in Agriculture in Taiwan
Proceedings of 9th International Congress of Agricultural Engineering, East Lansing, USA. St Joseph: ASAE.

HUANG B K & BOWERS G G (1977)
Solar Energy Utilisation using Greenhouse Bulk Curing and Drying System
Proceedings of Solar Crop Drying Conference, pp117-145, Raleigh, USA. Washington: USDA.

HUTCHINS M G (1982)
Optical Properties of Materials for Flat Plate Collectors
Helios, 14, March.

IBRAHIM M N (1978)
Utilisation of Solar Energy for Crop Drying in Malaysia
Proceedings of UNESCO Solar Drying Workshop, Manila, Philippines. Manila: BED.

IBRAHIM A A (1979)
Solar Heated Dehumidified Air in Processing Perishable Tropical Crops
Proceedings of 9th International Congress of Agricultural Engineering, Paper IV-2b-10, East Lansing, USA. St Joseph: ASAE.

ILYAS S M, GRIMM W & WIENEKE F (1981)
Effect of Some Important Parameters on the Performance of Simple Flat Plate Collectors
Proceedings of 3rd International Conference on Energy Use Management, 'Beyond the Energy Crisis: Opportunity and Challenge', West Berlin, West Germany. London: Pergamon Press.

ISHIBASHI T & ISHIDA M (1981)
Improved Flat Plate Solar Collector with V-Corrugated Transparent Insulator
Proceedings of ISES Solar World Forum, pp198-202, Brighton, UK. London: ISES.

ISLAM M N & FLINK J M (1982)
Dehydration of Potato. I - Air and Solar Drying at Low Air Velocities
Journal of Food Technology, 17, 373-385.

ISMAIL M S, LAH T A T & BUYONG A A (1982)
Solar Drying of Fruits and Vegetables
Agricultural Services Bulletin No 5, FAO, Rome, Italy.

JANSEN E F (1958)
Process for Inhibiting Enzyme Activity in Plant Tissue
US Patent 2,860,055, US Govt Printing Office, Washington, USA.

JINDAL V K & GUNASEKARAN S (1982)
Investigating Air Flow and Drying Rate due to Natural Convection in Solar Rice Dryers
Renewable Energy Review Journal, 4, 2, 1-8.

JOHNSTON J C (1979)
Solar Roofs Dry African Crops
Sunworld, 3, 6, 161-163.

KAPOOR S G & AGRAWAL H C (1973)
Solar Dryers for Indian Conditions
Proceedings of Conference 'The Sun in the Service of Mankind', pp1-11, Paris, France. Paris: UNESCO.

KEENER H M, SABBAH M A, MEYER G E & ROLLER W L (1977)
Plastic Film Solar Collectors for Grain Drying
Journal Article No 14-77, Ohio Agricultural Research and Development Centre, Wooster, USA. 21pp.

KELLER A (1970)
Selective Surfaces on Aluminium Foils
Proceedings of 1970 ISES Conference, Melbourne, Australia. Parkville: ISES.

KENT N L (1982)
Technology of Cereals - An Introduction for Students of Food Science and Agriculture (3rd Edition)
London, UK: Pergamon Press. 221pp.

KESARI J P & SOPONRONNARIT S (1981)
The Performance of a Low Cost Solar Rice Dryer Suitable in Wet Season in Asian Countries
Proceedings of ISES Solar World Forum, Brighton, UK. London: ISES

KITIC D & VIOLLAZ P E (1984)
Comparison of Drying Kinetics of Soybeans in Thin Layer and Fluidized Beds.
Journal of Food Technology 19, 399-408

KLINE G L (1981)
Solar Collectors for Multiple-use Applications on Farms
Proceedings of ISES Solar World Forum, Brighton UK, pp1044-1048, Brighton, UK. London: ISES

KOH H K, CHUNG D S, CONVERSE H H, FOSTER G H & AZER N Z (1973)
Silica Gel Regeneration by Solar Energy
Proceeding of 1973 Winter Meeting ASME., Chicago, USA. Chicago: ASME

KOK R & KWENDAKWENA N (1983)
The Construction and Testing of a Solar Food Dryer in Zambia
Paper No 83-4538, ASAE, St Joseph, USA. 14pp.

KRAMER A & TWIGG B A (1966)
Fundamentals of Quality Control in The Food Industry (2nd edition)
Westport, USA: AVI Publishing Co Inc. 541pp

KRANZLER G A (1980)
Solar Hop Drying
Paper PNW80-507, ASAE, St Joseph USA. 8pp

KREIDER J F & KREITH F (1981)
Solar Energy Handbook
New York, USA: McGraw-Hill Book Co. .1083pp

LARMOND E (1977)
Laboratory Methods for Sensory Evaluation of Food
Publication 1637, Dept of Agriculture, Ottawa, Canada. 74pp

LAWAND T A (1963)
Solar Dryers for Farm Produce
Technical Report T4, Brace Research Institute, Sainte Anne de Bellevue, Canada. 53pp

LAWAND T A (1966)
A Solar Cabinet Dryer
Solar Energy 19, 4, 158-164

LAWAND T A (1967)
The Operation of a Large Scale Solar Agricultural Dryer - Progress Report
Technical Report T33, Brace Research Institute, Sainte Anne de Bellevue, Canada. 12pp

LEE F A (1983)
Basic Food Chemistry (2nd edition)
Westport, USA: AVI Publishing Co Inc. 564pp

LITTLE I M D & MIRLESS J A (1974)
Project Appraisal and Planning for Developing Countries
London UK: Heinemann Press, U.K.

MACEDO I C & ALTEMANI C A C (1978)
Experimental Evaluation of Natural Convection Solar Air Heaters
Solar Energy, 20, 367-369

MAHMOUD B A, SHAH W H & SHAH F H (1981)
Comparative Studies of Solar Dehydrators
Pakistan Journal of Scientific and Industrial Research, 24, 2, 85-88

MAIER V P & SCHILLER F A (1960)
Studies on Domestic Dates. I, Methods for Evaluating Darkening
Food Technology, 14, 139-142

MAKOWER R U (1960)
Chemical Inactivation of Enzymes in Vegetables before Dehydration
Food Technology, 14, 160-164

MARTINO R (1976)
Run for the Sun: Solar Heating Opens a Vast New Market
Modern Plastics, May, 52-55

MARTOSUDIRJO S, KURISMAN & TARAGAN I (1979)
Improvement of Solar Drying Techniques in Post-harvest Technology - A Study of Onion Drying in Indonesia
Proceedings of Inter-Regional Symposium on Solar Energy for Development, Paper B-10, Tokyo, Japan. Tokyo: JSETA

MATTEI R (1984)
Sun Drying of Cassava for Animal Feed - a Processing System for Fiji.
FAO Field Document 3, RAS/83/001, FAO, Rome, Italy 39pp

McBEAN M G, JOSLYN M A & NURY F S (1970)
Dehydrated Fruit
Report, CSIRO, Sydney, Australia

McDOWELL J (1973)
Solar Drying of Crops and Foods in Humid Tropical Climates
Report CFNI-T-7-73, Caribbean Food and Nutrition Institute, Kingston, Jamaica. 42pp

McQUEEN H J, SHAPIRO, M M & FELDMAN D (1980)
Selection of Materials for Flat Plate Solar Collectors
Journal of Materials for Energy Systems, 2, 65-81

MENDOZA E R (1979)
Performance of a Low Cost Solar Crop Dryer
Proceedings of Inter-Regional Symposium on Solar Energy for Development, Paper B-7 Tokyo, Japan. Tokyo: JSETA

MENTING L C, HODGSTAD B & THIJSSEN H A C (1970)
Aroma Retention during the Drying of Liquid Foods
Journal of Food Technology, 5, 127-139

MEYER G E, KEENER H M & ROLLER W L (1975)
Solar Heated Air Drying of Soybean Seed and Shelled Corn
Paper 75-3002, ASAE, St Joseph, USA. 10pp

MILLER W M & BOWMAN G K (1978)
Fresh Citrus Fruit Drying with Heated and Desiccated Air
Proceedings of Florida State Horticultural Society, 91, 130-133

MIRZAEV M M, TAIROV Z, UMAROV G G & NABIKHANOV B (1982)
On the Investigation of Drying of Fruit and Grapes in Solar Installations
Geliotekhnika, 18, 6, 40-43

MISRA R N & KEENER H M (1980)
Engineering Analysis of Solar Assisted Low Temperature In-Bin Fall Grain Drying and Subsequent Long-term Storage in Ohio
Paper 80-3J42, ASAE, St Joseph, USA. 12pp

MISRA R N, KEENER H M & ROLLER W L (1979)
Storage versus No-storage of Solar Heat for Corn Drying under Ohio Conditions
Paper 79-3024, ASAE/Canadian Society of Agricultural Engineering, St Joseph, USA. 25pp

MORRISON D W & SHOVE G C (1975)
Bare Plate Solar Collector Grain Drying Bin
Paper 75-3513, ASAE, St Joseph, USA. 15pp

MOY J H, BACHMAN W & TSAI W V (1980)
Solar Drying of Taro Roots
Transactions of ASAE, 242-246

MREMA G C (1981)
Agricultural Mechanization and Farming Systems: Policies and Prospects
Proceedings of Farming Systems Research Conference, pp144-159. Washington,
USA. Washington: USAID

MREMA G C (1983)
Energy in Agriculture
Proceedings of Regional Workshop on Energy for Development in Eastern and
Southern Africa, pp207-321. Lund, Sweden: University of Lund

MREMA G C (1984a)
Land Use Planning for Agricultural Development
Proceedings of CRD-AFRICA Workshop on Agricultural and Rural Development,
'Principles and Programmes - Teaching and Research at University Level,
Arusha, Tanzania. (In Press)

MREMA G C (1984b)
Utilization of Bioenergy Resources: A Case Study of Tanzania
Report, World Resources Institute, Washington, USA

MUTHUVEERAPPAN V R, AMBALAVAN G & KAMARAJ G (1978)
An Experimental Investigation and Heat Transfer Study on One Ton Per Day
Solar Paddy Dryer
Proceedings of Conference 'The Sun - Mankind's Future Source of Energy'
pp1952-1957. New Delhi, India. Parkville, Australia: ISES. 2184pp

NAHAR N H & GARG H P (1981)
Selective Coatings on Flat Plate Solar Collectors
Renewable Energy Review Journal, 3, 1, June, 37-51

NAHWALI M (1966)
The Drying of Yams with Solar Energy
Technical Report T27, Brace Research Institute, Sainte Anne de Bellevue,
Canada. 17pp

NILES P W, CARNEGIE E J, POHL J G & CHERN J M (1976)
Design and Performance of an Air Collector for Industrial Crop Dehydration
Proceedings of Conference 'Sharing the Sun', pp88-99, Winnipeg, Canada.
Winnipeg: Solar Energy Society of Canada.

OJHA T P & MAHESHWARI R C (1979)
All Weather System of Crop Drying with Solar Collector and Agricultural Wastes
Proceedings of 9th International Congress of Agricultural Engineering, East
Lansing, USA. St Joseph: ASAE

ONORIO B R (1979)
A Solar Drying System for Fish Feed Production
Presented at South Pacific Commission 11th Regional Technical Meeting on Fisheries, Noumea, New Caledonia. 3pp

OTHIENO H, GRAINGER W & TWIDDELL I W (1981)
Application of Small Scale Solar Crop Dryers to Maize Drying in Kenya
Proceedings of 2nd Conference on Energy for Rural and Island Communities, Inverness, UK. London: Pergamon Press.

OZISIK M N, HUANG B K & TOKSOY M (1980)
Solar Grain Drying
Solar Energy, 24, 397-401

PABLO I S (1978)
The Practicality of Solar Drying of Tropical Fruits and Marine Products as Income Generation for Rural Development
Proceedings of UNESCO Solar Drying Workshop, Manila, Philippines. Manila: BED

PABLO I S (1980)
Solar Drying of Agri- and Marine Products
Presented at International Symposium on Recent Advances in Food and Science Technology, Taipeh, Taiwan. 8pp

PAINE F A (Ed) (1981)
Fundamentals of Packaging
Stanmore, UK: Institute of Packaging. 235pp

PATTERSON G & PEREZ P (1981)
Solar Drying in the Tropics
Santa Monica, USA: Meals for Millions/Freedom from Hunger Foundation. 13pp

PERRY R H & CHILTON C H (Eds) (1973)
The Chemical Engineers Handbook, (5th Edition)
Tokyo, Japan: McGraw-Hill Kogakusha Ltd

PETERSON W H (1973)
Solar Collectors for Agricultural Use
Presented at Grain Drying and Energy Management Workshop, Champaign, USA

PHILLIPS A L (1965)
Drying Coffee with Solar Heated Air
Solar Energy, 9, 4, 213-216

PONTING J D, WATTERS G G, FORREY R R, JACKSON R & STANLEY W L (1966)
Osmotic Dehydration of Fruits
Journal of Food Technology, 1, 10, 125-128

POTTER E F (1954)
A Modification of the Iodine Titration Methods for the Determination of Sulphur Dioxide in Dehydrated Cabbage
Food Technology, May, 269-270

PUIGGALI J R & VARICHON B (1982)
First Prototypes for Small Fruit and Vegetable Country Solar Dryers
(In) Drying '82, (Ed) Majumdar A S. London, UK: Hemisphere Publishing Corp

RAHMAN K M (1981)
Solar Drying Technology for Fruits and Vegetable Preservation
Bangladesh Quarterly, 2, 1, 7-10

RAMKRISHNA RAO M, BALACHANDA J & VASO KI (1978)
Spectral Selective Properties of Black Chrome and Nickel Electro-deposited
Coatings for Solar Absorbers
Proceedings of ISES Conference 'The Sun - Mankind's Future Source of Energy'
pp875-878, New Delhi, India. Parkville, Australia: ISES

RICHARDS A H (1976)
A Polyethylene Tent Fish Dryer for Use in Papua New Guinea's Sepik River Salt
Fish Industry
Proceedings at Seminar 'Sun Drying Methodology', Colombo, Sri Lanka. Colombo:
National Science Council

ROA G & MACEDO I C (1976)
Grain Drying in Stationary Bins with Solar Heated Air
Solar Energy, 18, 445-449

ROSS H H (1948)
A Textbook of Entomology
New York, USA: John Wiley & Sons

SACHAROV S (1976)
Handbook of Package Materials
Westport, USA: AVI Publishing co Inc. 243pp

SANDHU B S, MANNAN K D, DHILLONG S & CHEEMA L S (1979)
Design, Development and Performance of Multi-rack Natural Convection Dryer
Proceedings of ISES Silver Jubilee Congress, pp25-28, London, UK London:
Pergamon Press

SATCUNANATHAN S (1973)
A Crop Dryer Utilising a Two-pass Solar Air Heater
Proceedings of Conference 'The Sun in the Service of Mankind', Paper V27, Paris,
France. Paris: UNESCO

SATCUNANATHAN S & DEONARINE S (1973)
A Two-pass Solar Air Heater
Solar Energy, 15, 41-49

SCHLAG J H, RAY D C, SHEPPARD A P & WOOD J M (1976)
Improved Inexpensive Solar Collectors for Agricultural Requirement
Proceedings of Conference 'Sharing the Sun', pp 22-32, Winnipeg, Canada.
Winnipeg: Solar Energy Society of Canada

SCHOENAU G J & BESANT R W (1976)
The Potential of Solar Energy for Grain Drying in Western Canada
Sharing the Sun, 7, 33-49

SELCUK M K, ERSAY O & AKYURT M (1974)
Development, Theoretical Analysis and Performance Evaluation of Shelf-Type Solar Dryers.
Solar Energy, 16, 81-88

SHAW R (1981)
Solar Drying Potatoes
Appropriate Technology, 7, 4, 26-27

SHERWOOD T K (1929)
The Drying of Solids
Industrial and Chemical Engineering, 21, 1, 12-17

SHERWOOD T K (1936)
The Air Drying of Solids
Transactions of American Society of Chemical Engineers, 150-168

SINGH H & ALAM A (1981
Solar Cabinet Dryer for Chilli Drying
Seeds and Farms, VII, 7, 25-26, 31

SMITH H R (1956)
The Significance of Microanalytical Tests on Food
Washington USA: National Canners Association

SMITH C C (1981)
Development and Demonstration of Solar Malt Kilning
Proceedings of 3rd International Conference on Energy Use Management "Beyond the Energy Crisis - Opportunity and Challenge", West Berlin, West Germany.
London, UK: Pergamon Press

SMITH C C, ANDERSON G & CHAPMAN J C (1977)
Solar Drying of Potato Products
Proceedings of Symposium 'Changing Energy Use Futures', Los Angeles, USA.
New York: Pergamon Press

SUAREZ C, VIOLLAZ P E & CHIRIFE J (1980)
Diffusional Analysis of Air Drying of Grain Sorghum
Journal of Food Technology, 15, 523-531

TABOR H (1978)
Status Report on Selective Surfaces
Proceedings of ISES Conference 'The Sun - Mankind's Future Source of Energy' pp 829-835, New Delhi, India. Parkville, Australia: ISES. 2184pp

TDRI (1984)
Standard Tests adapted by TDRI

THOMPSON J E & TRICKLER C J (183)
Fans and Fan Systems
Chemical Engineering, March 21, 48-63

TRIM D S & CURRAN C A (1982)
A Comparative Study of Solar and Sun Drying of Fish in Ecuador
Report L60, TDRI, London, UK. 44pp

TRIM D S & KO H Y (1982)
Development of a Forced Convection Solar Dryer for Red Peppers
Tropical Agriculture (Trinidad), 49, 4, 319-323

TRIM D S & KAMAU I N (1984)
A New Parchment Drying System for Co-operative Factories II: System Commissioning
Kenya Coffee, 49, 577, 137-143

TRIM D S, BRENNDORFER B & KAMAU I N (1984)
A New Parchment Drying System for Co-operative Factories. I: System Design and Operating Principles
Kenya Coffee, 49, 577, 128-136

UMAROV G G & IKRAMOV A I (1978)
Features in the Drying of Fruit and Grapes in Solar Radiation Drying Apparatus
Gelioteknika, 14, 6, 55-57

UMAROV G G & TAIROV Z (1982)
A Combination Solar Unit for Drying Fruit and Grapes
Geliotekhnika, 18, 1, 61-63

UNIDO (1978)
Guide to Practical Project Appraisal: Social Cost - Benefit Analysis in Developing Countries
Project Formulation and Evaluation Series.

VAN ARSDEL, W B, COPLEY M J & MORGAN A I (1973a)
Food Dehydration, Volume 1: Drying Methods and Phenomena (2nd Edition).
Westport, USA: AVI Publishing Co Inc. 347pp

VAN ARSDEL W B, COPLEY M J & MORGAN A I (1973b)
Food Dehydration, Volume 2: Practices and Applications, (2nd Edition).
Westport, USA: AVI Publishing Co Inc. 529pp

VAN DRESSER P (1979)
Homegrown Sun Dwellings
Santa Fe, USA: Lightning Tree Publications. 136pp

VOIROL F (1972)
The Blanching of Vegetables and Fruit
Food Process Industries, August

WAGNER C J, COLEMAN R L & BERRY R E (1980)
Pretreatment for Solar and Hot-air Drying
Proceedings of Florida State Horticultural Society, 93, 336-338

WALTON L R, HENSON W H, McNEIL S G & BUNN J M (1980)
A Solar Energy System for Curling Burley Tobacco.
Transactions of ASAE, 192-196

WATERMAN J J (1976)
The Production of Dried Fish
Fisheries Technical Paper 160, FAO, Rome, Italy. 52pp

WEISER H H, MOUNTNEY G J & GOULD W A (1971)
Practical Food Microbiology and Technology, (2nd Edition)
Westport, USA: AVI Publishing Co Inc.

WEREKO-BROBBY C Y (1983)
The Appraisal of Renewable Energy Technologies for Developing Countries
Master of Business Administration Project, Middlesex Polytechnic London, UK

WHILLIER A (1964)
Black Painted Solar Air Heaters of Conventional Design
Solar Energy, 8, 1, 31-37

WHITE J A (1980)
Weatherability of Fibreglass Solar Collective Device
Polymers News, 3, 5, 239-245

WIENEKE F (1977)
Solar-aeration Drying of some Tropical Products
Presented at International Conference 'Rural Development Technology: an Integrated Approach' Bangkok, Thailand

WILHEIM W G (1980)
Low-cost Solar Collectors using Thin-film Plastic Absorbers and Glazings
Proceedings of 1980 Annual Meeting of American Section ISES, Phoenix, USA.
New York: ISES

WILLIAMS C N, BEENY J & WEBB B H (1969)
A Solar Heat Dryer for Crops and Other Products
Tropical Agriculture (Trinidad) 46, 1, 47-54

WILLIAMS E E, OKOS M R, PEART R M & BADENHOP A F (1976)
Solar Grain Drying and Collector Evaluation
Paper 76-3512, ASAE, St Joseph, USA

WILSON B W (1957)
Field Tests of Solar Energy Absorbers for Drying Vine Fruit
Report, CSIRO, Melbourne, Australia. 22pp

WOOLLEN A H (1969) (ED)
Food Industries Manual
London UK: Leonard Hill. 509pp

WRUBLESKI E M & CATANIA P J (1978)
Solar Grain Drying in Saskatchewan, Canada
Proceedings of ISES Congress 'Sun - Mankind's Future Source of Energy' pp 2089-2094. New Delhi, India. Parkville, Australia: ISES. 2184pp

ZEMANSKY M W (1968)
Heat and Thermodynamics
Tokyo, Japan: McGraw-Hill Kogakusha Ltd. 658pp

CONVERSION FACTORS AND USEFUL DATA

BASIC SI UNITS

Quantity	Name of unit	Unit symbol
Length	metre	m
Mass	kilogram	kg
Time	second	s
Electric current	ampere	A
Temperature	degree Kelvin	K
Luminous intensity	candela	cd
Substance	mole	mol

DERIVED SI UNITS HAVING SPECIAL NAMES

Physical quantity	SI unit	Unit symbol
Force	Newton	$N = kg\ m\ s^{-2}$
Energy	Joule	$J = N\ m$
Power	Watt	$W = J\ s^{-1}$
Pressure	Pascal	$Pa = N\ m^{-2}$

PREFIXES FOR UNIT MULTIPLES AND SUB-MULTIPLES

10^{-18}	atto	a	
10^{-15}	femto	f	
10^{-12}	pico	p	
10^{-9}	nana	n	
10^{-6}	micro	μ	
10^{-3}	milli	m	
10^{-2}	centi	c	
10^{-1}	deci	d	
10^{1}	deca	da	
10^{2}	hecto	h	
10^{3}	kilo	k	
10^{6}	mega	M	
10^{9}	giga	G	(US Billion)
10^{12}	tera	T	(UK Billion)

COMMON CONVERSION FACTORS

Length

1 inch (in)	: 25.40 mm
1 foot (ft)	: 0.3048 m
1 yard (yd)	: 0.9144 m
1 chain	: 20.12 m
1 mile	: 1.609 km

Area

1 in^2	: 645.2 mm^2
1 ft^2	: 0.0929 m^2
1 acre	: 0.4047 hectares
1 $mile^2$	: 2.590 km^2

Volume

1 in^3	: 0.0164 litre
1 ft^3	: 0.0283 m^3
1 UK gallon (gal)	: 4546 cm^3
1 US gal	: 3785 cm^3
1 US Bushel	: 0.352 m^3

Mass

1 ounce (oz)	: 28.35 g
1 pound (lb)	: 0.4536 kg
1 slug	: 14.59 kg
1 hundredweight (cwt)	: 50.80 kg
1 US ton	: 907.2 kg
1 tonne	: 1000 kg
1 ton	: 1016 kg

Velocity

1 ft minutes^{-1} (ft min^{-1})	: 0.0051 m s^{-1}
1 mile hours^{-1} (mile h^{-1})	: 0.4470 m s^{-1}

Volumetric Flow

1 ft^3 hr^{-1}	: 7.866 cm^3 s^{-1}
1 UK gal h^{-1}	: 1.263 cm^3 s^{-1}
1 ft^3 min^{-1} (cfm)	: 4.72 x 10^{-4} m^3 s^{-1}

Mass Flow

1 lb h^{-1}	: 0.1260 g s^{-1}
1 ton h^{-1}	: 0.2822 kg s^{-1}

Force

1 poundal (pdl)	: 0.1383 N
1 pound-force (lbf)	: 4.448 N
1 dyne (dyn)	: 10^{-5} N

Pressure

1 lb in $^{-2}$ (psi)	: 6.895 kPa
1 standard atmosphere	: 101.3 kPa
1 bar	: 100 kPa
1 inch water	: 249.1 Pa
1 torr (mm mercury)	: 133.3 Pa

Temperature Difference

1°F (R) : $5/9^{\circ}$C (K)

Temperature

$(^{\circ}F - 32) = {^{\circ}C} \times 1.8$

Energy

1 calorie (cal	: 4.187 J
1 erg	: 10^{-7}
1 British thermal unit (Btu)	: 1.055 kJ
1 kWh	: 3.600 MJ
1 therm	: 105.5 MJ

Power

1 horse power (hp) (British)	: 745.7 W
1 hp (metric)	: 735/5 W
1 Btu h^{-1}	: 0.2931 W

Calorific Value

1 Btu lb^{-1}	: 2.326 kJ kg^{-1}
1 cal g^{-1}	: 4.187 J g^{-1}
1 Btu ft^{-3}	: 37.26 kJ m^{-3}

Specific Heat

1 Btu lb^{-1} $^{\circ}$F^{-1} : 4.187 kJ kg^{-1} K^{-1}

Density

1 lb ft^{-3}	: 16.02 kg m^{-3}
1 lb in^{-3}	:27.68 g cm^{-3}

Insolation

1 Langley day^{-1}
(cal cm^{-2} day^{-1})
             : 0.418 MJ m^{-2} day^{-1}
             : 0.0116 kWh m^{-2} day^{-1}

USEFUL CONSTANTS

Bulk Densities

	lb ft^{-3}	kg m^{-3}
Wood	30-45	481-721
Straw	20	320
Peanuts	22	352
Walnuts	40	641
Potatoes	42	673
Cowpeas	48	769
Soybeans	48	769
Oats	32	513
Barley	39	625
Maize	48	769
Wheat	49	785
Rice	36	577

Calorific Values

	Btu lb^{-1}	MJ kg^{-1}
Wood	6470-8620	15 - 20
Coal	10780-15100	25 - 35
Oil	17240-19400	40 - 45
Peat	4310- 6470	10 - 15
Bagasse	3880	9

		Btu ft^{-3}	MJ m^{-3}
Gas	manufactured	510	19
	natural	1050	39
	liquid petroleum	1340	50

Specific Heats (at constant pressure)

	Btu lb^{-1} °F^{-1}	kJ kg^{-1} K^{-1}
Air	0.2400	1.005
Water	1.000	4.187
Steel	0.1070	0.4480
Wood	0.5000	2.093
Coal	0.3000	1.256
Cement	0.1860	0.7790
Glass	0.1800	0.7540

Specific heat of air
= $0.24 + 0.466 H$ (Btu lb^{-1} °F^{-1})
= $1 + 1.942h$ (kJ kg^{-1} K^{-1})
where h = absolute humidity

Densities (at STP)

	lb ft^{-3}	kg m^{-3}
Air	0.0800	1.280
Water	62.40	1,000
Mercury	847.00	13,570
Alcohol	50.00	801
Concrete	144.00	2,307
Steel	480.00	7,689
Glass	162.00	2,595

Variation of latent heat of water with temperature

Temperature (°C)	Latent heat (kJ.kg^{-1})
20	2384
40	2326
60	2280
80	2233
100	2210

ANALYTICAL TECHNIQUES

ADEQUACY OF BLANCHING

(Van Arsdel et al, 1973)

(a)   **Reagents**

Distilled water.
0.5% guaiacol in 50% ethyl alcohol solution.
0.8% hydrogen peroxide (2.8ml of 30% hydrogen peroxide per litre).   Keep in refrigerator in dark bottle, and renew solution each week or two.
Clean sand.

(b)   **Apparatus**

Test tubes, 18 mm or 23 mm in diameter.
75 mm or 100 mm in diameter funnels.
150 mm or 175 mm cotton milk filters.
Waring Blender or similar mixer, or porcelain mortar (4 to 6 in. diameter) and pestle.
50 ml graduated cylinder.
1 and 2 ml pipettes.
Timer or watch with second hand.
Test tube rack.
Balance which will weigh 10 g samples to 0.1 g (a triple-beam balance is recommended).   (If a blender is used, a larger sample will permit use of a less sensitive balance).

(c)   **Method**

(i)   Using a blender/mixer

   (1)   Weigh out a representative 100 - 200 g sample.

   (2)   Place in blender or mixer with 3 ml water to each gram of sample.

   (3)   Grind for 1 minute at moderate or high speed.

   (4)   Filter through cotton milk filter.

   (5)   Add 2 ml of filtrate to 20 ml of distilled water in test tube.

   (6)   Prepare a blank by adding 2 ml of filtrate to 22 ml of distilled water in a second test tube, mix, and use as a colour comparison tube. (Do not add guaiacol or peroxide to this tube).

   (7)   Add 1 ml of 0.5% guaiacol solution to first test tube without mixing.

(8)   Add 1 ml of 0.08% hydrogen peroxide to the same tube without mixing.

(9)   Mix contents thoroughly by inverting and watch for development of any colour differing from the blank, regardless of hue, but of sufficient intensity to show an obvious contrast. Development of colour is a positive test and indicates inadequate blanching. If no colour contrast develops within 3.5 minutes, consider the test negative and the product adequately blanched. If colour develops after 3.5 minutes, it is to be disregarded and the test still considered negative.

(ii)   Using mortar

(1)   Cut the tissue to be tested into small pieces and weigh out a representative 10 g sample.

(2)   Place 30 ml distilled water in a graduated cylinder.

(3)   Place sample in mortar with a little clean sand, add minimum amount of water from graduated cylinder to best consistency for thorough grinding, and grind for 3 minutes. Add remainder of water from cylinder and mix.

(4)   Proceed as under (i), 4 through 9 inclusive.

MOISTURE CONTENT

There are many methods of moisture determination (Van Arsdel et al, (1973)) but the two most common and useful are the <u>vacuum oven</u> method and the <u>air oven</u> method. However, the precise method used for specific commodities varies, particularly in the sample preparation, the air temperature and the drying time in the oven. Whatever method is used determinations should be carried out at least in duplicate.

1. **Vacuum Oven Method** (AOAC Method 22-012)
    (AOAC, (1980))

(a) **Apparatus**

Vacuum oven
Balance
Metal dishes with tightly fitting covers
Desiccator
Mill/mortar and pestle/blender

(b) **Method**

1. Prepare sample by pulping fresh produce in a blender or mortar and pestle, or grinding dried produce in a mill or mortar and pestle.

2. Dry metal dish plus cover. Weigh accurately (W_1).

3. Spread a 5-10 g sample evenly over the bottom of the metal dish and fit cover. Weigh accurately (W_2).

4. Place dish in vacuum oven at 70°C and dry to constant weight (about 6 hours). Remove to the desiccator, cool and weigh (W_3).

(c) **Calculation of results**

$$\text{Moisture content (\% wb)} = \frac{W_2 - W_3}{W_2 - W_1} \times 100$$

Note: This is the recommended method for fresh and dried fruits, but it can also be used for other commodities, such as vegetables or fish. The oven temperature may need to be adjusted if, for instance, volatiles are present, and the time to achieve constant weight will be different for each commodity, eg. 6 hours or 40 hours.

2. **Air Oven Method**
    (FAO, (1981))

The vacuum oven method is the most accurate, but if a suitable oven is not available, then this method can give sufficiently accurate results using cheaper and simpler equipment.

(a)   **Apparatus**

Air Oven
Balance
Metal dishes with tightly fitting covers
Desiccator

(b)   **Method**

1.   Prepare sample as for vacuum oven method.

2.   Dry metal dish plus cover overnight in an oven at 105 C. Remove from oven and place in a desiccator to cool. Weigh accurately (W_1).

3.   Place 2-5 g of ground sample into the dish and fit cover. Weigh accurately (W_2).

4.   Return dish to the oven and again desiccate to cool before weighing accurately.

5.   Remove from the oven and again desiccate to cool before weighing accurately (W_3).

(c)   **Calculation of results**

As for Vacuum Oven Method.

3.   **Air Oven Method for Grains** (AACC) - Method 44-18/19)
       (AAAC, (1976))

(a)   **Apparatus**

Air oven
Balance
Metal dishes with tightly fitting covers
Desiccator
Mill/Mortar and pestle

(b)   **Method**

For samples of more than 13% moisture conduct stages one and two, and for samples judged to contain 13% or less conduct stage two only.

Stage One

1.   Dry metal dish plus cover, weigh accurately (W_1).

2.   Spread damp grain evenly over the bottom of the metal dish. Weigh accurately (W_2). The exact amount of grain used is not critical but the layer thickness should be kept small enough to ensure that mould does not develop during the drying period, and

the sample should be large enough to ensure adequate material for grinding in stage two. A sample size of 50 g is usually adequate.

3. Place metal dishes (cover removed) in a warm, well-ventilated place (preferably on top of a heated oven) protected from dust and rodents, so that the grain will dry reasonably fast and reach approximately air-dry condition in 14-16 hours. In all cases, the moisture content must be reduced to 13% or less at this first stage. Weigh accurately (W_3).

Stage Two

1. Grind sample to pass sieve with circular openings of 1 mm diameter and mix thoroughly.

2. Weigh previously dried metal dish plus cover (W_4).

3. Spread a 2 g ($\pm$ 1 mg) sample evenly over the bottom of the metal dish, fit cover and weigh accurately (W_5).

4. Place dish (with cover removed) into the oven as quickly as possible and dry for 2 hours at 135° C.

5. Place covers on dishes, transfer to desiccator to cool, and weigh accurately (W_6).

(c) **Calculation of Results**

% moisture determined in stage one, $A = \dfrac{W_2 - W_3}{W_2 - W_1} \times 100$

% moisture determined in stage one, $B = \dfrac{W_5 - W_6}{W_5 - W_4} \times 100$

% total moisture (wet basis) $= A + \dfrac{(100 - A)\,B}{100}$

SALT CONTENT

(FAO, (1981))

(a) **Reagents**

0.1N silver nitrate
Potassium chromate indicator solution
(1% w/v solution in water)
Distilled water

(b) **Apparatus**

Balance
Blender/mortar and pestle
Volumetric flasks
Pipettes
Burettes
Funnels
Graduated cylinders

(c) **Method**

    (1)   Weigh accurately approximately 2 g of a representative sample. (Wg)

    (2)   Macerate in distilled water for 2 minutes.

    (3)   Transfer extract into a 250 ml volumetric flask and make up volume with distilled water.

    (4)   Titrate 25 ml aliquots of this against 0.1N silver nitrate using potassium chromate indicator (end point yellow to red). (V ml)

(d) **Calculation of results**

$$\% \text{ sodium chloride} = \frac{V \times 0.1^* \times 58}{W}$$

*   normality of silver nitrate; if a solution of different strength is used then the equation must be modified accordingly.

SULPHUR DIOXIDE

(Potter, (1953))

The method by Prater et al (1944) involves two titrations with iodine. One aliquot of the sample is titrated to measure the total reducing materials. Acetone is added to the other aliquot to bind the sulphur dioxide, and the reducing materials other than sulphite are then titrated. The difference between the titrations is a measure of the sulphur dioxide present. Unfortunately, the acetone/bisulphate complex is not completely stable and gives a fleeting end point. The method below oxidizes the sulphite to sulphate, thereby eliminating the fleeting end point.

(a)   **Reagents**

Distilled water
5N sodium hydroxide
5N hydrochloric acid
1% starch solution
0.05N iodine
3% hydrogen peroxide
0.05N potassium iodide

(b)   **Apparatus**

Beakers
Blenders
Pipettes
Burettes
Graduated cylinders
Volumetric flasks
Funnels
Balance
Stirrer

(c)   **Method**

(1)   In each of two 600 ml beakers suspend approximately 8 g of ground dehydrated material (M g) in 400 ml of water and add 5 ml of 5N sodium hydroxide.

(2)   Stir gently, being careful not to beat air into the solutions and let them stand for 20 minutes.

(3)   To one of the samples add 7 ml of 5N hydrochloric acid, stirring to avoid local concentration. Add 10 ml of 1% starch solution and titrate immediately with 0.05N iodine to a definite blue colour (V_1 ml). It is important that the acidified sample be titrated at once, before recombination occurs.

(4)   To determine the reducing materials other than sulphite, the second sample is acidified in the same manner, but instead of using a binding agent at this point to form a sulphite compex, add 2 ml of

3% hydrogen peroxide to oxidize the sulphite to sulphate. The sample is now titrated with iodine to a definite blue colour (V_2 ml).

(5)   Prepare a blank with water, alkali, acid, starch and hydrogen peroxide as above but with no sample. To this blank add 10 ml of 0.05N potassium iodide solution. If no blue colour develops within 30 seconds, this shows that the iodine titration solution is stable until well after the titration of the non-sulphite iodine reducing materials has been completed.

(d)   **Calculation of results**

1 ml of 1N iodine = 0.032 g SO_2

$$\therefore \quad ppm\ SO_2 = \frac{(V_1 - V_2) \times 0.05^* \times 0.032 \times 10^6}{M}$$

*   normality of iodine solution; if a solution of different strength is used then the equation must be amended accordingly.

ASCORBIC ACID

(University of Leeds, (1975))

The chemical estimation of absorbic acid depends upon its ability to reduce the oxidation-reduction indicator, 2:6 dichlorophenolindophenol to a colourless form, while it is itself oxidized to dehydroascorbic acid.

In acid solution the reaction is fairly, but not absolutely, specific for ascorbic acid. In biological material there may occur other reducing substances with redox potentials lower than that of chlorindophenol and hence capable of reducing the dye. These include products of alkaline or heat decomposition of sugars, phenolic compounds, glutathione, cysteine, and hydrogen sulphide. The rate of reduction of the dye by ascorbic acid, in acid solution, is greater than that by most of these substances and hence, if the titration is carried out rapidly, the reaction becomes fairly specific.

Ascorbic acid is stable in the intact cells of animals and plants, but it is rapidly oxidized by the oxygen of the air as soon as the cellular tissue is broken down, eg, when mincing or grinding the tissue. In minced plant material the oxidation is catalysed by a specific enzyme ie ascorbic acid oxidase, or by cupric ions. It is important in the determination of the ascorbic acid content of foods to prevent this destruction. Metaphosphoric acid is therefore added to the extracting fluid; it inactivates the oxidase, as well as the catalytic effect of cupric ions (by complex formation), and at the same time precipitates the proteins. Oxalic or acetic acids are often used.

(a) **Reagents**

Distilled water
0.2 mg ml^{-1} 2:6 dichlorophenolindophenol: prepare by dissolving 0.2 g in 100 ml hot water, filtering and diluting 10 times.

0.1 mg ml^{-1} Standard ascorbic acid: in 2% metaphosphoric acid
0.05% oxalic acid

(b) **Apparatus**

Conical flasks
Pipettes
Burettes
Funnels
Graduated cylinders
Beakers
Glass wool or centrifuge
Blender
Volumetric flasks

(c) **Method**

(1) Standardization of the dye solution. Pipette 5 ml of the standard ascorbic acid solution into a conical flask and titrate with the solution of dye until a faint pink colour persists (V_1 ml). The

chloroindophenol is thus standardized in terms of mg ascorbic acid/ml dye.

(2)   Blend 40 g of fruit/vegetable for 2 minutes with 200 ml oxalic acid. Filter through glass wool or centrifuge. Pipette 5 ml of filtrate into a conical flask and titrate with the dye (V_2 ml). Allow 40 ml for volume of fruit/vegetable when calculating results.

(d)   **Calculation of results**

$$\text{Ascorbic Acid content (mg ml}^{-1}) = \frac{100 \times 240 \times V_2 \times 0.5}{40 \times 5 \times V_1}$$

NON-ENZYMIC BROWNING (ALCOHOL SOLUBLE COLOUR (ASC) INDEX)

(Maier and Schiller, (1960))

The results of simple alcohol extraction methods as described here have been shown to correlate well with non-enzymic browning in many foods (Maier and Schiller, (1960)); Nury and Brekke, (1963)). The extraction procedure has been described by Chan and Cavaletto (1982).

(a)   **Reagents**

70% methanol
Distilled water

(b)   **Apparatus**

Filter papers
Filtercel
Volumetric flasks
Balance
Graduated cylinders
Vacuum filter
Spectrophotometer
Pipettes

(c)   **Method**

(1)   Mix 40 g of product (W g) with 100 ml 70% methanol and 2 g "Filtercel" for 3 mins.

(2)   Filter in vacuo the mixture through a layer of "Filtercel" on a Whatman No 2 filter paper.

(3)   Make filtrate up to 200 ml in a volumetric flask with 70% methanol, mix well and measure absorbance of sample (A) against 70% methanol blank at 400 nm.

(d)   **Calculation of results**

$$\text{ASC Index} = \frac{A}{W} \times 1000$$

TOTAL SUGARS AND REDUCING SUGARS

(TDRI, 1984)

This method is based on a colorimetric procedures employing the potassium ferricyanide – potassium ferrocyanide oxidation – reduction reaction. The yellow colour of alkaline ferricyanide, when heated with reducing sugars, diminishes in proportion to the quantity of sugar present due to the production of the colourless ferrocyanide. The determination of total relies upon the conversion of non-reducing sugars, eg sucrose, to reducing sugars, eg glucose and fructose, by quantitative hydrolosis using a dilute acid. In this manner the content of total sugars can be determined by analysis of reducing sugars after hydrolosis.

(a)　**Reagents**

Ferricyanide reagent

(i)　　Dissolve together, in about 10 ml of distilled water, 1.25 g potassium ferricyanide and about 1.0 g sodium carbonate. Make up to 25 ml with distilled water. This solution should be freshly prepared on each occasion.

(ii)　　Dissolve 8.75 sodium carbonate in water and make up to 100 ml in a volumetric flask. Store at room temperature.

(iii)　　To prepare ferricyanide reagent mix 25 ml of solution (i) and 100 ml of solution (ii) and make up to 1,000 ml with water. Use within 1 day of preparation.

0.5 mg ml^{-1} Standard reducing sugar solution. Weigh accurately 1.0 g. glucose and make up to 100 ml of distilled water in a Grade A volumetric flask. Take 5 ml of this solution and dilute to 100 ml with distilled water.

1N hydrochloric acid
10% sodium hydroxide solution
Phenophthalein indicator
Distilled water

(b)　**Apparatus**

Homogenizer
Graduated cylinders
Volumetric flasks
Centrifuge
Pipettes
Test tubes
Water bath
Spectrophotometer

(c)   **Method**

(1)   Sample extracts

Homogenize a suitable quantity of material with 50 ml distilled water for 3 minutes. Make extract up to 100 ml in volumetric flask and then centrifuge at approximately 10,000 rpm for 15 minutes. Remove supernatent for analysis of reducing sugars. For analysis of total sugars take 10 ml of supernatent prepared above and add 15 ml of 1N hydrochloric acid and 10 ml of distilled water. Boil the solution gently for 2 minutes. After cooling neutralize this solution by the addition of a solution of 10% sodium hydroxide using phenophthalein indicator. Make the neutralized solution up to 100 ml with water and use in the analysis for total sugars.

(2)   To duplicate test tubes (15 ml) add up to 2 ml of suitable diluted sample extract (or hydrolyzed and neutralized plant extract for total sugars determination).   Add 8 ml of freshly prepared ferricyanide reagent and make up to 10 ml with distilled water. Mix the solution well and place in a boiling water bath for exactly 15 mins. Cool tubes and contents rapidly by plunging them into an ice cooled water bath and mix the tube contents again. Immediately read the absorbance of samples at 380 nm using a blank containing no reducing sugar (ie 2 ml of water plus 8 ml of ferricyanide reagent).

(3)   At each sampling time a calibration plot for glucose should be prepared using 0.0, 0.2, 0.6, 1.0, 1.6 and 2.0 ml of diluted standard reducing sugar solution (0.5 mg ml^{-1}).   A graph may then be constructed in which absorbance of reaction mixtures at 380 nm are plotted against weight of glucose (reducing sugar). The values of absorbance obtained with test solutions when read off against this calibration plot will give values for the quantity of reducing sugar present in the reaction mixture, which after calculation will provide a value for the amount of reducing sugars (% glucose) or total sugars (% glucose or invert equivalents) in the original sample.

TOTAL ASH CONTENT

(TDRI (1984))

(a)   Reagents

Olive oil
Distilled water

(b)   Apparatus

Oven
Desiccator
Silica/platinum dish
Balance
Bunsen burner
Muffle furnace

(c)   Method

A silica or platinum dish is dried in an oven at about 105°C to constant weight (W_1). The dish is then left to cool in a desiccator.

Between 2 g and 5 g of sample is added to the dish which is then reweighed (W_2). A few drops of olive oil are added to the dish. The dish is then heated gently over a Bunsen burner flame, care being taken to stop the sample catching fire. When the sample has stopped bubbling and smoking, it is heated until it is well carbonized.

The dish is then placed into a muffle furnace at about 525°C for 2-3 hours. The dish is then removed and allowed to cool and then some distilled water added to the sample. The water is evaporated over a steam bath and the sample then dried on a hotplate, after which the dish is placed back in the muffle furnace until white ash is obtained, about a further 3-4 hours.

The dish is then placed into a vacuum desiccator and weighed again when cool (W_3). (Air must be let slowly into the desiccator after cooling, to avoid loss of sample).

(d)   Calculation of results

$$\text{Ash (\%)} = \frac{W_3 - W_1}{W_2 \quad W_1} \times 100$$

ACID INSOLUBLE ASH CONTENT

(TDRI 1984)

(a) **Reagents**

10% HCl
Distilled water

(b) **Apparatus**

Graduated cylinders
Bunsen burner
Funnels
Filter papers
Desiccator
Balance
Muffle furnace
Oven
Silica/Platinum dish

(c) **Method**

Using a previously ashed sample (Total Ash Content), 25 cm^3 of 10% HCl is added to the dish, which is then boiled gently over a Bunsen burner flame for 5 minutes. After this time, the solution is filtered with an ashless filter paper with hot distilled water.

The filter paper is then put back into the dish and burned off over a Bunsen burner flame until only white ash is left. Care must be taken to avoid the sample catching fire.

The dish is then placed into a vacuum desiccator, left to cool, and weighed (W_4).

(d) **Calculation of results**

$$\text{Acid Insoluble Ash (\%)} = \frac{W_4 - W_1}{W_2 \quad W_1} \times 100$$

PROTEIN

(TDRI 1984)

Micro-Kjeldahl Determination

(a)   Reagents

Caustic soda solution	(70 gm per 100 ml)
Hydrochloric acid	(0.1N)
Concentrated sulphuric acid	
Bromocresol green	(0.1% alcoholic)
Methyl red	(1% alcoholic)
Boric acid	(4% solution)
Selenium catalyst tablets	(BDH 1 g Na_2SO_4 - 0.05 g Se)
Silicone DC Antifoam MS A compound	

(b)   Apparatus

Micro-Kjeldahl flask
Markham still
Balance
Pipettes
Graduated cylinders
Conical flasks
Burettes
Funnels

(c)   Method

100-200 mg of the material* (M g) is weighed out into micro Kjeldahl flask (50 ml size). 3 ml of concentrated sulphuric acid are then added with one catalyst tablet and three glass balls. The flask is then heated on a mantle, slowly at first, as there is a lot of splashing. This necessitates close supervision until the digest becomes clear. After the liquid becomes a pale straw colour, the flask is heated for a further hour.

The digest is then allowed to cool and washed into the Markham still with a small amount of distilled water. The flask is rinsed a few times and the rinsings added to the diluted digest. The condenser is then immersed in 10 ml of boric acid contained in a conical flask (with five drops of bromocresol green and one drop of methyl red present). 15 ml of caustic soda solution is slowly added to the digest and the latter left steam distilling for 15 minutes after all the caustic soda has been added.

---

*   50-100 mg protein gives 7.5 ml - 15 ml titration

The solution in the conical flask is then titrated against 0.1N hydrochloric acid (V_1 ml) (the end point is reached when the solution becomes orange in colour). A blank should be prepared by heating a catalyst tablet with 3 ml of concentrated sulphuric acid and the liquid treated as for the digest above and then similarly titrated against 0.1 N hydrochloric acid (V_2 ml).

(d)   **Calculation of results**

$$\text{Nitrogen (\%)} = \frac{(V_1 - V_2) \times 0.1^* \times 11.4}{M}$$

*   normality of hydrochloric acid; if a solution of different strength is used the equation must be modified accordingly.

Protein (%) = 6.25 x Nitrogen (%)

Macro-Kjeldahl Determination
(TDRI 1984)

(a)   **Method**

1 g sample is weighed into a folded filter paper and placed in a macroKjeldahl flask with three glass balls, one catalyst tablet and 40 ml H_2SO_4; stand overnight. Prepare blank containing all the above (including filter paper) except for sample. Digest as for MicroKjeldahl. Dilute the digest to 100 ml in a volumetric flask but cool first in a conical flask under running water. All samples must be in duplicate.

FAT

(TDRI 1984)

Caution

A highly inflammable solvent is used to extract fat from the sample. Care should be taken therefore to ensure that the determination is not carried out in an area near naked flames, lighted cigarettes, matches etc.

(a)   Reagents

Petroleum spirit

(b)   Apparatus

Balance
Watchglass
Round-bottomed flask
Oven
Desiccator
Soxhlet extractor
Whatman extraction thimble
Paper clip
Funnels
Cotton wool

(c)   Method

The fat is best extracted from a dry sample. For the sake of convenience, the dry moisture sample is often used. Since results are usually expressed on a wet weight basis, the weight of the wet moisture samples (W_1 g) is used in calculation of the results; in this instance, there is no need to reweigh the sample before extraction. With tissue samples, the dried cake should be broken up immediately before transfer to the extraction thimble.

If the sample is already dry, 2 g of sample should be weighed in a watchglass on an analytical balance. Calculation of results is therefore on a dry weight basis.

Place a few anti-bumping granules in a clean, round flat-bottomed 250 ml flask. Place the flask in an oven, pre-heated to 100°C, to dry for at least 5 hours (preferably overnight). Remove the flask from the oven, place it in a desiccator to cool (approximately 30 minutes) and weigh on an analytical balance (W_2 g). Fit a clean dry Soxhlet extractor into the weighed flask and support with a clamp stand. Attach a Whatman extraction thimble (33 x 80 mm) firmly to the Soxhlet extractor with a paper clip. Place a wide-stemmed, glass powder funnel into the thimble and transfer the sample to the thimble through the funnel, washing through with petroleum spirit (40-60°C). Remove the funnel and plug the thimble with fat-free, non-absorbent cotton wool. Remove the paper clip and allow the thimble to settle. Replace the funnel in the extractor and add sufficient petroleum spirit until it syphons into the flask at least twice. This should use approximately 200 ml3 of this solvent.

Remove the funnel and clamp stand. Carefully place the flask and extractor on one heating mantle of the air bath. Carefully lower the reflux condenser into the extractor. Ensure that the water is running through the condenser. Set heater switch so that petroleum spirit in the flask just boils. Tap the flask gently to initiate boiling. Allow extraction to take place for 16 hours; during this time, check periodically that the flask is in no danger of boiling dry. After this time, switch off the mantle and allow to cool. Raise the condenser and take the extractor and flask away from the heating mantle. Remove the thimble with tongs and place it in a petri dish and leave to one side. If the extractor is more than half full with petroleum spirit, tilt the apparatus towards the syphon and allow the solvent to run into the flask. Separate the extractor and flask, pour any remaining solvent from the extractor into the flask. Place the solvent collection vessel (a modified Soxhlet extractor) into the flask. Return the apparatus to the heating mantle and lower the condenser. Switch on the heating mantle to the same setting as before. Tap the flask to initiate boiling. Allow the solvent to collect in the chamber and tap off periodically into a conical flask. This solvent can be used again. Turn off the heating mantle when most of the solvent has evaporated from the flask. Allow the flask to cool slightly; raise the condenser allowing the last drops of solvent to fall from the condenser into the collecting chamber. Remove the apparatus from the heating mantle and separate the flask and collecting vessel. Pour the last drops of solvent from the collecting vessel into the conical flask.

Place the nozzle from the air line into the neck of the flask, taking care that it does not come in contact with the fat. Gently turn on the air line to evaporate the remaining solvent. The nozzles from the air line can also be placed in the dish which contains the discarded extraction thimbles; once all the solvent has been evaporated from these they may be thrown away. After all the solvent has evaporated from the flask, place it into the oven to dry (approximately 5 hours). Remove the flask after this time, place in a desiccator to cool (approximately 30 minutes) and weigh on an analytical balance. (W_3 g)

(d)   **Calculation of results**

$$\text{Fat } (\%) = \frac{W_3 - W_2}{W_1} \times 100$$

THIOBARBITURIC ACID (TBA) METHOD

(TDRI (1984))

(a) Reagents

Thiobarbituric acid: 0.2883 g TBA (analar reagent) in 100 ml glacial acetic acid. The reagent is light-sensitive so prepare freshly on each occasion and store in a flask wrapped in aluminium foil. The TBA reagent is difficult to dissolve, so use a magnetic stirrer and slight heat. If left TBA may come out of solution so use a magnetic stirrer to redissolve.

(b) Apparatus

Blender/mortar and pestle
Parallel-necked round-bottomed flasks
Graduated cylinders
Volumetric flasks
Pipettes
Test tubes

Malonaldehyde distillation apparatus – Quickfit – see Figure A2.1

(1)   Condenser, 200 mm long 40/28 cone. Q – C x 7/06 (upside down)

(2)   500 ml round-bottomed flask, 3 parallel necks, centre socket 24/29 side sockets 19/16. FFR500/35/22P

(3)   Liebig condenser. 200 mm long 19/265 socket and cone. C x 1/12.

(4)   Stopper, closed ends, cone 24/29. SB24

(5)   Cone and screw cap, adaptor cone 19/26, diameter of hole in screw cap 7 – 8.5mm ST52/18

(6)   Hollow glass tubing, approx 6 mm external diameter

(7)   Recovery bend, sloping, 19/26 cone 14/23, socket 24/29, OXA31 (7 and 8 are not used in the lab. Instead part of a pipette (10 ml) is bent into a suitable angle to fit the apparatus. Corks and rubber tubing are used to make it fit properly. 8 does not fit exactly but it is the closest possible.

(9)   Tripod

(10)   Bunsen burner

(11)   Funnel

(12)   50 ml volumetric flask

(13)   2 retort stands and 3 clamps and boss heads

(c) **Method**

10 g (5 g if fatty) sample (W g) is macerated in 50 ml water for 2 minutes. Prepare duplicates of each sample. Wash sample into a parallel-necked 500 ml round bottomed flask using a further 47.5 ml water. Add 2.5 ml 4N HCl to bring pH 1.5b approx. (If the sample is very fatty and rancid, add antifoam. In this case, a blank of water, acid and antifoam must be run).

Add glass balls and place in position for malonaldehyde distillation apparatus as in Figure A2.1. Heat with bunsen burner.

Collect 50 ml of distillate in a volumetric flask in 10 minutes (this is the maximum time) from when boiling commences (ie first drop of distillate reaches the volumetric flask). Make sure the sample does not bubble too vigorously otherwise it will get into the distillation apparatus. If this happens, it will be necessary to start again. Wash apparatus well between each distillation. Store distillates at 0°C (it is possible to store them overnight if necessary).

Pipette 5 ml distillate into a test tube and add 5 ml TBA reagent. Prepare duplicates for each distillate. Shake and heat in boiling water for 35 minutes. Prepare a blank of 5 ml water and 5 ml TBA reagent (antifoam blank may be necessary using 5 ml of antifoam distillate).

(d) **Calculation of results**

$$\text{TBA* value} = \frac{(\text{Mean of all absorbance}) \times 7.8 \times 10}{W} \quad \text{if 5 ml distillate used}$$

$$= \frac{(\text{Mean of all absorbance}) \times 7.8 \times 50}{W} \quad \text{if 1 ml distillate used}$$

* as mg/kg malonaldehyde

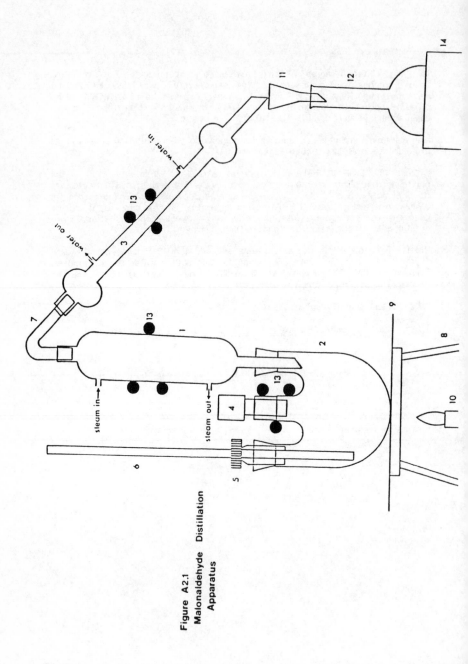

Figure A2.1
Malonaldehyde Distillation
Apparatus

TOTAL VOLATILE BASES (TVB)

(TDRI (1984))

(a) Reagents

5% w/v perchloric acid (54 ml of 60% PCA in 1000 ml H_2O)
2.5M potassium carbonate (345.525 g in 1000 ml H_2O)
N/70 Sulphuric acid (1 ml N H_2SO_4 + 69 ml H_2O)
N/70 Sodium hydroxide (1 ml 0.1 N NaOH + 6 ml H_2O)
Saturated potassium carbonate (120 g K_2CO_3 in 100 ml H_2O and filter off excess)
Tashiros Indicator: Stock solution – 0.2 g of methyl red + 0.4 g of methylene blue in 200 ml of ethanol. Prepare for use by mixing 1 volume of stock solution, 1 volume absolute alcohol and 2 volumes distilled water.
Gippert's wax; 2 parts (by weight), Beeswax, 1 part (by weight) Paraffin wax, 6 parts (by weight), Vaseline, melt together and mix thoroughly.

(b) Apparatus

Conway units
Pipettes
Burettes
Funnels
Conical flasks

(c) Method

Preparation of PCA extract. Weigh duplicate 12 g samples accurately (M g) into macerating vessels and add 80 ml ice-cold 5% w/v PCA. Homogenize for 1 minute at full speed. The homogenate is then transferred to a centrifuge tube and spun at 4,000 rpm for 15 minutes. The resulting supernatent should be clear. 20 ml of the supernatent are placed in a 50 ml beaker. This is neutralized to pH 5.5–6.5 by adding 2.5M potassium carbonate drop by drop from a burette while measuring the pH continously. The volume of potassium carbonate used is recorded. The precipitate is allowed to settle for 30 minutes in a refrigerator. The solution is then decanted and can be stored at -30°C until used.

The Conway units, 60 mm diameter, should be cleaned in chromic acid for 24 hours, washed and dried. The cover plates are coated with Gippert's wax and flamed to expel air bubbles.

2 ml of N/70 sulphuric acid is pipetted into the centre chamber of a Conway unit. 1 ml of the PCA extract is then pipetted into the outer chamber with 1 ml of potassium carbonate. The cover plate is pressed firmly on to the unit and left overnight. A blank must also be carried out; for this 1 ml distilled water is used in place of the PCA extract.

The solution is then titrated with the N/70 sodium hydroxide using 2 drops of Tashiros indicator (V_1 ml), the indicator going from reddish mauve to light green. The blank is similarly titrated (V_2 ml).

The samples and blanks are carried out in duplicate.

(d)   **Calculation of results**

Total Volatile Bases (mg N/100 g) $= \dfrac{(V_2 - V_1) \times 0.2^* \times 80 \times 100}{M}$

*   If a solution of concentration other than N/70 is used then equation must be amended accordingly.

HOWARD MOULT COUNT

(AOAC (1970))

(a) **Reagents**

Stabilizer solution - 0.5% sodium carboxymethylcellulose.
Place 500 ml boiling water in high-speed blender and cover. With blender running, add 2.5 g cellulose gum and 10 ml formaldehyde, and blend for about 1 minute. (Alternative stablizer solutions - 3-5% pectin or 1% algin). Add required quantity of stabilizer directly to water while agitating in high speed blender. Treat solution with vacuum or heat to remove air bubbles. Add 2 ml HC formaldehyde solution as preservative. Adjust to pH 7.0-7.5.

(b) **Apparatus**

(1) Microscope

(2) Howard mould-counting slide

Glass slide of one-piece construction with flat plane circle ca 19 mm diameter or rectangle 20 mm x 15 mm surrounded by moat and flanked on each side by shoulders 0.1 mm higher than plane surface. Cover glass is supported on shoulders and leaves depth of 0.1 mm between underside of cover glass and plane surface. Central plane, shoulders, and cover glass have optically worked surfaces. To facilitate calibration of microscope, newer slides are engraved with circle 1.382 mm diam or with 2 fine parallel lines 1.382 mm apart.

(3) Accessory disc for mould for counting.

Glass disc that fits into microscope eyepiece, rules into squares each side of which is equal to 1/6 of diam of field. Since limiting diaphragm is eyepiece field stop, rulings equal 1/6 of this diaphragm opening. Field viewed on slide with mould-counting microscope has diam of 1.382 mm at magnification of 90-125X.

(4) Method of illumination of compound microscope for mould counting.
Unless microscope has built-in light source, fasten lamp and microscope securely to baseboard so that they are used and maintained as unit. Adjust mirror pivot so that it is not easily moved, and hold microscope in place by screw or cleats.

(c) **Method**

In making mould counts, place 50 ml stabilizer solution in 100 ml graduated cylinder, add 50 ml ground sample by displacement, and mix thoroughly.

Clean Howard cell so that Newton's rings are produced between slide and cover glass. Remove cover and with knife blade or scalpel place portion of well-mixed sample upon central disc; with same instrument, spread evenly over disc, and cover with glass so as to give uniform distribution. Use only enough sample to bring material to edge of disc. (It is of utmost importance that the portion be taken from thoroughly mixed sample and spread evenly over slide disc. Otherwise, when coverslip is put in place, insoluble material, and consequently moulds, may be more abundant at centre of mount). Discard any mount showing uneven distribution of absence of Newton's rings, or liquid that has been drawn across moat and between cover and glass shoulder.

Place slide under microscope and examine with such adjustment that each field of view covers 1.5 mm^2. (This area, which is essential, may frequently be obtained by so adjusting draw-tube that diameter of field becomes 1.382 mm. When such adjustment is not possible, make accessory drop-in ocular diaphragm with aperture accurately cut to necessary size. Diameter of area of field view can be determined by use of stage micrometer. When instrument is properly adjusted, quantity of liquid examined per field is 0.15 mm^3). Use magnification of 90-125X. In those instances where identifying characteristics of mould filaments are not clearly discernible in standard field, use magnification of ca 200X (8 mm objective) to confirm identity of mould filaments previously observed in standard field.

For each of at least 2 mounts examine at least 25 fields taken in such a manner as to be representative of all sections of mount. Observe each field, noting presence or absence of mould filaments and recording results as positive when aggregate length of 1, 2 or 3 filaments present exceeds 1/6 of diameter of field. Calculate proportion of positive field from results of examination of all observed fields and report as % fields containing mould filaments.

PSYCHROMETRY AND USE OF PSYCHROMETRIC CHARTS

Psychrometry is the study of the properties of gas/vapour mixtures. However for the purpose of solar crop drying only the air/water vapour system is of interest. The psychrometric chart as Figure A3.1 is a graphical representation of the equilibrium relationship of gas/vapour systems.

Before the psychrometric chart is considered some basic definitions are important:

Absolute Humidity, h_a

The absolute humidity is defined as the weight of water vapour carried by unit weight of dry air. Units of absolute humidity are kg/kg.

In terms of water vapour pressures h_a can be expressed as:

$$h_a = \frac{m_w \cdot P_w}{m_a \cdot (P_a - P_w)}$$

where m_w = molecular weight of water (18 g mole^{-1})

m_a = molecular weight of air (28.8 g mole^{-1})

P_a = total atmospheric pressure (Pa)

P_w = partial pressure of water vapour (Pa)

When the partial vapour pressure of water is equal to its saturated vapour pressure, P_s, then the absolute humidity is the saturated humidity h_s.

Percentage Absolute Humidity, PS

This is the absolute humidity divided by the saturation humidity; it is sometimes termed the percentage saturation.

Percentage Relative Humidity, RH

This is the partial pressure of water vapour divided by the saturated vapour pressure of water at that temperature.

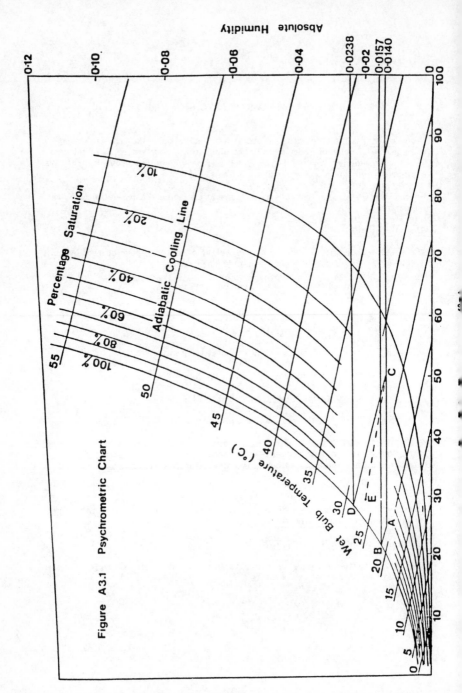

Figure A3.1   Psychrometric Chart

The terms percentage saturation and relative humidity are often used interchangeably and though this is not strictly correct the differences involved when dealing with conditions present in solar drying operations are small. The difference between the terms is most clearly seen if the two are defined in terms of partial pressures and vapour pressures.

$$PS = \frac{h}{h_S} \times 100 \ (\%) = \frac{P_W \cdot (P - P_S)}{P_S \cdot (P - P_W)} \times 100 \ (\%) \quad (A3.2)$$

$$RH = \frac{P_W}{P_S} \times 100 \ (\%)$$

Since the values of both P_S and P_W, although different, are very small compared with P, the difference between the terms $(P - P_S)$ and $(P - P_W)$ is extremely small. In this text percentage saturation and relative humidity will be treated as being interchangeable.

Wet-bulb Temperature

This is the temperature as measured by a thermometer, the bulb of which is wetted. When making this measurement considerable care must be taken (details are given in Chapter 17).

Adiabatic Cooling Lines

Evaporation of moisture into an air stream involves both heat and mass transfer. As moisture evaporates both the air stream and water surface lose sensible heat to provide the latent heat of vaporization of the water. If the temperature of the water is the adiabatic saturation temperature then the heat for evaporation will come from the air and therefore a relationship between gain in humidity and temperature drop can be found. This relationship is shown by the adiabatic cooling lines.

Other terms may be found on the psychrometric chart but the terms defined above are adequate for the purpose of evaluating and predicting dryer performance.

Example of Use of the Psychometric Chart

Using the psychometric chart the potential benefit of employing a solar collector to heat air can be evaluated. Assuming the ambient air has a temperature of 25°C and a RH of 70% and the collector can provide a temperature elevation of 25°C;

(i)   determine the humidity potential of the ambient air.

The intercept of the vertical dry bulb temperature line at 25°C and the 70% percentage saturation line denotes the condition of the ambient air, point A. Taking a horizontal line from this point to the absolute humidity axis enables the absolute humidity of the ambient air to be estimated.

Thus h_i =   0.0140 kg of moisture per kg of (dry) air

The saturation humidity of the air is determined by following an adiabatic cooling line from point A to the wet-bulb temperature line at point B and then along a horizontal line to the absolute humidity axis.

Thus h_{s1} = 0.0157 kg/kg

so then the potential of the ambient air to pick up moisture is:

$$h_1 \quad = \quad h_{s1} - h_i \quad\quad = \quad\quad 0.0157 - 0.0140$$
$$= \quad\quad 0.0017 \text{ kg/kg}$$

Therefore every kg of air has a capacity to "pick-up" 0.0017 kg of moisture from the commodity being dried. In practice it is unlikely that the air leaving the dryer will be saturated.

(ii)   determine the drying potential of the air after it has been heated to 50°C

During the heating process no moisture is added to the air and so there is no change in the absolute humidity. The condition of the air after being heated by 25°C to 50°C is found by moving horizontally on the chart from point A to intercept the line corresponding to a dry bulb temperature of 50°C. This is shown as point C. It can be estimated that this point corresponds to a relative humidity of 16%. Again, saturation humidity is found by following a line from point C parallel to the adiabatic cooling lines until the wet-bulb temperature line is intercepted - this is at point D. Following a horizontal line to the absolute humidity axis then gives the saturation humidity.

Thus h_{s2} = 0.0238 kg/kg

Therefore the potential of each kilogram of dry air to absorb moisture is as follows:

$$h_2 \quad = \quad h_{s2} - h_i \quad\quad = \quad\quad 0.0238 - 0.0140$$
$$= \quad\quad 0.0098 \text{ kg/kg}$$

The heated air therefore has a much greater capacity (0.0098 kg/kg) to absorb moisture than that of the ambient air (0.0017 kg/kg).

It is worth giving here a few words of caution. In the example quoted, in determining the theoretical drying capacity it has been assumed that the air would follow the adiabatic cooling line and exhaust from the dryer on the saturation line (points D or B). In practice it is likely to follow a slightly different path and exhaust at some other point, E (for the case of air heated to 50°C). In terms of design this means that whereas the theoretical outlet condition is 100% relative humidity a more realistic answer will be given by assuming no more than, say 80% saturation on exhaust and base the sizing of the dryer accordingly.

Note: The standard psychrometric charts are designed for use at an atmospheric pressure of 101.3 kPa, the standard pressure at sea level. However, atmospheric pressure varies considerably with altitude and corrections must be made when using the charts to allow for this as necessary. Generally up to about 1000m above sea level the standard charts will suffice. Above this altitude, corrections should be applied as discussed by Perry & Chilton (1973).

Sorption Isotherms and Useful Storage Data
(FAO, 1970)

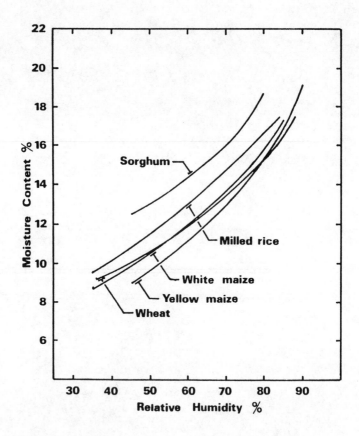

Figure A4·1   Moisture Sorption Isotherms for Wheat, Maize, Rice
and Sorghum at 25 °C

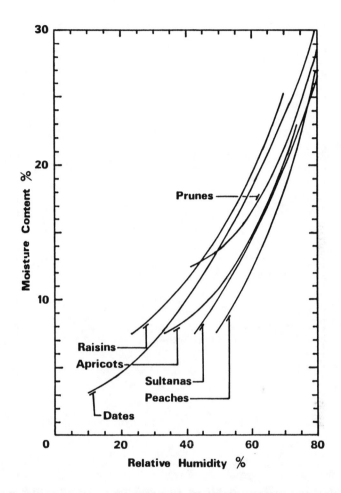

Figure A4·2   Moisture Sorption Isotherm for Various Dried
Fruits at 25°C

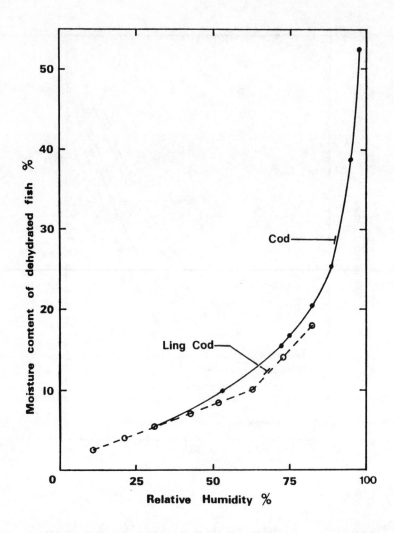

**Figure A4.5 Equilibrium Moisture Contents of Dehydrated Cod
and Ling Cod**

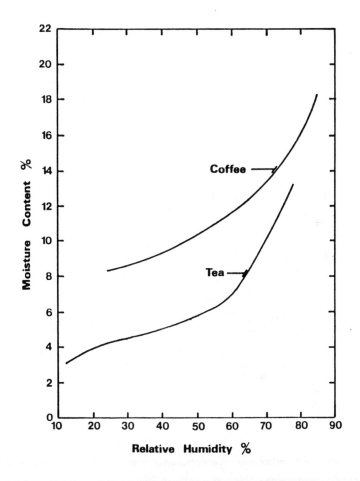

Figure A4·3   Moisture Content/Relative Humidity Equilibrium Curve for Coffee and Tea

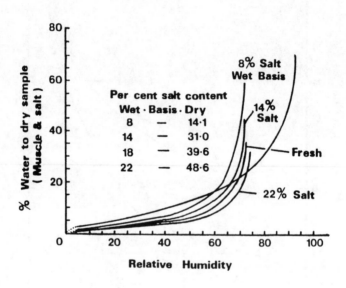

Figure A4·4   Equilibrium Water Content of Salt and Fresh Cod

Table A4.1   Advised Maximum Moisture Contents for Safe Storage of Cereals at 27°C

Cereal	Moisture content % (wet basis)
Wheat	13.5
Bulgar wheat	13.5
Wheat flour	12.0
Maize – yellow	13.0
– white	13.5
Maize meal	11.5
Milled rice	12.0
Sorghum	16.0

Note: The precise safe moisture content value differs to some extent between the varieties for all cereals. The variation in grain sorghums is particularly great. The values given are the average for each particular cereal, and where there is any doubt about particular varieties the equilibrium relative humidity of the grain, which must not exceed 70% for safe storage, should be used as the deciding factor.

Table A4.2   Maximum Permissible Moisture Contents for Safe Storage of Dried Fruits at 25°C

Fruit	Moisture Content % (wet basis)
Raisins	25.0
Sultanas	20.0
Prunes	21.5
Apricots	20.0
Peaches	18.0
Dates	24.0

TRIAL LOGSHEET

Trial No.   Dates: Venue:

		Dates		
		Day 1	Day 2	Day 3, etc
Start of drying				
End of drying				
Air flow m^3s^{-1}	High			
	Low			
	Mean			
Ambient Air Temperature °C	High			
	Low			
	Mean			
Air Temperature at Collector Outlet °C	High			
	Low			
	Mean			
Air Temperature at Drying Chamber Outlet °C	High			
	Low			
	Mean			
Ambient Air Relative Humidity %	High			
	Low			
	Mean			
Total Insolation, $J\ m^{-2}$				
Weight, or Moisture Content of Batch	Start			
	End			
Collection Efficiency %				
System Drying Efficiency %				
'Pick-Up' Efficiency %				

INSTRUMENT AND EQUIPMENT SUPPLIERS

All addresses in UK unless otherwise supplied:

1.   Photovoltaic panels

      BP Solar Systems Ltd
      Windmill Road
      Haddenham
      Aylesbury
      Bucks HP17 8JB

      Solapak Ltd
      Factory Three
      Cock Lane
      High Wycombe
      Bucks HP13 7DE

2.   Insolation measurement

      Enraf Nonius Ltd (Kipp & Zonen)
      165-167 Station Road
      Edgware
      Middx HA8 7JU

      Lintronic Ltd
      54-58 Bartholomew Close
      London EC1A 7HB

      Weather Measure Services Ltd
      The Old School House
      15 Bulkington Road
      Bedworth
      Warwicks CV12 9DG

3.   Temperature measurement

      A Gallenkamp & Co Ltd
      PO Box 290
      Technico House
      London EC2P 2ER

-    mercury, alcohol-in-glass thermometers
-    hand held digital thermometers
-    temperature recorders

Comark Electronics Ltd
Brookside Avenue
Rustington
West Sussex BN16 3LF

- hand held digital thermometers
- full range of thermocouples
- temperature recorders

Labfacility Ltd
26 Tudor Road
Hampton
Middx TW12 2NQ

- full range of thermocouples
- platinum resistance thermometers
- temperature recorders

Grant Instruments (Cambridge) Ltd
Barrington
Cambridge CB2 5QZ

- temperature recorders
- data loggers

Cristie Electronics Ltd
Rodney House
Church Street
Stroud
Glos GL5 1JL

- data loggers

4.   Air flow measurement

Weather Measure Services Ltd
The Old School House
15 Bulkington Road
Bedworth
Warwicks CV12 9DG

- cup anemometers

Casella London Ltd
Regent House
Britannia Walk
London N1 7ND

- cup anemometers
- vane anemometers

Airflow Developments Ltd
Lancaster Road
High Wycombe
Bucks HP12 3QP

- vane anemometers

-       hot wire anemometers
-       pilot static tubes

Gradko International Ltd
St Martins House
77 Wales Street
Winchester
Hants SO23 7RH

-       vane anemometers
-       cup anemometers

Wallac Controls Ltd
Crown House
Newbury
Berks RG14 5BY

-       hot wire anemometers

5.   Humidity measurement

Casella London Ltd
Regent House
Britannia Walk
London N1 7ND

-       whirling hygrometers
-       digital humidity meters
-       hair hygrometers

Kane-May Ltd
Burrowfield
Welwyn Garden City
Herts AL7 4BR

-       digital humidity meters

C B Scientific Ltd
New Mills Estate
Post Office Road
Inkpen
Newbury
Berks RG15 0PS

-       digital humidity meters

Negretti & Zambra (Environmental) Ltd
Stock Lake
Aylesbury
Bucks HP20 1DR

-       whirling hygrometers

6.   Pressure measurement

   Airflow Developments Ltd
   Lancaster Road
   High Wycombe
   Bucks HP12 3QP

   -     manometers

7.   Weight measurement

   Ohaus
   Florham Park
   New Jersey 07932
   USA

   -     sliding weight balances
   -     spring balances

   Balance Consultancy
   Avon Court
   Castle Street
   Trowbridge
   Wiltshire

   -     electronic balances

   Sartorius Instruments Ltd
   18 Avenue Road
   Sutton
   Surrey SM2 6JD

   -     mechanical and electronic balances

8.   Moisture measurement

   Hedinair Ltd
   Beaver Centre
   Selinas Lane
   Dagenham
   Essex RM8 1QH

   -     ovens

   W C Hereaus GmbH
   Werksgruppe Elektrowarme
   D 6450 Hanau
   West Germany

   -     ovens
   -     vacuum ovens

   Foss Electric (UK) Ltd
   The Chantry
   Bishopthorpe

York YO2 1QF

- infratesters

Opancol Ltd
1 Berens Road
London NW10 5DX

- moisture meter

Kappa Janes Ltd
27 Stewart Avenue
Shepperton
Middx TW17 0EQ

- moisture meters

G Lufft GmbH & Co
Altenbergstrasse 3
Postfach 692
D 7000 Stuttgart 1
West Germany

- water activity meters

9. pH measurement

Gallenkamp & Co Ltd
PO Box 290
Technico House
Christopher Street
London EC2P 2ER

- hand held meters
- bench meters

Camlab Ltd
Nuffield Road
Cambridge CB4 1TH

- hand held meters
- bench meters

Northern Instruments (Leeds) Ltd
72 Armley Lodge Road
Leeds LS12 2HT

- hand held meters
- bench meters

10. Colour measurement

Kirstol Ltd
Cheethams Mill

Park Street
Stalybridge
Cheshire SK15 2BT

-        Hunter colour measuring system

The Tintometer Ltd
The Colour Laboratory
Waterloo Road
Salisbury
Wilts SP1 2JY

-        Munsell colour measuring system

EVALUATION OF DRYER PERFORMANCE

It is necessary to evaluate the thermodynamic performance of a solar dryer. Examination of logged results show that the dryer dries 100kg of fresh peppers at 80% (wb) moisture to the required degree of dryness, 5% (wb) in 3 days. The dryer has a collector of effective area 15 m^2 and a fan that maintains an air flow of $0.5 m^3 s^{-1}$. Climatic data show a mean level of insolation of 20 MJ m^{-2} per 12 hour day. Ambient air conditions indicate a mean daily temperature of 25°C with a relative humidity of 70% and the temperature of the air entering the drying chamber has been monitored as a mean of 35°C.

What are the system drying efficiency and the pick-up efficiency of the dryer?

Solution

The system drying efficiency, η_d is obtained from equation 4.1 viz.

$$\eta_d = \frac{W \, \Delta H_L}{I_d \cdot A_c}$$

where W   = moisture evaporated, kg

ΔH_L = latent heat of vaporization of water, 2320 kJ kg^{-1}

I_d = total daily insolation incident upon collector
       = 20,000 kJ m^{-2} day^{-1}

A_c = area of collector, 15 m^2

W is calculated as follows:

Moisture initially present = 100 x 0.8 = 80 Kg

. ˙ . Bone dry weight of peppers = 20 kg

Moisture present in dried peppers = $\frac{20 \times 0.05}{0.95}$ = 1.05 kg

. ˙ . Moisture evaporated in dryer, W = 80 - 1.05
                                      = 78.95 kg

Total insolation upon collector over 3 days = 20 x 3 = 60 MJm^{-2}

. ˙ . η_d = $\frac{78.95 \times 2320}{15 \times 60 \times 1000}$ =   0.204

System Drying Efficiency = 20.4%

The pick-up efficiency η_p is calculated from equation 4.4 viz.

$$\eta_p = \frac{W}{V . \rho . t . (h_{as} - h_i)}$$

where v = volumetric air flow rate, 0.5 m³s⁻¹

ρ = air density = 1.28 kg m⁻³

t = drying time = 3 days = 129,600 s

h_{as} = adiabatic saturation humidity

h_i = absolute humidity of inlet air

From the psychrometric chart, h_i at 25°C and 70% RH is 0.014 kg kg⁻¹. h_{as} is also found from the psychrometric chart by following a line of constant humidity from h_i to its intercept with the 35°C line and then along the line of constant enthalpy to its intercept with the 100% saturation curve, giving a value of 0.0186 kg kg⁻¹

$$\therefore \quad \eta_p = \frac{78.95}{0.5 \times 1.28 \times 129,600 . (0.0186 - 0.014)} = 0.207$$

Pick-up Efficiency = 20.7%

DETERMINATION OF EFFECTIVE INSOLATION LEVELS

Consider two solar collectors at the same location:

(i)   at a slope of $10°$ from the horizontal facing due south,

(ii)   at the same slope, but facing $45°$ west of due south.

Both collectors are at a latitude of $15°N$. If at mid-day on November 21 the insolation measured on a horizontal surface is $600\ Wm^{-2}$, what is the insolation on the collector surfaces?

Solution

i)   Consider first the surface facing due south

The following angles are known:

Slope angle, β	$= 10°$
Latitude, ϕ	$= 15°$
Surface azimuth angle, γ	$= 0°$
Hour angle, ω	$= 0°$

The declination angle δ is calculated as follows:

for November 21 the day number n = 325 then

$$\delta = 23.45 \sin (0.9863(284 + 284 + 325))$$

$$= 23.45 \sin 600.66$$

$$= 20.44°$$

Equation 5.3 can now be used.

For a collector facing due South

$\gamma = 0$. Since $\cos \gamma = 1$ and $\sin \gamma = 0$ equation 5.3 simplifies to:

$$
\begin{aligned}
\cos \theta &= \sin \delta \ \sin \phi \ \cos \ \beta - \sin \delta \ \cos \phi \ \sin \beta \\
&+ \cos \delta \ \cos \phi \ \cos \beta \ \cos \omega \\
&+ \cos \delta \ \sin \phi \ \sin \beta \ \cos \omega
\end{aligned}
$$

$\cos \theta$ $= \sin (-20.44) \sin (15) \cos (10)$

$\qquad - \sin (-20.44) \cos (15) \sin (10)$

$\qquad + \cos (-20.44) \cos (15) \sin (10) \cos (\ )$

$\qquad + \cos (-20.44) \sin (15) \sin (10) \cos (\ )$

$\qquad = (-0.349) \times 0.259 \times 0.98 - (-0.349) \times 0.966 \times 0.174$

$\qquad + 0.937 \times 0.966 \times 0.985 \times 1 + 0.937 \times 0.259 \times 0.174 \times 1$

$\qquad = -0.0890 + 0.0586 + 0.8913 + 0.0421$

$\qquad = 0.903$

∴ $\theta = 25.4°$

NB A simpler method of determining the angle of incidence at mid–day for a collector facing due north or south is shown in Appendix 9.

To determine the intensity of insolation on a sloping surface from data for a horizontal surface, the angle of incidence of insolation on the horizontal surface must be evaluated.

For a horizontal surface since $\beta = 0$ and hence $\cos \beta = 1$ and $\sin \beta = 0$ equation 5.3 reduces to:

$\cos \theta_h =$ $\sin \delta \sin \phi + \cos \delta \cos \phi \cos \omega$

$\qquad = \quad \sin (-20.44) \sin. \ (15) + \cos (-20.44) \cos (15) \cos$

$\qquad = \quad ((0-0.349) \times 0.259) + (0.937 \times 0.966 \times 1) + (0.937) \ (0.966) \times 1$

$\qquad = \quad -0.090 + 0.905 = 0.815$

$\theta_h = \quad 35.5°$

The level of insolation on the sloping surface, I_s, can now be calculated using equation 5.1

$I_s \quad = \quad I_h \ . \ \dfrac{\cos \theta}{\cos \theta_h}$

$\qquad = \quad 600 \ . \ \dfrac{\cos 25.4}{\cos 35.5}$

$\qquad = \quad 600 \times \dfrac{0.903}{0.815} = 665 \ W \ m^{-2}$

(ii)   For the collector facing 45° west of south.

As before, the following angles are known:

Slope angle, β	$= 10°$
Latitude, ϕ	$= 15°$
Surface azimuth angle, γ	$= 45°$
Hour angle, ω	$= 0°$

and since the day number n is as before the angle of declination δ is -20.40.

Again using equation 5.3:

$$\cos \Theta = \sin(-20.44) \; \sin(15) \; \cos(10)$$

$$- \sin(-20.44) \; \cos(15) \; \sin(10)$$

$$+ \cos(-20.44) \; \cos(15) \; \cos(10) \; \cos(0)$$

$$+ \cos(-20.44) \; \sin(15) \; \sin(10) \; \cos(45) \; \cos(0)$$

$$+ \cos(-20.44) \; \sin(10) \; \sin(45) \; \sin(0)$$

$$= (-0.349) \times 0.259 \times 0.985$$

$$- (-0.349) \times 0.966 \times 0.174 \times 0.707$$

$$+ 0.937 \times 0.966 \times 0.985 \times 1$$

$$+ 0.937 \times 0.259 \times 0.174 \times 0.707 \times 1$$

$$+ 0.937 \times 0.174 \times 0.707 \times 0$$

$$= -0.089 \; -0.041 + 0.892 + 0.030 + 0$$

$$= 0.874$$

$$\therefore \; \Theta = 29.1°$$

From equation 5.1

$$I_S = 600 \cdot \frac{\cos 29.1}{\cos 35.4}$$

$$= 600 \times \frac{0.874}{0.815} = \underline{644 \text{ W m}^{-2}}$$

These calculations show little difference between the intensities of insolation on the two surfaces. This is because the slope angle, β, is small; had β been greater then the difference made by the different azimuth angles γ would have been greater.

DESIGN OF A SOLAR COLLECTOR

It is necessary to design a flat plate solar collector to provide a required air flow of $1 \, \text{m}^3\text{s}^{-1}$ at a temperature of $40°C$.

The following information is known:

(i)   The drying season runs from the beginning of November to the end of January

(ii)   Average ambient temperature during the drying season is $30°C$.

(iii)   The dryer is to be situated at a latitude of $10°N$.

(iv)   Available insolation data is limited but the following values for average total daily radiation on a horizontal surface are known:

    November   20.9 MJ $\text{m}^{-2}\text{day}^{-1}$
    December   19.2 MJ $\text{m}^{-2}\text{day}^{-1}$
    January   20.1 MJ $\text{m}^{-2}\text{day}^{-1}$

Solution

For this example the design procedure will consist of the following steps;

(i)   Determine the optimum collector slope,

(ii)   Calculate the intensity of insolation on a surface of this slope,

(iii)   Decide which of the types of collectors appears most suitable for this operation,

(iv)   Determine the collector area required,

(v)   Bearing in mind the effect of air velocity on collector performance determine the dimensions (width, depth and length) of the collector,

(i)   Determining optimum collector slope.

From a general knowledge of the apparent movement of the sun it can be seen that during the drying season the sun will be overhead at or near the Tropic of Capricorn. Thus for a dryer situated in the northern hemisphere a south facing collector will receive most insolation.

To calculate the optimum slope angle, take December 15 as the midpoint of the drying season.

Angle of declination, δ is calculated from the equation

$$\delta = 23.45 \sin (0.9863.(284+n)) \qquad (A9.1)$$

For December 15, n = 349

Hence δ = 23.45 sin (0.9863(284 + 349))

               = 23.45 sin (624)

               = 23.45 x (-0.995) = -23.3°

To maximise the level of insolation on a collector the simplest approach is to situate the collector so that it is perpendicular to insolation at mid-day in the middle of the dry season.

Though equation 5.3 could be used to calculate the optimum slope, a consideration of the geometry of the situation offers a simple solution.

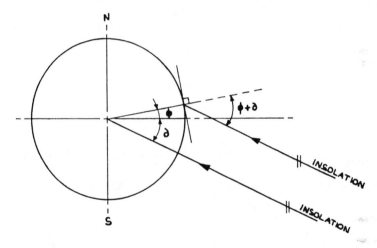

Figure A9.1 Angle of Incidence on a South Facing Roof at Mid-day

Looking at the angles subtended at the centre of the globe in Figure A9.1 it can be seen that the angle between the incident radiation and a perpendicular to the earth's surface at a latitude of 10°N is the sun of the declination angle δ and the angle of latitude ϕ. Thus for a horizontal surface at this latitude, the angle of incidence θ , at solar noon is given by,

$$\theta \;=\; \delta + \phi \qquad\qquad (A9.2)$$
$$= 10 \;+\; 23.3 \;=\; 33.3° \text{ (as a slope from the vertical)}$$

and so for a surface to be perpendicular to insolation at this time it must face south at a slope from the horizontal of 33.3°, as shown in Figure A9.1.

(It is important to note that this approach to determining θ, the angle of incidence, is only valid at solar noon and for a collector facing either due north or south.)

Thus a surface of slope 33.3° facing south has been shown to be the optimum for receiving insolation. In practice a variation of a few degrees will make only a small difference in collector performance.

(ii)   Calculation of the Intensity of Insolation on the Collector Surface.

Due to the limited amount of information available and the variation in intensity of insolation with climatic conditions precise prediction of the intensity of insolation on the collector surface is not possible. To provide data for the sizing of the solar collector an average value of insolation will be estimated.   The prcedure here is to first calculate the intensity of insolation on a horizontal surface and then upon the collector surface. The insolation data available is an average total amount of insolation over a period of a day on a horizontal surface. Instantaneous insolation on a surface is approximately proportional to the cosine of the angle of incidence, Θ. Equation 5.3 can be used to calculate the angle of incidence for insolation on a horizontal surface, Θ_h. Since the slope angle is zero, equation 5.3 simplifies to:

$$\cos \Theta_h = \sin \delta . \sin \phi + \cos \delta . \cos \phi . \cos \omega \qquad (A9.3)$$

δ is calculated from equation A9.1:

δ = -19.1° on November 15
δ = -23.3° on December 15
δ = -21.3° on January 15

A reasonable estimate of the mean value of Θ_h over the day can be made by assuming a 12 hour day and dividing it into four 3 hour periods and calculating Θ_h for each period. With a 12 hour day the hour angle, ω, varies from -90° at 0600 to +90° at 1800. For the 1st period 0600-0900, the mean value of   w is -67.5°, and hence for November 15:

$$
\begin{aligned}
\cos \Theta_h &= \sin(-19,1).\sin(10) + \cos(-19.1).\cos(10).\cos(-67.5) \\
&= ((-0.327) \times 0.174) + (0.944 \times 0.984 \times 0.383) \\
&= -0.057 + 0.356 \\
&= 0.299
\end{aligned}
$$

Similarly $\cos \Theta$ for the period 0900-1200 on November 15 is calculated as 0.803. It cam be appreciated that by symmetry Θ_h for 0600-0900 is identical to Θ_h for 1500-1800, and Θ_h for 0900-1200 is identical to Θ_h for 1200-1500.

The insolation on a horizontal I_h surface for the period 0600-0900 on November 15 is calculated thus:

$$I_h = \frac{20.9 \times 0.299}{0.299 + 0.803 + 0.803 + 0.299}$$

$$= \frac{6.249}{2.204} = 2.84 \text{ MJ m}^{-2}$$

$$\text{and} \quad I_h = \frac{2.84 \times 1000 \times 1000}{3 \times 60 \times 60} = 263 \text{Wm}^{-2}$$

and for the period 0900-1200:

$$I_h = 7.61 \text{ MJ m}^{-2}$$

$$\text{and} \quad I_h = 705 \text{ W m}^{-2}$$

Data for December 15 and January 15 are likewise calculated and shown in Table A9.1.

Equation 5.3 is used again to calculate the angle of incidence upon the collector surface Θ. For the period 0600-0900 on November 15:

$$\cos \Theta = \sin(-19.1).\sin(10).\cos(33.3)$$

$$- \sin(-19.1).\cos(10).\sin(33.3).\cos(0)$$
$$+ \cos(-19.1).\cos(10).\cos(33.3).\cos(-76.5)$$
$$+ \cos(-19.1).\cos(33.3).\sin(0).\sin(-67.5)$$

$$= (-0.327) \times 0.174 \times 0.836$$
$$- (-0.327) \times 0.985 \times 0.549 \times 1$$

$$+ 0.945 \times 0.174 \times 0.549 \times 1$$
$$+ 0.945 \times 0.549 \times 0 \times 0.924$$

$$= -0.048 + 0.177 + 0.924$$

$$= 0.461$$

and for the period 0900-1200, $\cos \Theta = 0.931$.

Equation 5.1 is used to determine the intensity of insolation on the collector surface:

$$I_c = \frac{I_h.\cos \Theta}{\cos \Theta_h}$$

For the period 0600-0900 on November 15:

$$I_c = 263 \times \frac{0.461}{0.299} = 405 \text{ W m}^{-2}$$

and for the period 0900-1200, $I_c = 817 \text{ W m}^{-2}$.

Data for December 15 and January 15 are likewise calculated and shown in Table A9.2.

From Table A9.2 it is clear that there is a considerable variation in the level of insolation incident upon the collector. This will result in a significant variation in the amount of heat which the collector can impart to the air flowing through it. A compromise must be made between a collector which can provide the required air flowrate and temperature under the low insolation conditions (which would be large and thus expensive) and one which only meets the design requirement when insolation is high (which would have a lower cost, but might result in excessively long drying times). Factors which will govern how this compromise is made include:

- 243 -

Time	Mean	$\cos \Theta$	I_h MJ m^{-2}	I_h W m^{-2}
Nov 15				
0600–0900	−67.5	0.299	2.84	263
0900–1200	−22.5	0.803	7.61	705
1200–1500	22.5	0.803	7.61	705
1500–1800	67.5	0.299	2.84	263
Dec 15				
0600–0900	−67.5	0.277	2.54	235
0900–1200	−22.5	0.767	7.05	653
1200–1500	22.5	0.767	7.05	653
1500–1800	67.5	0.277	2.54	235
Jan 15				
0600–0900	−67.5	0.288	2.70	250
0900–1200	−22.5	0.785	7.35	681
1200–1500	22.5	0.785	7.35	681
1500–1800	67.5	0.288	2.70	250

TABLE A9.2

Time	$\cos \Theta_h$	$\cos \Theta$	$\dfrac{\cos \Theta}{\cos \Theta_h}$	I_c W m^{-2}
Nov 15				
0600–0900	0.299	0.461	1.54	405
0900–1200	0.803	0.931	1.15	810
1200–1500	0.803	0.931	1.15	810
1500–1800	0.299	0.461	1.54	405
Dec 15				
0600–0900	0.277	0.480	1.73	409
0900–1200	0.767	0.937	1.22	797
1200–1500	0.767	0.937	1.22	797
1500–1800	0.277	0.480	1.73	406
Jan 15				
0600–0900	0.288	0.471	1.63	408
0900–1200	0.785	0.934	1.19	810
1200–1500	0.785	0.934	1.19	810
1500–1800	0.288	0.471	1.63	408

(i)   cost of collector materials
(ii)   effect of extended drying times on product quality
(iii)   whether dryer is used continuously or intermittently

For the purpose of this exercise it will be taken that an average of 10°C temperature rise is required. Thus the average of the insolation levels I_c in Table A9.2 will be used as the basis for sizing, viz I_c (average) = 606 W m^{-2}

(iii)   **Selection of Collector Type**

For this case selection of collector type is not a clear cut decision, the temperature elevation 10°C is quite high for a bare plate collector. A covered collector will be more expensive. In such a situation a design of both a bare plate and a single cover collector and an approximate costing will help in making a decision.

For this example it will be assumed that a single cover collector has been selected and that glass is available for the cover.

(iv)   **Determination of collector area**

The procedure here is to first estimate the collection efficiency $_c$, and then the collector area.

The collection efficiency is determined from equation 6.4:

$$\eta_c = \frac{1}{1 + U_L/h} . (1 - \exp(-U_0/G_a.C_p)). \frac{G_a C_p}{U_0} . f_{ca}$$

where U_L = collector heat loss coefficient, 6.99 W m^{-2} K^{-1}

h = heat transfer coefficient between absorber and flowing air 22.7 W m^{-2} K^{-1}

U_0 = overall heat transfer coefficient, 5.3 W m^{-2} K^{-1}

G_a = mass flowrate per unit collector area 40.8 kg s^{-1}m^{-2}

C_p = specific heat of air, 1.005 kJ.kg^{-1} K^{-1}

f_{ca} = effective transmissivity absorptivity product from Table 6.2.

Hence

$$\eta_c = \frac{1}{1 + \frac{6.99}{22.7}} \times (1 - \exp \frac{-5.3}{40.8 \times 1.005}) \times \frac{40.8 \times 1005}{5.3} \times 0.88$$

$$= 0.765 \times 0.121 \times 7.737 \times 0.88$$
$$= 0.63$$

From equation 6.1

$$\eta_c = \frac{V.\rho.C_p.\Delta T}{A_c \; I_c}$$

and rearranging

$$A_c = \frac{V.\rho.C_p.\Delta T}{\eta_c.I_c}$$

$$= \frac{1 \times 1.28 \times 1005 \times 10}{0.63 \times 606}$$

$$= 33.7 \; m^2$$

The mass flowrate of air per unit area of collector G_a is then calculated:

$$G_a = \frac{V.\rho}{A_c}$$

$$= \frac{1 \times 1.28}{33.7}$$

$$= 0.038 \; kg \; s^{-1} \; m^{-2}$$

A correction factor for the air flow is now determined by linear interpolation from Table 6.3:

$$\text{Correction factor} = \frac{38.0 - 13.6}{40.8 - 13.6} . (1 - 0.88) + 0.88$$

$$= 0.99$$

Thus corrected η_c = 0.99 x 0.63 = 0.62

and corrected A_c = $\dfrac{1 \times 1.28 \times 1.005 \times 10 \times 1000}{0.62 \times 606}$ = 34.2 m^2

$\therefore$ Collector Area = 34 m^2

(v)   Determination of Collector Dimensions

This last step is to some extent an iterative procedure, dimensions are chosen and if these prove suitable when factors such as pressure drop and heat transfer coefficients are considered then the chosen dimensions can be used; if the chosen dimensions are not suitable then new values are selected until acceptable ones are found.

As a first estimate, assume collector dimensions of 8.5 m x 4 m x 0.05 m. Equation 6.5 is used to determine the heat transfer coefficient h;

$$Nu = 0.02 \; Re^{0.8}$$

where

$$Re = \frac{\rho.v.L}{\mu}$$

$$\rho = 1.28 \text{ kg m}^{-3}$$

$$L = \text{hydraulic diameter of the duct}$$

$$= \frac{2 \times (\text{width} \times \text{depth})}{(\text{width} + \text{depth})}$$

$$= \frac{2 \times (4 \times 0.05)}{4 + 0.05} = 0.099 \text{ m}$$

$$v = \frac{\text{volumetric air flow}}{\text{cross-sectional area of flow}}$$

$$= \frac{1}{4 \times 0.05} = 5 \text{ ms}^{-1}$$

$$\mu = 1.8 \times 10^{-5} \text{ kg m}^{-1} \text{ s}^{-1}$$

$$\therefore \quad Re = \frac{1.28 \times 5 \times 0.099}{1.8 \times 10^{-5}} = 35.2 \times 10^3$$

Hence $Nu = 0.02 \times (35.2 \times 10^3) \, 0.8 = 86.7$

Now $Nu = \frac{h.L}{k}$

$$\therefore \quad h = \frac{k.Nu}{L} = \frac{0.025 \times 86.7}{0.099} = 21.9 \text{ W m}^{-2} \text{ K}^{-1}$$

The value of h is in good agreement with the assumed value made in calculating the collection efficiency.

The pressure drop through the collector ΔP, is calculated from equation 12.3

$$\Delta P = \frac{f.L.G_d^2}{2.\rho.R_h}$$

where f $=$ friction factor, which is determined from Figure 12.2 as 0.007

G_d $=$ mass flowrate of air per unit duct area, 6.4 kg s^{-1} m^{-2}

R_h $=$ hydraulic radius

$$= \frac{0.099}{4} = 0.0248 \text{ m}$$

Hence $\Delta P = \frac{0.007 \times 8.5 \times 6.4^2}{2 \times 1.28 \times 0.0248} = 38 \text{ Pa}$

Even if the collector is to be situated on the suction side of the fan such a pressure drop should pose no problems for an axial flow fan.

The collector dimensions chosen are therefore appropriate for the duty in question.

SOLAR COLLECTOR LITERATURE

Author(s)(Date of Publication)	Collector Type				Materials	
	Forced Convection	Natural Convection	Bare Plate	Covered Collector	Cover	Absorber
BESANT et al (1980)	*		*	*		
BLAGA (1978)				*	*	
BOWMAN (1962)					*	
BUELOW & BOYD (1957)	*			*		
BUELOW (1961)	*		*	*		
BUELOW (1962)	*		*	*		
de BUSSY (1981)						*
CARNEGIE (1978)	*			*		
CARNEGIE (1979)]	*			*		
CHAU et al (1980)	*			*		*
CHODA & READ (1970)	*			*		
CHRISTIE (1970)				*		*
CLOSE (1963)	*			*		
DAVIDSON (1980)	*		*	*		
EDLIN (1958)						
HUTCHINS (1982)					*	*
IBRAHIM (1979)	*			*		
ILYAS et al (1982)	*		*	*		*

Author(s)(Date of Publication)	Collector Type				Materials	
	Forced Convection	Natural Convection	Bare Plate	Covered Collector	Cover	Absorber
ISHIBASHI & ISHIDA (1981)	*			*		
KEENER et al (1977)	*			*	*	*
KELLER (1970)						*
KLINE (1981)	*			*	*	*
MACEDO & ALTEMANI (1978)		*				*
MARTINO (1976)						*
McQUEEN et al (1980)					*	*
NAHAR & GARG (1981)						*
NILES et al (1976)	*		*	*		
PETERSON (1980)	*		*	*		
RAMAKRISHNA RAO et al (1978)				*		
SATCUNANATHAN (1973)	*			*		
SCHLAG et al (1976)	*				*	
TABOR (1978)			*			*
WHILLIER (1964)	*			*		*
WHITE (1977)					*	
WILHELM (1980)	*			*	*	*

SOLAR DRYING LITERATURE

Commodities

A	green leafy vegetables	B	tubers and root crops
C	other vegetables	D	fruit
E	grains and cereals	F	spices
G	beverages	H	fish and meat

Type of Dryer

1   Direct dryers employing natural convection with combined collector and chamber

2   direct dryers employing natural convection with separate collector and drying chamber

3   indirect dryers employing natural convection with separate collector and drying chamber

4   indirect dryers employing forced convection with separate collector and drying chamber

5   hybrid dryers

SOLAR DRYER LITERATURE

Author(s) (Date of Publication)	Commodity Dried									Type of Dryer				
	A	B	C	D	E	F	J	H	J	1	2	3	4	5
ABU AHMED et al (1981)								*		*				
AHMED (1979)								*		*				
AKYURT & SELCUK (1973)			*		*	*							*	*
ALAM et al (1978)													*	
ANEDELINA (1978)								*					*	
ANON (1975)				*										
ANON (1978 a)	*	*	*	*	*	*	*	*	*	*			*	
ANON (1978 b)								*		*				
ANON (1980)												*		
ANSCHUTZ et al (1980)					*								*	
BAILEY & WILLIAMSON (1965)					*								*	
BHATIA & GUPTA (1970)				*						*				
BHATTACHARYYA & MAZUMDAR (1976)		*									*			
BIREWAR (1978)									*		*			
BISWAS & TANDON (1978)					*								*	
BOLIN et al (1980)				*									*	
BOOTHUMJINDA et al (1980)					*					*				

Author(s) (Date of Publication)	Commodity Dried									Type of Dryer				
	A	B	C	D	E	F	G	H	J	1	2	3	4	5
BOSE (1978)				*	*		*						*	
BOSE (1980)							*							*
BOWREY et al (1980)				*										*
BUELOW (1961)					*								*	*
CALDERWOOD (1982)					*									*
CATANIA et al (1980)					*								*	
CHAKRABORTY (1976)								*					*	
CHAKRABORTY (1978)								*					*	
CHANG (1978)									*					*
CHAU & BAIRD (1980)					*									*
CHEEMA (1978)			*	*						*	*			
CHEEMA & RIBERIO (1978)			*							*	*			
CLARK (1981)	*	*	*							*	*			
CLARK (1982)	*	*	*	*						*	*			
CLARK & SAHA (1982)					*						*			
CUNDIFF (1980)									*					*
DAVIDSON (1980)					*								*	*
DAVIS & LIPPER (1961)					*								*	*

Author(s) (Date of Publication)	Commodity Dried									Type of Dryer				
	A	B	C	D	E	F	G	H	J	1	2	3	4	5
DENG et al (1979)								*		*			*	
DIOUF (1980)								*		*				
DOE (1979 a)								*		*				
DOE (1979 b)							*						*	
DOE et al (1977)								*		*			*	
ENO & FELDERMAN (1980)					*					*			*	
EXELL (1980)					*									
EXELL & KORNSAKOO (1978)					*					*				
EXELL et al (1979)					*		*			*			*	
EZEKWE (1981)					*					*				
FILINO HARAHAP & MUSTADJAB (1978)					*								*	
FOSTER & PEART (1976)					*		*					*	*	
GHOSH (1973)					*					*	*			
GRAINGER et al (1981)				*						*				
GUTIERREZ et al (1979)				*	*					*				
HARIGOPAL & TONAPI (1980)			*											*
HELLICKSON (1981)					*									*
HOWARTH (1978)		*								*				
HSIEH & CHANG (1979)	*				*				*					*

	A	B	C	D	E	F	G	H	J	1	2	3	4	5
HUANG et al (1975)	*								*					*
HUANG & BOWERS (1977)					*			*					*	*
IBRAHIM (1978)					*				*				*	
ISLAM & FLINK (1982)		*											*	
ISMAIL et al (1982)					*			*				*		
JOHNSTON (1979)			*		*									*
KAPOOR & AGRAWAL (1973)			*	*			*			*			*	
KESARI & SOPONRONNARIT (1981)														
KOK & KWENDAKWEMA (1983)	*		*								*			
KRANZLER (1980)							*	*				*	*	*
LAWAND (1963)			*											
LAWAND (1966)			*	*										
MAHMOOD et al (1979)	*		*			*								
MARTOSUDIRJO et al (1979)														
MEYER et al (1975)					*					*	*		*	
MIRZAEV (1982)				*						*	*			
MISRA & KEENER (1980)					*						*		*	*
MISRA et al (1979)					*								*	*
MORRISON & SHOVE (1975)					*								*	
MOY et al (1980)		*								*	*			

- 255 -

Author(s) (Date of Publication)	Commodity Dried									Type of Dryer				
	A	B	C	D	E	F	G	H	J	1	2	3	4	5
MUTHUVEERAPPAN et al (1978)					*								*	
NAHWALI (1966)		*												*
OJHA & MAHESHWARI (1979)					*					*				
ONORIO (1979)								*	*			*	*	
OTHIENO et al (1981)					*									
OZISIK et al (1980)					*								*	
PABLO (1978)				*				*		*		*		
PABLO (1980)			*	*				*		*				
PETERSON (1973)					*									*
PETERSON (1980)					*									*
PHILLIPS (1965)							*							*
PUIGGALI & VARICHON (1983)				*								*		
RAHMAN (1981)				*						*			*	
RICHARDS (1981)					*			*		*			*	
ROA & MACEDO (1976)					*					*	*			
SANDHU et al (1979)		*	*										*	
SATCUNANATHAN (1973)		*	*	*					*					
SCHOENAU (1976)					*									*
SCHOENAU & BESANT (1976)					*								*	*
SELCUK et al (1974)				*									*	

Author(s) (Date of Publication)	Commodity Dried									Type of Dryer				
	A	B	C	D	E	F	G	H	J	1	2	3	4	5
SHAW (1981)		*								*				
SINGH & ALAM (1981)						*			*		*			
SMITH (1981)							*							*
SMITH et al (1977)		*											*	*
TRIM & CURRAN (1982)								*		*	*			
TRIM & KO (1982)						*							*	
TRIM & KAMAU (1984)							*							*
TRIM et al (1984)							*							*
UMAROV & IKRAMOV (1978)				*						*				
UMAROV & TAIROV (1982)				*									*	
WAGNER et al (1980)			*										*	
WALTON et al (1980)									*				*	
WIENEKE (1977)							*			*		*		
WILLIAMS et al (1969)		*											*	
WILLIAMS et al (1976)					*								*	*
WILSON (1957)				*									*	
WRUBLESKI & CATANIA (1978)					*									*

ESTIMATION OF NATURAL CONVECTION AIR FLOW RATES

Ambient air at a temperature of $25°C$ and 60% RH is heated to $40°C$ in a solar chimney dryer to be used to dry rice, as shown in Figure A12.1:

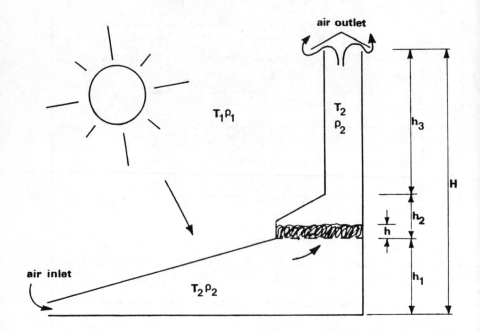

Figure A12.1

The drying chamber height is 0.6m and the height between the ground and the base of the drying chamber is 1.0 m. For an air flow of 5.5 $mm.s^{-1}$ through a 0.2 m deep rice bed, what chimney height would be necessary to achieve the required temperature rise? What would be the effect on the air flow of increasing the chimney height by one third and by decreasing it by one third? If the weather becomes cloudy reducing the dryer temperature to $30°C$, what would be the resulting air flow?

Solution

Assumptions made in determining the equations relating chimney height to air flow are:

(i) at all points inside the solar dryer the air temperature and therefore the air density is uniform,

(ii)   there is no leakage of air from the sides of the dryer and the warm air leaves only from the chimney outlet,

(iii)   the drying of grain takes place by convection only (not by direct radiation),

(iv)   the resistance to air flow through the dryer components, ie the collector, drying chamber and chimney is negligible in comparison with the resistance of the grain bed.

The resistance to air flow for grain is obtained from equation 12.1:

$$v = a (\Delta P/h_b)^b$$

where v =   volumetric air flow rate per unit cross-sectional area of grain bed ($m^3 \ s^{-1} \ m^{-2}$)

ΔP =   pressure drop across grain bed (Pa)

h_b =   grain bed thickness (m)

a, b =   empirical constants

In a natural convection solar dryer, the pressure difference across the grain bed is solely due to the density difference between the hot air inside the dryer and the ambient air, ie

$$\Delta P = (\rho_1 - \rho_2) g.H. \qquad (A12.1)$$

where $\rho_1 \ \rho_2$ =   air densities at temperatures T_1 and T_2 respectively ($kg \ m^{-3}$)

g =   acceleration due to gravity (9.81 ms^{-2})

H =   height of hot air column (m)

Over the temperature range 25-90°C air density can be calculated from the expression:

$$\rho = 1.11363 - 0.00308T \qquad (A12.2)$$

Substituting for ρ in equation A12.1 gives:

$$\Delta\rho = 0.00308 \ \Delta T.g.h. \qquad (A12.3)$$

Substituting for $\Delta\rho$ in equation A12.1:

$$v = a (0.00308 \ \Delta T.g.H/h_b)^b$$

Experimental values of a and b have been reported by Vindal and Gunasekaran (1982) for natural convection of air flow through rice beds of 0.0008 and 0.87 respectively.

Hence, v = $0.0008 (0.00308 . \Delta T.g. H/h_b)^{0.87}$

or v = $3.81 . 10^{-5} (\Delta T.H/h_b)^{0.87}$ (A12.4)

(i)   Calculation of chimney height

H_1 =   1.0 m

H_2 =   0.6 m

v =   0.0055 ms^{-1}

ΔT =   40 − 25 = 15°C

Substituting these values into equation A12.4:

$$0.0055 = 3.81 \times 10^{-5} (15.H/0.2)^{0.87}$$
$$= 3.81 \times 10^{-5} \times 42.29 \times H^{0.87}$$
$$= 1.63 \times 10^{-3} \times H^{0.87}$$

From which H = 4.05 m

The chimney height, $H_3 = H - (H_2 + H_1)$

=   4.05 − (0.6 + 1.0)

=   2.45 m

(ii)   Calculation of effect upon air flow if chimney height increased by one third

(New) H_3 = 2.45 × 1.33 = 3.27 m
∴ H = 1.0 + 0.6 + 3.27 = 4.87 m

Substituting for H in equation A12.4:

v $= 3.81 \times 10^{-5} (15 \times 4.87/0.2)^{0.87}$

$= 3.81 \times 10^{-5} \times 109.6$

$= 0.0065$ ms^{-1}, an increase of 18%

(iii)   Calculation of effect upon air flow if chimney height decreased by one third

(New) H_3 = 2.45 × 0.67 = 1.63 m

∴ H = 1.0 + 0.6 + 1.63 = 3.23 m

Substituting for H in equation A12.4:

v $= 3.81 \times 10^{-5} (15 \times 3.23/0.2)^{0.87}$

$$= 3.81 \times 10^{-5} \times 118.7$$

$$= \underline{0.0045 \text{ ms}^{-1}, \text{ a decrease of } 18\%}$$

(iv) Calculation of air flow through the rice bed when dryer air temperature is reduced to 30°C

$$\Delta T \quad = 30 - 25 = 5°C$$

Substituting for ΔT in equation A12.4:

$$v \quad = 3.81 \times 10^{-5} (5 \times 4.05/0.2)^{0.87}$$

$$= 3.81 \times 10^{-5} (5 \times 4.05/0.2)^{0.87}$$

$$= \underline{0.0021 \text{ ms}^{-1}}$$

Note In this example the chimney neither looses nor gains heat. In practice many solar dryers are constructed in a manner such that the chimney behaves as an absorber. The chimney therefore heats up and transfers this heat to the dryer exhaust air thereby increasing its temperature and the draught developed.

CALCULATION OF AIR FLOW THROUGH DRYING BEDS

A forced convection solar dryer with a separate collector and drying chamber (2 m x 2 m x 1.5 m deep) is being used to dry 3 tonnes of a cereal crop having a bulk density of 780 kg m^{-3}. It is known that the resistance to air flow per metre depth of this crop is 325 Pa. Estimate the air flow through the bed and the fan power required.

Solution

(i)   Air flow estimation

Resistance to air flow for grain is obtained from equation 12.1:-

$$v = a(\Delta P/h_b)^b$$

where v =   volumetric air flow per unit cross-sectional area of grain bed ($M^3s^{-1}m^{-2}$)

ΔP =   pressure drop across the grain bed (Pa)

h_b =   grain bed depth (m)

a, b =   empirical constants

a and b are determined as 0.0003 and 1 respectively.

$\therefore$ v =   0.0003 ($\Delta P/h$)   (A13.1)

Now, 3 tonnes of the crop with bulk density of 780 kg m^{-3}, would occupy a volume of 3000/780 = 3.85 m^3. The drying chamber is of cross section 2 m x 2 m.

Hence h_b = 3.85/(2 x 2) = 0.96 m

and ΔP = 325 x 0.96 = 312 Pa

Substituting for ΔP and h in equation A13.1

$$v = 0.0003 (312/0.96) = 0.1 \text{ ms}^{-1}$$

$\therefore$ Volumetric air flow V = 0.1 x 2 x 2 = 0.4 m^{3}s^{-1}

(ii)   Estimation of fan power

The air power (static) of a fan is obtained from the expression:

Air power = V . ΔP (A13.2)

Substituting for V and ΔP

Air power = 0.4 x 312

= <u>125 W</u>

Taking into consideration a mechanical efficiency of the fan of 60% the motor for the fan should be 125/0.6 = 210 W.

DISCOUNT FACTORS

The value (equivalent to values at time 0) of a sum of 1.000 occurring in a given future year, when discounted at a given interest rate.

Discount Rate

Year	0	2	4	5	6	7	8	9	Year
0	1.0000	1.0000	1.0000	1.0000	1.0000	1.0000	1.0000	1.0000	0
1	1.0000	0.9804	0.9615	0.9524	0.9434	0.9346	0.9259	0.9174	1
2	1.0000	0.9612	0.9246	0.9070	0.8900	0.8734	0.8573	0.8417	2
3	1.0000	0.9423	0.8890	0.8638	0.8396	0.8163	0.7938	0.7722	3
4	1.0000	0.9238	0.8548	0.8227	0.7921	0.7629	0.7350	0.7084	4
5	1.0000	0.9057	0.8219	0.7835	0.7473	0.7130	0.6806	0.6499	5
6	1.0000	0.8880	0.7903	0.7462	0.7050	0.6663	0.6302	0.5963	6
7	1.0000	0.8706	0.7599	0.7107	0.6651	0.6227	0.5835	0.5470	7
8	1.0000	0.8535	0.7307	0.6768	0.6274	0.5820	0.5403	0.5019	8
9	1.0000	0.8368	0.7026	0.6446	0.5919	0.5439	0.5002	0.4604	9
10	1.0000	0.8203	0.6756	0.6139	0.5584	0.5083	0.4632	0.4224	10
11	1.0000	0.8043	0.6496	0.5847	0.5268	0.4751	0.4289	0.3875	11
12	1.0000	0.7885	0.6246	0.5568	0.4870	0.4440	0.3971	0.3555	12
13	1.0000	0.7730	0.6006	0.5303	0.4688	0.4150	0.3677	0.3262	13
14	1.0000	0.7579	0.5775	0.5051	0.4423	0.3878	0.3405	0.2992	14
15	1.0000	0.7430	0.5553	0.4810	0.4173	0.3624	0.3152	0.2745	15
16	1.0000	0.7284	0.5339	0.4581	0.3936	0.3387	0.2919	0.2519	16
17	1.0000	0.7142	0.5134	0.4363	0.3714	0.3166	0.2703	0.2311	17
18	1.0000	0.7002	0.4936	0.4155	0.3503	0.2959	0.2502	0.2120	18
19	1.0000	0.6864	0.4746	0.3957	0.3305	0.2765	0.2317	0.1945	19
20	1.0000	0.6730	0.4564	0.3769	0.3118	0.2580	0.2145	0.1784	20
21	1.0000	0.6598	0.4388	0.3589	0.2942	0.2415	0.1987	0.1637	21
22	1.0000	0.6468	0.4220	0.3419	0.2775	0.2257	0.1839	0.1502	22
23	1.0000	0.6342	0.4057	0.3256	0.2168	0.2109	0.1703	0.1378	23
24	1.0000	0.6217	0.3901	0.3101	0.2470	0.1971	0.1577	0.1264	24
25	1.0000	0.6095	0.3751	0.2953	0.2330	0.1842	0.1460	0.1160	25
26	1.0000	0.5976	0.3607	0.2812	0.2198	0.1722	0.1352	0.1064	26
27	1.0000	0.5859	0.3468	0.2678	0.2074	0.1609	0.1252	0.0976	27
28	1.0000	0.5744	0.3335	0.2551	0.1956	0.2504	0.1159	0.0895	28
29	1.0000	0.5631	0.3207	0.2429	0.1846	0.1406	0.1073	0.0822	29
30	1.0000	0.5521	0.3083	0.2134	0.1741	0.1314	0.0994	0.0754	30
33	1.0000	0.5202	0.2740	0.1999	0.1462	0.1072	0.0789	0.0582	33
35	1.0000	0.5000	0.2534	0.1813	0.1301	0.0937	0.0676	0.0490	35
38	1.0000	0.4712	0.2253	0.1566	0.1092	0.0765	0.0537	0.0378	38
40	1.0000	0.4529	0.2083	0.1420	0.0872	0.0668	0.0460	0.0318	40
43	1.0000	0.4268	0.1852	0.1227	0.0816	0.0545	0.0365	0.0246	43
45	1.0000	0.4102	0.1712	0.1113	0.0726	0.0476	0.0313	0.0207	45
48	1.0000	0.3865	0.1522	0.0961	0.0610	0.0389	0.0249	0.0160	48
50	1.0000	0.3715	0.1407	0.0872	0.0543	0.0339	0.0213	0.0134	50

DISCOUNT FACTORS

Discount Rate

Year	10	11	12	13	14	15	16	17	Year
0	1.0000	1.0000	1.0000	1.0000	1.0000	1.0000	1.0000	1.0000	0
1	0.9091	0.9009	0.8929	0.8850	0.8772	0.8696	0.8621	0.8547	1
2	0.8264	0.8116	0.7972	0.7831	0.7695	0.7561	0.7432	0.7305	2
3	0.7513	0.7312	0.7118	0.6931	0.6750	0.6575	0.6407	0.6244	3
4	0.6830	0.6587	0.6355	0.6133	0.5921	0.5718	0.5523	0.5337	4
5	0.6209	0.5935	0.5674	0.5428	0.5194	0.4972	0.4761	0.4561	5
6	0.5645	0.5346	0.5066	0.4803	0.4556	0.4323	0.4104	0.3898	6
7	0.5132	0.4817	0.4523	0.4251	0.3996	0.3759	0.3538	0.3332	7
8	0.4665	0.4339	0.4039	0.3762	0.3506	0.3269	0.3050	0.2848	8
9	0.4241	0.3909	0.3606	0.3329	0.3075	0.2843	0.2630	0.2434	9
10	0.3855	0.3522	0.3220	0.2946	0.2697	0.2472	0.2267	0.2080	10
11	0.3505	0.3173	0.2875	0.2607	0.2366	0.2149	0.1954	0.1778	11
12	0.3186	0.2858	0.2567	0.2307	0.2076	0.1869	0.1685	0.1520	12
13	0.2900	0.2575	0.2292	0.2042	0.1821	0.1625	0.1452	0.1299	13
14	0.2633	0.2320	0.2046	0.1807	0.1597	0.1413	0.1252	0.1110	14
15	0.2394	0.2090	0.1827	0.1599	0.1401	0.1229	0.1079	0.0949	15
16	0.2176	0.1883	0.1631	0.1415	0.1229	0.1069	0.0930	0.0811	16
17	0.1978	0.1696	0.1456	0.1252	0.1078	0.0929	0.0802	0.0693	17
18	0.1799	0.1528	0.1300	0.1108	0.0955	0.0808	0.0691	0.0592	18
19	0.1635	0.1377	0.1161	0.0981	0.0830	0.0703	0.0596	0.0506	19
20	0.1486	0.1240	0.1037	0.0868	0.0728	0.0611	0.0514	0.0433	20
21	0.1351	0.1117	0.0926	0.0768	0.0638	0.0531	0.0443	0.0370	21
22	0.1228	0.1007	0.0826	0.0680	0.0560	0.0462	0.0382	0.0316	22
23	0.1117	0.0907	0.0738	0.0601	0.0491	0.0402	0.0329	0.0270	23
24	0.1015	0.0817	0.0659	0.0532	0.0431	0.0349	0.0284	0.0231	24
25	0.0923	0.0736	0.0588	0.0471	0.0378	0.0304	0.0245	0.0197	25
26	0.0839	0.0663	0.0525	0.0417	0.0331	0.0264	0.0211	0.0169	26
27	0.0763	0.0597	0.0468	0.0369	0.0291	0.0230	0.0182	0.0144	27
28	0.0693	0.0538	0.0419	0.0326	0.0255	0.0200	0.0157	0.0123	28
29	0.0630	0.0485	0.0374	0.0289	0.0224	0.0174	0.0135	0.0105	29
30	0.0573	0.0437	0.0334	0.0256	0.0196	0.0151	0.0116	0.0090	30
33	0.0431	0.0319	0.0238	0.0177	0.0132	0.0099	0.0075	0.0056	33
35	0.0356	0.0259	0.0189	0.0139	0.0102	0.0075	0.0055	0.0041	35
38	0.0267	0.0190	0.0135	0.0096	0.0069	0.0049	0.0036	0.0026	38
40	0.0221	0.0154	0.0107	0.0075	0.0053	0.0037	0.0026	0.0019	40
43	0.0166	0.0112	0.0076	0.0052	0.0036	0.0025	0.0017	0.0012	43
45	0.0137	0.0091	0.0061	0.0041	0.0027	0.0019	0.0013	0.0010	45
48	0.0103	0.0067	0.0043	0.0028	0.0019	0.0012	0.0008	0.0005	48
50	0.0085	0.0054	0.0035	0.002	0.0014	0.0009	0.0006	0.0004	50

DISCOUNT FACTORS

Discount Rate

Year	18	19	20	21	22	23	24	25	Year
0	1.0000	1.0000	1.0000	1.0000	1.0000	1.0000	1.0000	1.0000	0
1	0.8475	0.8403	0.8333	0.8264	0.8197	0.8130	0.8065	0.8000	1
2	0.7182	0.7062	0.6944	0.6830	0.6719	0.6610	0.6504	0.6400	2
3	0.6086	0.5934	0.5787	0.5645	0.5507	0.5374	0.5245	0.5120	3
4	0.5158	0.4987	0.4823	0.4665	0.4514	0.4369	0.4230	0.4096	4
5	0.4371	0.4190	0.4019	0.3855	0.3700	0.3552	0.3411	0.3277	5
6	0.3704	0.3521	0.3349	0.3186	0.3033	0.2888	0.2751	0.2621	6
7	0.3139	0.2959	0.2791	0.2633	0.2486	0.2348	0.2218	0.2097	7
8	0.2660	0.2487	0.2326	0.2176	0.2038	0.1909	0.1789	0.1678	8
9	0.2255	0.2090	0.1938	0.1799	0.1670	0.1552	0.1443	0.1342	9
10	0.1911	0.1756	0.1615	0.1486	0.1369	0.1262	0.1164	0.1074	10
11	0.1619	0.1476	0.1346	0.1228	0.1122	0.1026	0.0938	0.0859	11
12	0.1372	0.1240	0.1122	0.1015	0.0920	0.0834	0.0757	0.0687	12
13	0.1163	0.1042	0.0935	0.0839	0.0754	0.0678	0.0610	0.0550	13
14	0.0985	0.0876	0.0779	0.0693	0.0618	0.0551	0.0492	0.0440	14
15	0.0835	0.0736	0.0649	0.0573	0.0507	0.0448	0.0397	0.0352	15
16	0.0708	0.0618	0.0541	0.0474	0.0415	0.0364	0.0320	0.0281	16
17	0.0600	0.0520	0.0451	0.0391	0.0340	0.0296	0.0258	0.0225	17
18	0.0508	0.0437	0.0376	0.0323	0.0279	0.0241	0.0208	0.0180	18
19	0.0431	0.0367	0.0313	0.0267	0.0229	0.0196	0.0168	0.0144	19
20	0.0365	0.0308	0.0261	0.0221	0.0187	0.0159	0.0135	0.0115	20
21	0.0309	0.0259	0.0217	0.0183	0.0154	0.0129	0.0109	0.0092	21
22	0.0262	0.0218	0.0181	0.0151	0.0126	0.0105	0.0088	0.0074	22
23	0.0222	0.0183	0.0151	0.0125	0.0103	0.0086	0.0071	0.0059	23
24	0.0188	0.0154	0.0126	0.0103	0.0085	0.0070	0.0057	0.0047	24
25	0.0160	0.0129	0.0105	0.0085	0.0069	0.0057	0.0046	0.0038	25
26	0.0135	0.0109	0.0087	0.0070	0.0057	0.0046	0.0037	0.0030	26
27	0.0115	0.0091	0.0073	0.0058	0.0047	0.0037	0.0030	0.0024	27
28	0.0097	0.0077	0.0061	0.0048	0.0038	0.0030	0.0024	0.0019	28
29	0.0082	0.0064	0.0051	0.0040	0.0031	0.0025	0.0020	0.0015	29
30	0.0070	0.0054	0.0042	0.0033	0.0026	0.0020	0.0016	0.0012	30
33	0.0042	0.0032	0.0024	0.0019	0.0014	0.0011	0.0008	0.0006	33
35	0.0030	0.0023	0.0017	0.0013	0.0009	0.0007	0.0005	0.0004	35
38	0.0019	0.0013	0.0010	0.0007	0.0005	0.0004	0.0003	0.0002	38
40	0.0013	0.0010	0.0007	0.0005	0.0004	0.0003	0.0002	0.0001	40
43	0.0008	0.0006	0.0004	0.0003	0.0002	0.0001	0.0001	0.0001	43
45	0.0006	0.0004	0.0003	0.0002	0.0001	0.0001	0.0001	0.0000	45
48	0.0004	0.0002	0.0002	0.0001	0.0001	0.0000	0.0000		48
50	0.0003	0.0002	0.0001	0.0001	0.0000				50

DISCOUNT FACTORS

Discount Rate

Year	28	30	33	35	38	40	45	50	Year
0	1.0000	1.0000	1.0000	1.0000	1.0000	1.0000	1.0000	1.0000	0
1	0.7813	0.7692	0.7510	0.7407	0.7246	0.7143	0.6897	0.6667	1
2	0.6104	0.5917	0.5653	0.5487	0.5251	0.5102	0.4756	0.4444	2
3	0.4768	0.4552	0.4251	0.4064	0.3805	0.3644	0.3280	0.2963	3
4	0.3725	0.3501	0.3160	0.3011	0.2757	0.2603	0.2262	0.1975	4
5	0.2910	0.2693	0.2403	0.2230	0.1998	0.1859	0.1560	0.1317	5
6	0.2274	0.2072	0.1807	0.1652	0.1448	0.1328	0.1076	0.0878	6
7	0.1776	0.1594	0.1358	0.1224	0.1049	0.9049	0.0742	0.5085	7
8	0.1388	0.1226	0.1021	0.0906	0.0760	0.0678	0.0512	0.0390	8
9	0.1084	0.0943	0.0768	0.0671	0.0551	0.0484	0.0353	0.0260	9
10	0.0847	0.0725	0.0577	0.0497	0.0399	0.0346	0.0243	0.0173	10
11	0.0662	0.0558	0.0434	0.0368	0.0289	0.0247	0.0168	0.0116	11
12	0.0517	0.0429	0.0326	0.0273	0.0210	0.0176	0.0116	0.0077	12
13	0.0404	0.0330	0.0245	0.0202	0.0152	0.0126	0.0080	0.0051	13
14	0.0316	0.0254	0.0185	0.0150	0.0110	0.0090	0.0055	0.0034	14
15	0.0247	0.0195	0.0139	0.0111	0.0080	0.0064	0.0038	0.0023	15
16	0.0193	0.0150	0.0104	0.0082	0.0058	0.0046	0.0026	0.0015	16
17	0.0150	0.0116	0.0078	0.0061	0.0042	0.0033	0.0018	0.0010	17
18	0.0118	0.0089	0.0059	0.0045	0.0030	0.0023	0.0012	0.0007	18
19	0.0092	0.0068	0.0044	0.0033	0.0022	0.0017	0.0009	0.0005	19
20	0.0072	0.0053	0.0033	0.0025	0.0016	0.0012	0.0006	0.0003	20
21	0.0056	0.0040	0.0025	0.0018	0.0012	0.0009	0.0004	0.0002	21
22	0.0044	0.0031	0.0019	0.0014	0.0008	0.0006	0.0003	0.0001	22
23	0.0034	0.0024	0.0014	0.0010	0.0006	0.0004	0.0002	0.0001	23
24	0.0027	0.0018	0.0011	0.0007	0.0004	0.0003	0.0001	0.0001	24
25	0.0021	0.0014	0.0008	0.0006	0.0003	0.0002	0.0001	0.0000	25
26	0.0016	0.0011	0.0006	0.0004	0.0002	0.0002	0.0001		26
27	0.0013	0.0008	0.0005	0.0003	0.0002	0.0001	0.0000		27
28	0.0010	0.0006	0.0003	0.0002	0.0001	0.0001			28
29	0.0008	0.0005	0.0003	0.0002	0.0001	0.0001			29
30	0.0006	0.0004	0.0002	0.0001	0.0001	0.0000			30
33	0.0003	0.0002	0.0001	0.0000	0.0000				33
35	0.0002	0.0001	0.0000						35
38	0.0001	0.0000							38
40	0.0001								40
43	0.0000								43
45									
48									
50									

ANNUITY FACTORS

The value (equivalent to values at time 0) of continuous annual payments of 1.0000 for a given number of years, when discounted at given discount rates.

Discount Rate

Year	0	2	4	5	6	7	8	9	Year
0	-	-	-	-	-	-	-	-	0
1	1.0000	0.9804	0.9615	0.9524	0.9434	0.9346	0.9259	0.9174	1
2	2.0000	1.9416	1.8861	1.8594	1.8334	1.8080	1.7833	1.7591	2
3.	3.0000	2.8839	2.7751	2.7232	2.6730	2.6243	2.5771	2.5313	3
4	4.0000	3.8077	3.6299	3.5460	3.4651	3.3872	3.3121	3.2397	4
5	5.0000	4.7135	4.4518	4.3295	4.2124	4.1002	3.9927	3.8897	5
6	6.0000	5.6014	5.2421	5.0757	4.9173	4.7665	4.6229	4.4859	6
7	7.0000	6.4720	6.0021	5.7864	5.5824	5.3893	5.2064	5.0330	7
8	8.0000	7.3255	6.7327	6.4632	6.2098	5.9713	5.7466	5.5348	8
9	9.0000	8.9826	7.4353	7.1078	6.8017	6.5152	6.2469	5.9952	9
10	10.0000	9.7868	8.1109	7.7217	7.3601	7.0236	6.7101	6.4177	10
11	11.0000	10.5753	8.7605	8.3064	7.8869	7.4987	7.1390	6.8052	11
12	12.0000	11.3484	9.3851	8.8363	8.3838	7.9427	7.5361	7.1607	12
13	13.0000	12.1062	9.9856	9.3936	8.8527	8.3577	7.9038	7.4869	13
14	14.0000	12.8493	10.5631	9.8986	9.2950	8.7455	8.2442	7.7862	14
15	15.0000	13.5777	11.1184	10.3797	9.7122	9.1079	8.5595	8.0607	15
16	16.0000	14.2919	11.6523	10.8378	10.1059	9.4466	8.8514	8.3126	16
17	17.0000	15.6785	12.1657	11.2741	10.4773	9.7632	9.1216	8.5436	17
18	18.0000	16.3514	12.6593	11.6896	10.8276	10.0591	9.3719	8.7556	18
19	19.0000	17.0112	13.1339	12.0853	11.1581	10.3356	9.6036	8.9501	19
20	20.0000	17.6580	13.5903	12.4622	11.4699	10.5940	9.8181	9.1285	20
21	21.0000	18.2922	14.0292	12.8212	11.7641	10.8355	10.0168	9.2922	21
22	22.0000	18.9139	14.4511	13.1630	12.0416	11.0612	10.2007	9.4424	22
23	23.0000	19.5235	14.8568	14.4886	12.3034	11.2722	10.3711	9.5800	23
24	24.0000	20.1210	15.2470	13.7986	12.5504	11.4693	10.5288	9.7066	24
25	25.0000	19.5235	15.6221	14.0939	12.7834	11.6536	10.6748	9.8226	25
26	26.0000	20.1210	15.9828	14.3752	13.0032	11.8258	10.8100	9.9290	26
27	27.0000	20.7069	16.3296	14.6430	13.2105	11.9867	10.9352	10.0266	27
28	28.0000	21.2813	16.6631	14.8981	13.4062	12.1371	11.0511	10.1161	28
29	29.0000	21.8444	16.9837	15.1411	13.5907	12.2777	11.1584	10.1983	29
30	30.0000	22.3965	17.2920	15.3725	13.7648	12.4090	11.2578	10.2737	30
33	33.0000	23.0886	18.1476	16.0025	14.2302	12.7538	11.5139	10.4644	33
35	35.0000	24.9986	18.6646	16.3742	14.4982	12.9477	11.6546	10.5668	35
38	38.0000	26.4406	19.3679	16.8679	14.8460	13.1935	11.8289	10.6908	38
40	40.0000	27.3555	19.7928	17.1591	15.0463	13.3317	11.9246	10.7574	40
43	43.0000	28.6616	20.3708	17.5459	15.3062	13.5070	12.0432	10.8380	43
45	45.0000	29.4902	20.7200	17.7741	15.4558	13.6055	12.1084	10.8812	45
48	48.0000	30.6731	21.1951	18.0772	15.6500	13.7305	12.1891	10.9336	48
50	50.0000	31.4822	21.4822	18.2559	15.7619	13.8007	12.2335	10.9617	50

ANNUITY FACTORS

Discount Rate

Year	10	11	12	13	14	15	16	17	Year
1	0.9091	0.9009	0.8929	0.8850	0.8772	0.8696	0.8621	0.8547	1
2	1.7355	1.7125	1.6901	1.6681	1.6467	1.6257	1.6052	1.5852	2
3	2.4869	2.4437	2.4018	2.3612	2.3216	2.2832	2.2459	2.2096	3
4	3.1699	3.1024	3.0373	2.9745	2.9137	2.8550	2.7982	2.7432	4
5	3.7098	3.6959	3.6048	3.5172	3.4331	3.3522	3.2743	3.1993	5
6	4.3553	4.2305	4.1114	3.9976	3.8887	3.7845	3.6847	3.5892	6
7	4.8684	4.3122	4.5638	4.4226	4.2883	4.1064	4.0386	3.9224	7
8	5.3349	5.1461	4.9676	4.7988	4.6389	4.4873	4.3436	4.2072	8
9	5.7590	5.5370	5.3283	5.1317	4.9464	4.7716	4.6065	4.4506	9
10	6.1446	5.8892	5.6502	5.4262	5.2161	5.0188	4.8332	4.6586	10
11	6.4951	6.2065	5.9377	5.6869	5.4527	5.2337	5.0286	4.8364	11
12	6.8137	6.4924	6.1944	5.9176	5.6603	5.4206	5.1971	4.9884	12
13	7.1034	6.7500	6.4235	6.1218	5.8424	5.5831	5.3423	5.1183	13
14	7.3667	6.9819	6.6282	6.3025	6.0021	5.7245	5.4675	5.2293	14
15	7.6061	7.1909	6.8109	6.4624	6.1422	5.8474	5.5755	5.3242	15
16	7.8237	7.3792	6.9740	6.6039	6.2651	5.9542	5.6685	5.4053	16
17	8.0216	7.5488	7.1196	6.7291	6.3729	6.0472	5.7487	5.4746	17
18	8.2014	7.7106	7.2497	6.8399	6.4674	6.1280	5.8178	5.5339	18
19	8.3649	7.8393	7.3658	6.9380	6.5504	6.1982	5.8775	5.5845	19
20	8.5136	7.9633	7.4694	7.0248	6.6231	6.2593	5.9288	5.6278	20
21	8.6487	8.0751	7.5620	7.1016	6.6870	6.3125	5.9731	5.6648	21
22	8.7715	8.1757	7.6446	7.1695	6.7429	6.3587	6.0113	5.6964	22
23	8.8832	8.2664	7.7184	7.2297	6.7921	6.3988	6.0442	5.7234	23
24	8.9847	8.3481	7.7843	7.2829	6.6351	6.4338	6.0726	5.7465	24
25	9.0770	8.4217	7.8431	7.3300	6.8729	6.4641	6.0971	5.7662	25
26	9.1609	8.4881	7.8957	7.3717	6.9061	6.4906	6.1182	5.7831	26
27	9.2372	8.5478	7.9426	7.4086	6.9352	6.5135	6.1364	5.7975	27
28	9.3066	8.6016	7.9844	7.4412	6.9607	6.5335	6.1520	5.8099	28
29	9.3696	8.6501	8.0218	7.4701	6.9830	6.5509	6.1656	5.8204	29
30	9.4269	8.6938	8.0552	7.4957	7.0027	6.5660	6.1772	5.8294	30
33	9.5694	8.8005	8.1354	7.5560	7.0482	6.6005	6.2034	5.8493	33
35	9.6442	8.8552	8.1755	7.5856	7.0700	6.6166	6.2153	5.8582	35
38	9.7327	8.9186	8.2210	7.6183	7.0937	6.7338	6.2278	5.8673	38
40	9.7791	8.9511	8.2438	7.6344	7.1050	6.6418	6.2335	5.8713	40
43	9.8340	8.9886	8.2696	7.6522	7.1173	6.6503	6.2394	5.8755	43
45	9.8628	9.0079	8.2825	7.6609	7.1232	6.6543	6.2421	5.8773	45
48	9.8969	9.0302	8.2972	7.6705	7.1296	6.6585	6.2450	5.8792	48
50	9.9148	9.0417	8.3045	7.6752	7.1327	6.6605	6.2463	5.8801	50

ANNUITY FACTORS

Discount Rate

Year	18	19	20	21	22	23	24	25	Year
1	0.8475	0.8403	0.8333	0.8264	0.8197	0.8130	0.8065	0.8000	1
2	1.5656	1.5465	1.5278	1.5095	1.4915	1.4740	1.4568	1.4400	2
3	2.1742	2.1399	2.1065	2.0739	2.0422	2.0114	1.9813	1.9520	3
4	2.6901	2.6386	2.5887	2.5404	2.4936	2.4483	2.4043	2.3616	4
5	2.1272	3.0576	2.9906	2.9260	2.8636	2.8035	2.7454	2.6893	5
6	3.4976	3.4098	3.3255	3.2446	3.1669	3.0923	3.0205	2.9514	6
7	3.8115	4.7057	3.6046	3.5079	3.4155	3.3270	3.2423	3.1611	7
8	4.0776	3.9544	3.8372	2.7256	3.6193	3.5179	3.4212	3.3289	8
9	4.3030	4.1633	4.0310	3.9054	3.7863	3.6731	3.5655	3.4631	9
10	4.4941	4.3389	4.1925	4.0541	3.9232	3.7993	3.6819	3.5705	10
11	4.6560	4.4865	4.3271	4.1769	4.0354	3.9018	3.7757	3.6565	11
12	4.7932	4.6105	4.4392	4.2785	4.1274	3.9854	3.8514	3.7251	12
13	4.9095	4.7147	4.5327	4.3624	4.2028	4.0530	3.9124	3.7801	13
14	5.0081	4.8022	4.6106	4.4317	4.2646	4.1082	3.9616	3.8241	14
15	5.0916	4.8759	4.6755	4.4890	4.3152	4.1530	4.0013	3.89593	15
16	5.1624	4.9377	4.7230	4.5364	4.3567	4.1894	4.0333	3.8874	16
17	5.2223	4.9897	4.7746	4.5755	4.3908	4.2190	4.0591	3.9099	17
18	5.2732	5.0333	4.8122	4.6079	4.4187	4.2431	4.0799	3.9279	18
19	5.3162	5.0700	4.8435	3.6346	4.4415	4.2627	4.0967	3.9424	19
20	5.3527	5.1009	4.8696	4.6567	4.4603	4.2786	4.1103	3.9539	20
21	5.3837	5.1268	4.8913	4.6750	4.4756	4.2916	4.1212	3.9631	21
22	5.4099	5.1486	4.9094	4.6900	4.4882	4.3021	4.1300	3.9705	22
23	5.4321	5.1668	4.9245	4.7025	4.4985	4.3106	4.1371	3.9764	23
24	5.4509	5.1822	4.9371	4.7128	4.5070	4.3176	4.1428	3.9811	24
25	5.4669	5.1951	4.9476	4.7213	4.5139	4.3232	4.1474	3.9849	25
26	5.4804	5.2060	4.9563	4.7284	5.5196	4.3278	4.1511	3.9879	26
27	5.4919	5.2151	4.9636	4.7342	4.543	4.3316	4.1542	3.9903	27
28	5.5016	5.2228	4.9697	4.7390	4.5281	4.3346	4.1566	3.9923	28
29	5.5098	5.2292	4.9747	4.7430	4.5312	4.3371	4.1585	3.9938	29
30	5.5168	5.2347	4.9789	4.7463	4.5338	4.3391	4.1601	3.9950	30
33	5.5320	5.2462	4.9878	4.7531	4.5390	4.3431	4.1632	3.9975	
35	5.5836	5.2512	4.9915	4.7559	4.5411	4.3447	4.1644	3.9984	35
38	5.5452	5.2561	4.9951	4.7585	4.5435	4.3462	4.1655	3.9992	38
40	5.5482	5.2582	4.9966	4.7596	4.5439	4.3467	4.1659	3.9995	40
43	5.5510	5.2602	4.9980	4.7606	4.5446	4.3472	4.1663	3.9997	43
45	5.5523	5.2611	4.9986	4.7610	4.5449	4.3474	4.1664	3.9998	45
48	5.5536	5.2619	4.9992	4.7614	4.5451	4.3476	4.1665	3.9999	48
50	5.5541	5.2623	4.9995	4.7616	4.5452	4.3477	4.1666	3.9999	50

ANNUITY FACTORS

Discount Rate

Year	28	30	33	35	38	40	45	50	Year
1	0.7813	0.7692	0.7519	0.7407	0.7246	0.7143	0.6897	0.6667	1
2	1.3916	1.3609	1.3172	1.2894	1.2497	1.2245	1.1653	1.1111	2
3	1.8684	1.8161	1.7423	1.6959	1.6302	1.5889	1.4933	1.4074	3
4	2.2410	2.1663	2.0618	1.9969	1.9060	1.8492	1.7195	1.6049	4
5	2.5320	2.4356	2.301	2.2200	2.1058	2.0352	1.8755	1.7366	5
6	2.7594	2.6427	2.4828	2.3852	2.2506	2.1680	1.9831	1.8244	6
7	2.9370	2.8021	2.6187	2.5075	2.3555	2.2628	2.0573	1.8829	7
8	3.0758	2.9247	2.7208	2.5982	2.4315	2.3306	2.1085	1.9220	8
9	3.1842	3.0190	2.7976	2.6653	2.4866	2.3790	2.1438	1.9480	9
10	3.2689	3.0915	2.8553	2.7150	2.5265	2.4136	2.1681	1.9653	10
11	3.3351	3.1473	2.8987	2.7519	2.5555	2.4383	2.1849	1.9769	11
12	3.3868	3.1903	2.9314	2.7792	2.5764	2.4559	2.1965	1.9846	12
13	3.4272	3.2233	2.9559	2.7994	2.5916	2.4685	2.2045	1.9897	13
14	3.4587	3.2487	2.9744	2.8144	2.6026	2.4775	2.2100	1.9931	14
15	3.4834	3.2682	2.9883	2.8255	2.6106	2.4839	2.2138	1.9954	15
16	3.5026	3.2832	2.9987	2.8337	2.6164	2.4885	2.2164	1.9970	16
17	3.5177	3.2948	3.0065	2.8398	2.6206	2.4918	2.2182	1.9980	17
18	3.5294	3.3037	3.0124	2.8442	2.6236	2.4941	2.2195	1.9986	18
19	3.5386	3.3105	3.0169	2.8476	2.6258	2.4958	2.2203	1.9991	19
20	3.5458	3.3158	3.0202	2.8501	2.6274	2.4970	2.2209	1.9994	20
21	3.5514	3.3198	3.0227	2.8519	2.6285	2.4979	2.2213	1.9996	21
22	3.5558	3.3230	3.0246	2.8533	2.6294	2.4985	2.2216	1.9997	22
23	3.5592	3.3254	3.0260	2.8543	2.6300	2.4989	2.2218	1.9998	23
24	3.5619	3.3272	3.0271	2.8440	2.6304	2.4992	2.2219	1.9999	24
25	3.5640	3.3286	3.0279	2.8556	2.6307	2.4994	2.2220	1.9999	25
26	3.5656	3.3297	3.0285	2.8560	2.6310	2.4996	2.2221	1.9999	26
27	3.5669	3.3305	3.0289	2.8563	2.6311	2.4997	2.2221	2.0000	27
28	3.5679	3.3312	3.0293	2.8565	2.6313	2.4998	2.2222	2.0000	28
29	3.5687	3.3317	3.0295	2.8567	2.6313	2.4999	2.2222	2.0000	29
30	3.5693	3.3321	3.0297	2.8568	2.6314	2.4999	2.2222	2.0000	30
33	3.5704	3.3328	3.0301	2.8570	2.6315	2.5000	2.2222	2.0000	33
35	3.5708	3.3330	3.0302	2.8571	2.6315	2.5000	2.2222	2.0000	35
38	3.5711	3.3332	3.0302	2.8571	2.6316	2.5000	2.2222	2.0000	38
40	3.5712	3.3332	3.0303	2.8571	2.6316	2.5000	2.2222	2.0000	40
43	3.5713	3.3333	3.0303	2.8571	2.6316	2.5000	2.2222	2.0000	43
45	3.5714	3.3333	3.0303	2.8571	2.6316	2.5000	2.2222	2.0000	45
48	3.5714	3.3333	3.0303	2.8571	2.6316	2.5000	2.2222	2.0000	48
50	3.5714	3.3333	3.0303	2.8571	2.6316	2.5000	2.2222	2.0000	50

ECONOMIC PROJECT EVALUATION

A small scale rural farmer producing 2,000 kg of maize per year is offered the choice of two designs of solar crop dryers. The first is a simple natural convection device which for an investment of $10,000 will reduce post-harvest losses and boost annual marketable produce from 1,000kg to 1,500kg at a retail price of $5.00per kg. The second dryer is a photovoltaic-powered forced convection device costing $25,000 but capable of providing up to 2,500kg of marketable produce per year at $5.000 per kg. The farmer is offered two options to take up the extra drying capacity of the sophisticated dryer:

a)   To boost annual production by 500kg at a further investment of $1,000 per annum; or

b)   To lease out the capacity to other producers at a hire rate of $2.00 per kg for 8 years and then at $3.50 per kg for the next 7 years.

The economic life of the simple dryer is 10 years, whilst the sophisticated dryer will last for 15 years. The simple dryer is constructed entirely from local materials, but the photovoltaic modules and fans of the second have to be imported at a cost of $10,000. The discount rate offered for the $10,000 to construct the simple dryer is 8%; whilst that for the expensive dryer is 13%, to take account of the importation cost of the photovoltaic modules and fans. However, because the second dryer offered an opportunity of increased food production, the Ministry of Agriculture offered a grant of $5,000 to the farmer if he increased his own food production and $2,000 if the dryer was used by other producers.

Which of the three options would maximise the farmer's wealth (benefits)?

(i)   Cash Flow Statements

The cash flow statements for the three options available to the farmer are set out in Tables A16.1, A16.2 and A16.3. The most important point to note here is that the gross revenues used are only those accruing from the application of the solar dryers, and not the value of the total sales of products. For example, in the case of the simple dryer, the total value of sales of 1,500kg of produce will be $7,500, which total includes $2,500 from the extra 500 kg recovered from post-harvest losses. The $2,500 represents the relevant gross benefit for the appraisal. The same rules are used to arrive at the revenues for the other two options.

(ii)   Calculation of Payback

The Payback periods for three options are set out in Table A16.4. The respective periods required to recoup the initial capital investments are:

a.	Simple Dryer	=	6 years
b.	Forced Dryer 1	=	4 years
c.	Forced Dryer 2	=	5 years

Table A16.1: Cash Flow Statement for Simple Solar Dryer

YEARS	0	1	2	3	4	5	6	7	8	9	10
CAPITAL COSTS ($)											
Land	500										
Solar Dryer	10,000										
OPERATING COSTS ($)											
Materials	-	-	-	-	-	-	-	-	-	-	-
Labour	500	500	500	500	500	500	500	500	500	500	500
Maintenance	200	200	200	200	200	200	200	200	200	200	200
TOTAL COSTS ($)	10,500	700	700	700	700	700	700	700	700	700	700
REVENUE ($)	-	2,500	2,500	2,500	2,500	2,500	2,500	2,500	2,500	2,500	2,500
NET CASH FLOW ($)	(10,500)	1,800	1,800	1,800	1,800	1,800	1,800	1,800	1,800	1,800	1,800

Table A16.2: Cash Flow Statement for Forced Convection Dryer, Option I

YEARS	0	1	2	3	4	5	6	7	8	9	10	11	12	13	14	15
CAPITAL COSTS ($)																
Land	500															
Solar Dryer	25,000															
OPERATING COSTS ($)																
Materials	–	1,000	1,000	1,000	1,000	1,000	1,000	1,000	1,000	1,000	1,000	1,000	1,000	1,000	1,000	1,000
Labour	–	750	750	750	750	750	750	750	750	750	750	750	750	750	750	750
Maintenance	–	400	400	400	400	500	600	600	400	400	400	700	500	400	400	400
TOTAL COSTS ($)	25,500	2,150	2,150	2,150	2,150	2,250	2,250	2,350	2,350	2,150	2,150	2,450	2,250	2,150	2,150	2,150
REVENUE ($)	5,000	7,500	7,500	7,500	7,500	7,500	7,500	7,500	7,500	7,500	7,500	7,500	7,500	7,500	7,500	7,500
NET CASH FLOW ($)	(20,500)	5,350	5,350	5,350	5,350	5,250	5,150	5,150	5,350	5,350	5,350	5,050	5,250	5,350	5,350	5,350

Table A16:3 Cash Flow Statement for Forced Convection Dryer, Option II

YEARS	0	1	2	3	4	5	6	7	8	9	10	11	12	13	14	15
CAPITAL COSTS ($)																
Land	500	–	–	–	–	–	–	–	–	–	–	–	–	–	–	–
Solar Dryer	25,000	–	–	–	–	–	–	–	–	–	–	–	–	–	–	–
OPERATING COSTS ($)																
Materials	–	–	–	–	–	–	–	–	–	–	–	–	–	–	–	–
Labour	–	500	500	500	500	500	500	500	500	500	500	500	500	500	500	500
Maintenance	–	400	400	400	400	500	600	600	400	400	400	700	500	400	400	400
TOTAL COSTS ($)	25,500	900	900	900	900	1,000	1,100	1,100	900	900	900	1,200	1,000	900	900	900
REVENUE ($)	2,000	6,000	6,000	6,000	6,000	6,000	6,000	6,000	6,000	6,750	6,750	6,750	6,750	6,750	6,750	6,750
NET CASH FLOW ($)	(23,500)	5,100	5,100	5,100	5,100	5,000	4,900	4,900	5,100	5,850	5,850	5,550	5,750	5,850	5,850	5,850

Table A16.4: Calculations of Payback Period

End of Year	SIMPLE DRYER			FORCED CONVECTION DRYER I			FORCED CONVECTION DRYER II		
	CC	AP	CP	CC	AP	CP	CC	AP	CP
0	10,500	–	–	20,500	–	–	23,500	–	–
1		1,800	1,800		5,350	5,350		5,100	5,100
2		1,800	3,600		5,350	10,700		5,100	10,200
3		1,800	5,400		5,350	16,050		5,100	15,300
4		1,800	7,200		5,350	21,400		5,100	20,400
5		1,800	9,000		5,350	26,650		5,000	25,400
6		1,800	10,800						
7									
8									
9									
10									
11									
12									
13									
14									
15									

CC = Capital Cost ($)
AP = Annual Profit ($)
CP = Cumulative Profit ($)

The more expensive dryers both have a payback period of less than 6 years and will therefore be preferred to the simple dryer if the objective was solely to recoup the absolute value of capital investment. Since Option I of the forced convection dryer gives a shorter payback period (4 years), it will be a better choice than Option II.

A very important point here is that the gross capital investments by the farmer for the forced dryers have been adjusted to take account of the incentives of $5,000 and $2,000.

(iii)   Accounting Rates of Return

Table A16.5 sets out the calculation of the rates of return on total assets employed for the three options. Applying the equation 19.1 for the accounting rate of return, and assuming a straightline depreciation gives the following rates.

    a)   Simple Dryer

$$R_a \quad = \quad \frac{1,800 - 1,050}{10,500} \qquad = \underline{7.1\%}$$

    b)   Forced Convection Dryer - I

$$R_a \quad = \quad \frac{5,290 - 1,367}{20,500} \qquad = \underline{19.1\%}$$

    c)   Forced Convection Dryer - II

$$R_a \quad = \quad \frac{5,390 - 1,567}{23,500} \qquad = \underline{16.3\%}$$

Both methods show the first option of the forced convection dryer as the best choice, though the relative advantage is much smaller when R_a, the rate of return, is evaluated on the basis of total assets employed. The wide difference between the rate calculated from the two methods emphasises the point made earlier about the inconsistencies in the approach.

(iv)   Calculation of Net Present Values

Given that the annual net benefits from the simple dryers are constant at £1,800, the net present value (NPV) for the project can be calculated from the Annuity Table (Appendix 15). At a discount rate of 8% over the project's economic life of 10 years,

$$\text{NPV} \quad = \quad 10,500 + (1,800 \times 6.710) \quad = -10,500 + 12,078$$
$$= \$\underline{1,578}$$

Table A16.6 shows the NPV calculations for all three projects using the appropriate discount factors.

The first option of the forced convection dryer, that of increased production, has the highest net present value of all three projects, and should therefore be the farmer's most preferred choice, as it provides the greatest benefits.

- 277 -

Table A16.5: Rate of Return on Total Assets

Year	SIMPLE DRYER Total Capital ($)	SIMPLE DRYER Net Profit ($)	FORCED CONVECTION DRYER-I Total Capital ($)	FORCED CONVECTION DRYER-I Net Profit ($)	FORCED CONVECTION DRYER-II Total Capital ($)	FORCED CONVECTION DRYER-II Net Profit ($)
0	10,500	-	20,500	-	23,500	-
1	-	1,800	-	5,350	-	5,100
2	-	1,800	-	5,350	-	5,100
3	-	1,800	-	5,350	-	5,100
4	-	1,800	-	5,250	-	5,100
5	-	1,800	-	5,150	-	5,000
6	-	1,800	-	5,150	-	4,900
7	-	1,800	-	5,350	-	4,900
8	-	1,800	-	5,350	-	5,100
9	-	1,800	-	5,350	-	5,850
10	-	1,800	-	5,050	-	5,550
11	-	-	-	5,250	-	5,750
12	-	-	-	5,350	-	5,850
13	-	-	-	5,350	-	5,850
14	-	-	-	5,350	-	5,850
15	-	-	-	5,350	-	5,850
		18,000		79,350		80,850

a. Average profit

$$\frac{18,000}{10} = \$1,800 \text{ Average profit} = \frac{79,350}{15} = \$5,290 \text{ Average profit} = \frac{80,850}{15} = \$5,390$$

b. Rate of return

$$\frac{\$1,800}{10,500} = 17.1\% \text{ Rate of Return} = \frac{\$5,290}{20,500} = 25.8\% \text{ Rate of return} = \frac{\$5,390}{23,500} = 22.9\%$$

Table A16.6: Net Present Values

Year	SIMPLE DRYER Net Benefits ($)	Discount Factor (8%)	Present Value ($)	FORCED CONVECTION DRYER-I Net Benefits ($)	Discount Factor (13%)	Present Value ($)	FORCED CONVECTION DRYER-II Net Benefits ($)	Discount Factor (13%)	Present Value ($)
0	(10,500)	1.000	(10,500)	(20,500)	1.000	(20,500)	(23,500)	1.000	(23,500)
1	1,800	0.926	1,667	5,350	0.885	4,735	5,100	0.885	4,514
2	1,800	0.857	1,543	5,350	0.783	4,189	5,100	0.783	3,534
3	1,800	0.794	1,429	5,350	0.693	3,708	5,100	0.693	3,126
4	1,800	0.735	1,323	5,350	0.613	3,280	5,100	0.613	3,126
5	1,800	0.681	1,226	5,250	0.543	2,851	5,000	0.543	2,715
6	1,800	0.630	1,134	5,150	0.480	2,472	4,900	0.480	2,352
7	1,800	0.584	1,051	5,150	0.425	2,189	4,900	0.425	2,083
8	1,800	0.540	972	5,350	0.376	2,012	5,100	0.376	1,918
9	1,800	0.500	900	5,350	0.333	1,782	5,850	0.333	1,948
10	1,800	0.463	833	5,350	0.295	1,578	5,850	0.295	1,726
11				5,050	0.261	1,318	5,550	0.261	1,449
12				5,250	0.231	1,213	5,750	0.231	1,328
13				5,350	0.204	1,091	5,850	0.204	1,193
14				5,350	0.181	986	5,850	0.181	1,059
15				5,350	0.160	856	5,850	0.160	936

Net Present Value = $1,578   Net Present Value = $13,742   Net Present Value = $10,373

Nevertheless, the farmer could still opt for the cheapest dryer and still increase his overall wealth, if for example they were unable or unwilling to make large investments of new capital.

Now if the subsidies were not available from the Agriculture Ministry, the NPV of the two forced convection dryer options would be:

For Option I   NPV = - 25,500 + 34,243 = $8,743

For Option II   NPV = - 25,500 + 33,873 = $8,373

Without the incentives, there is only a marginal difference between increased production and renting out of spare capacity. In such a case, the farmer may decide to give up the marginally better option which entails more hard work and opt for the lease of spare capacity. This may be so, even if the overall national need is to increase food production.

Individual versus Group Welfare

The Government's objective in promoting the development of solar dryers may have been to reduce post-harvest losses without increasing the fuel importation bill. However, from the farmer's point of view, the most beneficial technology is not that which has no foreign component, but rather the one in which the element of foreign cost is about 40% of total cost. It is arguable that the $10,000 cost for the photovoltaic modules and fans would be higher than the equivalent amount of fossil fuel to dry the products in more conventional forms.

Another factor to note is the cheapest system is not necessarily the best choice for the farmer. The principal criterion is that of overall wealth maximisation, and as long as the farmer is able to afford the cost of borrowing the money, the choice of dryer will be on the potential economic benefits to him and not really on the merits of energy saving potential.

The incentives show the potential effect of indirect actions (externalities) on project viability. What if the Government had introduced a penal import tax of say 100% of the value of imported goods or given greater incentives to farmers using the simple locally available dryers? In the first case,

For Option I NPV = -25,500 - 10,000 + 34,243 = -$1,257

For Option II, NPV = -25,500 - 10,000 + 33,873 = -$1,627

In this situation, the simple dryer will be the only viable choice for the farmer.

If there was a straight forward incentive of $7,500 for the simple dryer, then:

NPV =   -10,500 + 7,500 + (1,800 x 6.710)
     =   -3,000 + 12,078
     = $9,078

whereas the NPV's for the two forced convection dryer options, if unsubsidised, are as previously calculated $8,743 and $8,373 respectively.

Again, the simple dryer will be the most attractive option.

It is therefore very important to be aware of both the socio-economic objectives (and the associated incentives or penalties) as well as the financial conditions for particular project options. It is here that the preparation of cash flow statements is most useful in setting out the relative effects of various externalities on the time value of money.

INDEX

A